WINGS

WINGS

ONE HUNDRED YEARS OF BRITISH AERIAL WARFARE

PATRICK BISHOP

ISIS
LARGE PRINT
Oxford

First published in Great Britain 2012
by
Atlantic Books
an imprint of Atlantic Books Ltd.

Published in Large Print 2013 by ISIS Publishing Ltd.,
7 Centremead, Osney Mead, Oxford OX2 0ES
by arrangement with
Atlantic Books Ltd.

British Library Cataloguing in Publication Data
Bishop, Patrick (Patrick Joseph)
Wings.
  1. Aeronautics, Military - - Great Britain - - History.
  2. Great Britain. Royal Flying Corps - - History.
  3. Great Britain. Royal Air Force - - History.
  4. Air warfare - - History.
  5. Great Britain - - History, Military.
  6. Large type books.
  I. Title
  358.4'00941–dc23   358·4009

ISBN 978–0–7531–5326–0 (hb)
ISBN 978–0–7531–5327–7 (pb)

Printed and bound in Great Britain by
T. J. International Ltd., Padstow, Cornwall

To Tim Harris

Contents

CRA

Preface

The Last Dogfight

The encounter lasted little more than three minutes. It took place in the violet-blue skies of a midwinter dusk, over the Falkland Islands, 8,000 miles from Britain. It happened more than thirty years ago and it is very unlikely that anything like it will happen again.

On 8 June 1982, at 3.50p.m. local time, a Sea Harrier fighter jet piloted by Flight Lieutenant David Morgan took off from the flight deck of the aircraft carrier HMS *Hermes*, on station about ninety miles north-east of Port Stanley, the capital of East Falkland. Another Sea Harrier, with Lieutenant Dave Smith at the controls, followed two minutes later. The pair set course for Choiseul Sound, the sea channel separating a stretch of wilderness called Lafonia from the rest of East Falkland, where they were to mount a CAP — a combat air patrol.

Earlier in the day two ships moving soldiers forward for the final assault on Port Stanley had been attacked by Argentine air force jets while the troops waited to disembark. There were no aeroplanes to protect them and no missile batteries in place. The bombs killed more than fifty men. CAPs had been flown over the areas since the catastrophe. While there was still light there was still time for another Argentinian attack.

As Morgan approached the scree-covered hillsides of the island, which were turning purple in the setting sun, he saw "a huge vertical column of oily black smoke" rising from the bay at Fitzroy settlement, where the stricken ships lay. The rescue operation was still under way and landing craft crawled back and forth, loaded with wounded. Morgan wrote later that he was "gripped by an awful sense of foreboding".

The two jets settled into a pattern, ploughing a parallel furrow a couple of miles above the scene, cruising at 240 knots (276 mph), flying for ten minutes into the sunset, then turning back again. Sea Harriers were equipped with Blue Fox radar for looking downwards. It was designed for use over the Arctic Ocean against the Soviet air force but over land it was "useless". Instead the pair relied on their eyes. The dusk was in layers, shading from light to dark as it neared the earth's surface. Staring into it was tiring. After a few minutes both pilots began to experience "empty field myopia", losing their middle and long-range vision. Morgan and Smith fought it by focussing on each other, then on their forward radar screens, before resuming their visual search.

As they headed west along Choiseul Sound Morgan noticed a small landing craft making its way eastwards. He radioed the air controller aboard one of the ships in the area, who told him it was a "friendly", transporting troops to the inlet at Bluff Cove, further up the coast.

2

As he passed it on each leg of the patrol he looked down and "imagined the crew, cold and tired in their tiny boat and . . . wondered if they had any idea we were watching over them."

For forty minutes they flew back and forth, nursing their fuel, not talking, "both feeling a burgeoning impotence" at their detachment from the scene below. At about 4.40p.m. Morgan made another turn to the west and checked his fuel gauge. He had four minutes flying time left before he would have to head back to the mother ship, *Hermes*. The landing craft was still butting eastwards, with white water breaking over its bow.

Then Morgan noticed a shape emerging out of the dying light of the western sky.

"A mere mile to the east of the tiny vessel was the camouflaged outline of a . . . fighter, hugging the sea and heading directly for the landing craft, which had become a very personal part of my experience for the last forty minutes," he remembered later.

He jammed open the throttle lever, shouted to Smith to follow him down and pushed his Harrier into a sixty-degree dive as the air-speed indicator shot up from 240 to more than 600 knots. As they hurtled downwards the jet closed on the landing craft. It was a delta-winged A-4 Skyhawk, and he watched it open fire, "bracketing the tiny matchbox of a craft" with 20 mm cannon fire. Then a dark shape detached from the wing. Morgan was relieved to see the bomb explode at least a hundred feet beyond the vessel. But then he saw another A-4 running in behind the first attacker. The

3

second pilot did not miss and he watched "the violent, fire-bright petals of the explosion, which obliterated the stern".

Morgan felt rage grip him. "All-consuming anger welled in my throat," he recalled, "and I determined, in that instant, that this pilot was going to die."

It seemed to him that "the world suddenly became very quiet. I was completely focused and was acutely aware that this was the moment for which all my training had prepared me."

He had flown many hours of mock-combat, but never encountered a real enemy. He hauled his Harrier down and behind the second Argentinian. Edging into his peripheral vision on the left, he suddenly picked up another Skyhawk skimming low over the wave-tops. He decided to go for this one first. He "rolled out less than half a mile behind the third fighter, closing like a runaway train".

The radar that detected targets and relayed them to the "head-up display" (HUD) beamed onto the cockpit windscreen. As it picked up the aircraft an electronic pulse sounded in Morgan's earphones that became an "urgent, high-pitched chirp" when it located the heat of the Skyhawk's engine. This was the signal for the pilot to lock on the Sidewinder.

"My right thumb pressed the lock button on the stick and instantly the small green missile cross in the HUD transformed itself into a diamond sitting squarely over the back end of the Skyhawk," Morgan remembered. The weapon was ready to fire.

"I raised the safety catch and mashed the red, recessed firing button with all the strength I could muster." There was a fractional delay as the missile's thermal battery ignited. Then "the Sidewinder was transformed from an inert, eleven-feet-long drainpipe into a living, fire-breathing monster as it accelerated to nearly three times the speed of sound and streaked towards the enemy aircraft."

The shock of the departing missile flung Morgan's aircraft onto his starboard wing-tip. As he righted the Harrier, he saw the missile racing for the Skyhawk's flaming jet pipe, "leaving a white corkscrew of smoke against the slate grey sea". After two seconds "what had been a living, vibrant flying machine was completely obliterated as the missile tore into its vitals and ripped it apart." The pilot, Ensign Alfredo Vazquez, "had no chance of survival and within a further two seconds the ocean had swallowed all trace of him and his aeroplane as if they had never been".

There was no time for reflection. Another target was directly in front of him, only a mile away. It was the Skyhawk which had bombed the landing craft and it was turning to the left. Morgan locked on and fired. The jet was flown by Lieutenant Juan Arrarás. He seemed to realize the mortal danger behind him and swung hard to the right, forcing the missile to reverse its course. It made no difference. The Sidewinder closed on the Skyhawk, impacting behind the cockpit in a flash of white light.

"The air was filled with the aluminium confetti of destruction, fluttering seawards," Morgan wrote. "I watched, fascinated, as the disembodied cockpit yawed rapidly starboard through ninety degrees and splashed violently into the freezing water." At that moment "a parachute snapped open, right in front of my face".

Arrarás had managed to eject from the disembodied cockpit. He "flashed over my left wing, so close that I saw every detail of the rag-doll figure, its arms and legs thrown into a grotesque star shape by the deceleration of the silk canopy". Morgan felt a flash of "relief and empathy" for his enemy, then concentrated on his next target.

Both his missiles were gone. That left the Harrier's two 30 mm guns. What he took to be the last remaining Skyhawk was ahead of him. He lifted the safety slide on the trigger. The head-up display had disappeared from the windscreen and he had only his own skill and eyesight to rely on when taking aim. As he closed on the Skyhawk it "broke rapidly towards me. I pulled the blurred outline to the bottom of the blank windscreen and opened fire." The cannon shells pumped out at a rate of forty per second. In the darkness he could not see whether or not they were hitting. Then, "suddenly over the radio came an urgent shout from Dave Smith: 'Pull up! Pull up! You're being fired at!' "

Morgan had seen only three Skyhawks. He had failed to spot a fourth, piloted by Lieutenant Hector Sanchez, which was now bearing down on him. He "pulled up into the vertical, through the setting sun, and in a big, lazy, looping manoeuvre, rolled out at 12,000 feet, heading north-east for *Hermes* with my heart racing."

Smith, meanwhile, dived low and chased the third Skyhawk over the water. At a mile range he fired a Sidewinder. Seven seconds later it struck the aircraft of First Lieutenant Danilo Bolzan. There was a brilliant white flash as the missile exploded. Looking behind, Morgan saw it disappear "in a huge yellow-orange fireball as it spread its burning remains over the sand dunes on the north coast of Lafonia."

Two Argentinian pilots, Bolzan and Vazquez, were now dead. Arrarás, whose rag-doll figure had flashed past Morgan's cockpit, had also perished, killed by the impact of the low-level ejection. Though they had won the battle, the British pilots' survival was uncertain. They were dangerously low on fuel and *Hermes* was ninety miles away. If they ran out of petrol they would have to eject into the freezing sea and pray that a helicopter would find them. They climbed high, gaining the maximum height to glide down into a landing.

"At forty thousand feet the sun was still a blaze of orange," wrote Morgan, "but as I descended the light became progressively worse. By the time I had descended to ten thousand feet the world had become an extremely dark and lonely place."

To add to the hazards a storm was brewing and *Hermes* was lying in heavy rain and gusting wind. There was no fuel to spare for a careful approach using his on-board radar to guide him. He called the carrier and asked the Controller to talk him down, onto the centre line of the flight deck. He was descending through thick turbulent cloud with three miles left to run when his fuel warning lights flashed. A few seconds later he "saw a glimmer of light emerging through the rain and at eight hundred feet the lights fused into the recognizable outline of the carrier". He "slammed the nozzle lever into the hover stop, selected full flap and punched the undercarriage button to lower the wheels". The Sea Harrier was a jump jet, capable of stopping dead in mid-air and hovering. Morgan's aircraft came to an airborne halt on the port side of the deck. He manoeuvred it sideways onto the centre line, then "closed the throttle and banged the machine down on the rain-streaked deck". As he taxied forward to park he heard Dave Smith landing behind him.

So ended the last air-to-air action engaged in by British pilots. It hardly merits the description "dogfight", as the Argentinian pilots, despite their manifest courage, then as in previous encounters, never properly "came out to play", to use the characteristic euphemism of the British jet jockeys. It came at the end of a brief air war that still carried a whiff of classic aerial combat of the First and Second World Wars.

As a young war correspondent who had sailed to the South Atlantic with the Task Force I had a grandstand view of some of the fighting. I witnessed the heroism of the Argentinian pilots as they took their Mirages and Skyhawks in low over San Carlos Water through a curtain of corkscrewing missiles and fizzing tracer. On the long trek to Stanley my blood stirred when a pair of Harriers screamed protectively overhead. They seemed to us, shivering in the sleet and mud, the direct descendants of the Fighter Boys of 1940. And that is how they self-consciously saw themselves. Ground controllers still vectored pilots onto targets by informing them that there was "trade" in the offing — just as they did in the Battle of Britain. Pilots still called out "Tally Ho!" before launching their attacks.

Having downed a few pints of beer after his victory, David Morgan retreated through the eerie red glow of the night-lighting in the *Hermes* passageways to the deserted briefing room, where he sat for a while. His "feelings of satisfaction and pride were tempered by a melancholy that I could not identify". He remembered a poem, "Combat Report" by John Pudney, who had served as an RAF intelligence officer in the Second World War. Something compelled him to write it out in felt-tip pen on the briefing board. The last lines seemed right for what he had just seen and done.

> "I let him have a sharp four-second squirt,
> Closing to fifty yards. He went on fire."
> Your deadly petals painted, you exert
> A simple stature. Man-high, without pride,
> You pick your way through heaven and the dirt.
> "He burned out in the air: that's how the poor
>   sod died."

That done, he sat down on the bench at the front of the room. He became aware that "there was moisture running down both my cheeks".

The air war ended two days later. British pilots would never again fight another like it. High technology was already in the process of edging human agency from the aerial battlefield. When Britain went to war with Iraq nine years later, British pilots rarely saw an enemy plane, and the seven fixed-wing aircraft brought down were the victims of missiles. In the Balkans conflict of 1992–1995, the Serbian air force posed little threat, nor did the Iraq air force during the 2003 invasion, or the Libyan air force during NATO operations in 2011. In the Afghan conflict there is no risk at all from enemy aircraft as the Taliban do not have an air force.

British and American pilots sit in the skies, launching incredibly expensive weapons, utilizing the most sophisticated technology against men with rifles who wear sandals to go to war. In this conflict, I also had a ringside seat.

In the summer of 2008, in Helmand Province, I was with the Parachute Regiment on an operation to clear a route south of the Kajaki Dam in preparation for the delivery of a new turbine for the powerhouse generator. As we moved down the track we came under sporadic fire from insurgents hidden in mud-walled compounds. A pattern was soon established. The RAF Joint Tactical Air Controller on the ground with the Paras radioed the map co-ordinates of the troublesome enemy to a distant air base. There was a pause while permission was obtained for a strike. Then a few minutes later the location would erupt in flames from a laser-guided bomb launched from an aircraft flying at a height that made it invisible. Military aviation has come a very long way in a very short time. This is the story its journey.

CHAPTER ONE

Pilots of the Purple Twilight

In the space of three generations flight has flooded and ebbed from the world's imagination. Aeroplanes are part of the backdrop of life and travelling in them has become mundane and usually tedious. Yet a hundred years ago the sight of a rickety contraption of wire and canvas, fluttering and swooping above the fields with a strangely clad figure perched precariously inside, was guaranteed to create great — even wild — excitement.

In June 1910, only twenty months after the first aeroplane made a paltry, 450 yard hop over British soil, *Flight* magazine reported that "it is becoming the fashion to consider any open-air function quite incomplete unless there is an exhibition of flying to give tone to it". The editorial was commenting on an incident that had taken place a few days before. At an agricultural show in the city of Worcester a Blériot monoplane "ran amok". At the controls was Mr Ernest Dartigan. He was assistant to a Captain Clayton, who had been due to give a "series of spectacular flights" but had injured himself in a crash the previous day.

Rather than disappoint the 14,000 people gathered at the showground, Dartigan had rolled the Blériot out to taxi up and down on the grass. The results were disastrous. Dartigan quickly lost control and the aeroplane charged into the crowd, killing a woman and injuring several others.

At the subsequent inquest, Clayton admitted that he was not a captain at all, but had adopted the title "for business purposes". Neither he nor Dartigan possessed a certificate of competence from the Royal Aero Club. The pseudo-aviator did not shoulder the blame alone, however. A Worcestershire County Council official who witnessed the accident told the court that the "conduct of the crowd was foolhardy in the extreme. [They] insisted upon crowding around the aeroplane and badly hampered the movements of the man who was in control, in spite the efforts of police and officials to keep them back."

This little tragedy tells us quite a lot about those early days. It reveals the ad hoc nature of primitive aviation, glorious or foolhardy according to your point of view. Everything was necessarily innovatory and improvised. "Captain" Clayton might have crocked himself in a prang, but the show went on nonetheless. The pressure that Dartigan felt to perform is also revealing. He seems to have considered himself duty bound to give the crowds what they came for. One suspects he also saw an opportunity to indulge his own fantasies. With Clayton indisposed, a splendid opportunity arose for his assistant to shine. From the outset, aviation was in the hands of those with a tendency to show off — frequently with the same sad results as on this occasion.

And then there is the woman whose eagerness to get close to the action proved fatal. There were many more like her in the crowd. Photographs of early displays show broad-brimmed bonnets scattered abundantly among the flat hats and homburgs. Women did not want to just watch what was happening. They were eager to take part. Almost from the beginning adventurous females were clamouring to "go up", despite the obvious dangers, first as passengers, then as pilots. At the same time as the Worcester air show, the first flying school was opening its doors at Brooklands motor-racing circuit in Weybridge, Surrey. Mrs Hilda Hewlett, a forty-six-year-old mother of two who was the first woman to gain a Royal Aero Club certificate, co-owned it with her French lover.

What was it that drew the crowds? In part they had come to witness what was manifestly a great step forward in the history of mankind. The skeletal monoplanes and biplanes, constructed from homely materials of wood, canvas and wire, had realized the ancient human dream of defying gravity. They were oddly beautiful and the men who flew them seemed to earthbound mortals like elevated beings.

The spectators also enjoyed the frisson of danger. Newspapers — then as now eager to create alarm — presented flying as a suicidal activity. Some claimed that the crowds went to air shows in the base hope that someone would come a cropper. The chances were high. Early aviators showed an almost insane disregard for risk.

Even in this company of daredevils Sam Cody, a naturalized American who was the first man to fly in Britain, stood out. In a routine accident in the spring of 1912, while instructing Lieutenant Fletcher in his biplane, nicknamed the "Cathedral" on account of its comparatively impressive size, Cody was "thrown out and fell a considerable distance, sustaining injuries to his head and legs". He continued in this nerveless fashion until he met his death in August 1913 over Laffan's Plain near Aldershot, in an accident apparently caused by a panicky passenger, who wrapped his arms around him so tightly that he was unable to operate the controls.

Pilots seemed to consider even the most basic safety measures unmanly. In August 1912 an Australian aviator called Lindsay Campbell was killed in a crash at Brooklands. Medical evidence at the inquest recorded he had fractured his skull. Campbell had not been wearing a helmet. A correspondent to *Flight* noted that "aviators, and especially English aviators, have a constitutional objection to wearing helmets for the reason apparently that . . . it is too much a concession to the idea of danger."

Aviation was married to death from the start, but there was nothing morbid about the instant fascination felt by the public. The instinct that pulled in the air-show crowds and that swelled the ranks of aero-modelling clubs, inducing people to subscribe to a crop of aviation magazines, was optimistic and life-affirming. It was the sense of possibility, the feeling that the frontiers of existence were expanding, that gave them a thrill. They recognized, even if they did not understand, the enormity of what was happening and accepted that for things to progress, risks would have to be taken. A great enterprise was worth sacrifices. Men would die, but not for nothing.

Few of those doing the flying had much idea of where aviation would lead. It was enough that humans could now take to the air. All most of them asked of an aeroplane was that it allowed them to get as close to the sensation of flight as the laws of nature allowed. In 1946, two years before his death, Orville Wright was guest of honour at a military conference in New York. The American air ace Eddie Rickenbacker hailed him as a visionary who had foreseen how aeroplanes would transform the twentieth century. But Wright told Rickenbacker that he was talking nonsense.

"Wilbur and I had no idea aviation would take off in the way it has," he said. "We had no idea that there'd be thousands of aircraft flying around the world. We had no idea that aircraft would be dropping bombs. We were just a couple of kids with a bike shop who wanted to get this contraption up in the air."

Poignantly, given what was to come, the Wright brothers believed that their invention might actually reduce the incidence of war. They cherished the thought that "governments would realize the impossibility of winning by surprise attacks . . . no country would enter into war with another of equal size when it knew

15

that it would have to win by simply wearing out the enemy."

The joy that aircraft excited was almost immediately matched by unease. Long before the Wright brothers got airborne, a great English poet had glimpsed one direction in which the aeroplane would take us. In 1835 Alfred, Lord Tennyson, wrote a poem, *Locksley Hall*, in which the narrator tells how he

> . . . dipt into the future far as human eye could
> see,
> Saw the Vision of the world, and all the wonder
> that would be;
>
> Saw the heavens fill with commerce, argosies of
> magic sails,
> Pilots of the purple twilight, dropping down with
> costly bales . . .

However, it was not this benign presentiment of celestial trade routes that would be remembered so much as the couplet that followed. For he also

> Heard the heavens fill with shouting, and there
> rain'd a ghastly dew
> From the nations' airy navies grappling in the
> central blue.

This was a remarkable prophecy — that once the opportunity arose, the sky would become a battlefield. It would come to pass only eleven years after that first callow skip over the sands of Kitty Hawk. The yearning to fly was very old, but the itch to fight was older. Aviation's passage from innocence to experience was depressingly swift.

It was apparent immediately that the invention of the aeroplane raised important military possibilities. In terrestrial warfare possession of the high ground brought benefits, notably the ability to calculate the enemy's strength and work out what he was up to. Hovering over the earth increased the purview dramatically. After hot-air balloons appeared in France in 1783 they were soon put to military purposes. Gasbags, tethered to the earth, were seen intermittently around battle-fields throughout the nineteenth century. Spotters, equipped with spyglasses, yelled down to the ground details of what they could see of enemy movements and dispositions. Unlike balloons, aeroplanes could move about under their own power and seemed able to do the job of reconnaissance better.

Their arrival, however, provoked unease among a significant section of the British military establishment. The army was slow to accept change. Reconnaissance had always been the preserve of the elite cavalry regiments. This attitude was summed up in a story that their officers were concerned that noisy aeroplanes would "frighten the horses".

Initially it seemed as if aircraft might turn out to be merely a passing craze. Early aero-engines were weak and unreliable, prone to chronic overheating. As performance improved, however, the realization grew

17

that aeroplanes would shape the future — political, economic, social and military.

In July 1909 Louis Blériot flew across the Channel in a monoplane of his own design. It looked like a dragonfly, or a Leonardo da Vinci drawing. Wonder at this achievement was matched by apprehension. Leading the pessimists was H. G. Wells whose science-fiction novels had given him the standing of a seer. The day afterwards he judged Blériot's feat to be a blow to British prestige. "We have fallen behind in the quality of our manhood," he wrote in the *Daily Mail*. "Within a year we shall have — or rather they will have — aeroplanes capable of starting from Calais . . . circling over London, dropping a hundredweight or so of explosive upon the printing machines of the *Daily Mail* and returning securely to Calais for another similar parcel."

The *Mail*'s proprietor Lord Rothermere was a noisy advocate of "air-mindedness". It was he who had put up the £1,000 prize that inspired Blériot's attempt. The fact that a Frenchman had won it seemed proof of his conviction — echoed by Wells — that national virility was drooping. Britain was lagging behind in the air race and an urgent effort was needed to catch up.

The perils of complacency were apparent across the water that Blériot had conquered. A few weeks after the historic flight a Grande Semaine d'Aviation was held at Reims. It was a heady event, watched by hundreds of thousands. Spectators drank the local champagne, dined in a 600-seat restaurant and cheered on the aviators, on occasion becoming so excited they swept through the barriers to mob their heroes. Fliers arrived from all over the world to take part in races offering lavish prize money. An American, Glenn Curtiss, whose receding hairline and chin made him look more like a bank clerk than a knight of the air, triumphed in the main event, a time-trial, beating Blériot with an average speed of less than 50 mph.

The show nonetheless established France's dominance in the air. All but two of the twenty-two aviators were French. Most of the power plants in use were Gnome rotary engines, developed by the Paris-based Seguin brothers. These engines did what the name suggests, revolving around a fixed crankshaft. The propeller was simply attached to the rotating engine. Despite the oddness of the concept to modern eyes, they were efficient and comparatively light. The Seguins used nickel-steel alloy, machined to give the optimum power-to-weight ratio, and the fact that air cooled the spinning cylinders removed the need for water jackets. Among the spectators was David Lloyd George, then Chancellor of the Exchequer. He left with the conviction that "flying machines are no longer toys and dreams . . . they are an established fact."

Above all they were a military fact. By the end of that year the French army had 200 aircraft in service. The Germans — Britain's rivals in a crippling naval arms race — were exploring another field of aviation. Count Ferdinand von Zeppelin, a southern German professional soldier, had seen military reconnaissance balloons in action while attached to the Union army during the American Civil War. Over the next four decades he advanced the concept, developing an airship constructed around a rigid aluminium frame covered with fabric, kept aloft by hydrogen cells, controlled from an underslung gondola and shaped like a cigar to provide aerodynamic efficiency. Zeppelin's airship was intended as an instrument of war and the German military bought its first one in 1908. The following year they went into commercial service.

It wasn't just the French and the Germans. The Italians had shown far greater energy and imagination than the British in their response to flight, establishing their own military aviation service, equipped with balloons, in 1884. In October 1911 they became the first to employ aeroplanes in war, flying bombing sorties against the Turks during a colonial squabble in Libya, which, although of minimal effectiveness, produced wild projections from the growing claque of air-power advocates of what warplanes might achieve.

It was only in that year that the British government moved to make up for lost ground. In April 1911 an Air Battalion was formed inside the Royal Engineers. Until then military aeronautics had been confined to a small unit which experimented with balloons and man-lifting kites from headquarters at Farnborough, near the army's headquarters in Aldershot, Surrey. Its balloon factory produced small, non-rigid airships and from 1910 a handful of experimental aeroplanes. The chief designer — and test pilot — was Geoffrey de Havilland, a vicar's son and engineering maestro, who went on to become one of the great names of British aviation. The Aircraft Factory, as it became, was superintended by

Mervyn O'Gorman, a dapper Irish civil engineer, described by a contemporary as a "thruster, possessing brains, flamboyance, courage and imagination".

The Air Battalion was staffed by mechanics drawn from the Royal Engineers. The task of piloting aircraft was deemed to be a job for officers. Initially there were no aeroplanes for the volunteers to fly. The quality of the early training was apparent in a report in *Flight* of 25 June 1910. "At last an official start has been made with the instruction of British Army officers in the art of flying," it ran. "On Monday evening the Hon C. S. Rolls [of Rolls Royce fame] visited the balloon factory at Farnborough and explained to a number of officers . . . the workings of his Short-Wright machine which has been at the balloon factory for some time." However, "no attempt at flight was made." Instead "the motors were started up and the method of handling the machine was demonstrated."

The Short-Wright was one of only a handful of assorted flying machines available, and if O'Gorman had his way the factory — despite its name — would not be making up the short-fall. He regarded his establishment as a research and design centre rather than a production line, so training craft had to be bought in from private aviation companies.

The navy had viewed the birth of aviation coolly. When the Wright brothers approached the Admiralty in 1907 with a view to selling them their invention they were told that "in their Lordships" opinions aeroplanes

21

would not be of any practical use to the naval service'[1]. Events made continued indifference impossible. It was obvious to the open-minded that aircraft had the potential to transform warfare at sea.

The navy's preoccupation with the activities of their German rivals meant their attention was first focused on airships. Concern at the appearance of the Zeppelin had led to the Admiralty ordering a rigid airship of its own, *Naval Airship No. 1*, popularly known as the *Mayfly*, and built by Vickers at Barrow-in-Furness. The nickname would turn out to be tragically appropriate, given its ephemeral life span. The specifications kept changing as the navy sought to load it with more and more equipment. The framework, made from a new alloy, duralumin, was too weak to bear the extra weight. On 24 September 1911, when the *Mayfly* was towed out of her shed, stern first, for what was supposed to be her maiden flight, she crumpled and sank, her back broken by three tons of surplus equipment.

The disaster ensured that for the time being, naval interest and expenditure was confined to aeroplanes. Experiments carried out by the American navy had given a glimpse of future possibilities. In November 1910, Eugene Ely flew a biplane designed by Glenn Curtiss, the American pilot who had been garlanded at the 1909 Reims air show and was now establishing himself as an aviation trailblazer. The machine took off from a wooden ramp, tacked onto the forecastle of the

---

[1] To be fair to the navy, the War Office, and French and American governments also declined the offer.

light cruiser USS *Birmingham*. The aeroplane clipped the water and Ely put down as soon as he could. The two-and-half-mile flight was nonetheless proclaimed by Curtiss to be an event of huge significance. He predicted that, henceforth, the great battleships, laden with armour and bristling with guns that dominated naval strategy, were heading for extinction.

"The battles of the future will be fought in the air," he declared. Battleships, encumbered as they were with masts, towers and turrets, were not configured to launch air fighters and "without these to defend them . . . would be blown apart". It was a bold assertion, but as events would prove, fundamentally correct. Curtiss tried to prove his point with demonstrations showing how aircraft could drop dummy bombs with a high degree of accuracy on a simulated large warship target.

Having taken off from a ship, Ely went on to achieve the far trickier task of landing on one, putting down a modified Curtiss plane on a wooden platform constructed on the USS *Pennsylvania* in San Francisco Bay in January 1911. The cruiser was at anchor and the closing speed on landing had been dangerously fast. Ely arranged for twenty-two manila lines to be stretched across the deck, weighted with sandbags, to snag on hooks welded on the undercarriage of his aeroplane. Thus was born the transverse arrester, a system that in its essentials would last to modern times.

The navy's venture into the air was speeded up by the intervention of an outsider. Frank McClean, an engineer and amateur aviator, offered for pilot training the use of two of his Short biplanes, which he kept at the Royal Aero Club aerodrome in Eastchurch on the Isle of Sheppey (where the Short brothers who had switched from balloon to aircraft-making conveniently had a factory). Applications were invited from interested officers: they had to be unmarried and wealthy enough to pay their own instruction costs. Two hundred applied for the four places available and Eastchurch became the cradle of early naval aviation. The base began to fill up with mechanics — engine-room artificers, carpenters, ship-wrights and wireless operators, all volunteers, to provide the vital expertise to support the men in the air.

The project had the blessing of the Admiralty's political master, Winston Churchill. In 1912 Churchill made his first flight and had instantly caught the benign contagion of air enthusiasm. "I am bound to confess that my imagination supplied me at every moment with the most realistic anticipation of a crash," he wrote afterwards. "However, we descended in due course with perfect safety . . . having been thoroughly bitten, I continued to fly on every possible occasion when my duties permitted." Fortunately, these were not too numerous. Churchill was keen but inept and his instructors came to dread his appearances.

Despite Ely's feats, operating aircraft from ships was a delicate operation, requiring optimum conditions of wind, weather and sea. While the experiments were going on Curtiss was already developing another concept: the "hydroaeroplane", later shortened by Churchill to the handier "seaplane". This was one of Curtiss's standard aircraft — a "pusher" with the propeller mounted behind the cockpit — fitted with a central wooden float instead of an undercarriage and two stabilizing floats under each wing-tip. On 17 February 1911 Curtiss took off from a shore base at North Island off San Diego, California, and flew out to the USS *Pennsylvania*, where he landed alongside. The aircraft was hoisted on-board, then placed back in the water. Curtiss took off and flew back to North Island without mishap. This provided a simple demonstration of how aviation could be of great practical use to navies. The Government provided funds, which resulted in a Curtiss amphibian machine that could operate with floats or wheels. Equipped with a 75-hp engine (also Curtiss-designed) it could carry an observer, had a range of sixty miles and could reach 1,000 feet, vastly increasing a commander's knowledge of what lay in the surrounding waters.

British naval aviators were heading in the same direction. Lieutenant Arthur Longmore, one of the original Eastchurch trainees, managed to land, on improvised rubberized airbags, on the River Medway. In May 1912 his colleague Lieutenant Charles Samson took off from a platform built on the foredeck of a warship while she was underway. Later HMS *Hermes* was fitted out as a parent ship for seaplanes. They took off on wheels, set into their floats, and landed on the water to be collected and winched ashore.

The Short brothers came up with an innovation that helped to overcome a basic problem that arose from trying to marry aeroplanes to ships. They invented the Short Folder Seaplane with hinged wings which reduced the span from fifty-six feet to twelve. One of this type was on *Hermes* as part of the "Red" force during the Fleet's 1913 manoeuvres. Equipped with a radio transmitter, it was able to send back valuable information on "enemy" positions.

The army had already used aircraft in their manoeuvres the previous autumn. They opened on Monday, 16 September 1912 in the flatlands east of Cambridge. There were two divisions on either side. Red Force, under Sir Douglas Haig, was the attacker. Blue Force, under Sir James Grierson, defended. Both had aircraft to support them — a balloon and seven aeroplanes each. More had been intended, but summer had seen a spate of fatal accidents. Most of the crashes had involved monoplanes. The decision was made to drop single-wing aircraft, relatively quick and nimble though they were, in favour of more stable biplanes.

The afternoon before the war game began, the commander of Blue Force's cavalry element delivered some unwelcome news to Grierson. He reported that, as the forces were positioned so far apart, his men would be unable to provide information about the enemy's whereabouts until at least twenty-four hours after the exercise began. Grierson turned to Major Robert Brooke-Popham, who had obtained his Royal Aero Club certificate only two months before, but was commanding the tiny air component.

"Do you think the aeroplanes could do anything?" he asked.

Brooke-Popham assured him they could.

The following day, at 6a.m., his pilots and observers took off into clear blue skies. Three hours later they were back with "complete, accurate and detailed information concerning the disposition of all the enemy troops". From then on Grierson relied almost entirely on aircraft for reconnaissance. To the chagrin of the cavalrymen, aircraft were sometimes asked to verify information they had galloped hard to bring in. Blue Force won the war game.

The different needs of the army and navy sent their air arms in diverging directions, but in April 1912 an attempt was made to bring them together. The Committee of Imperial Defence announced the birth of a new formation, the Royal Flying Corps (RFC). It comprised a military wing and a naval wing, and a training centre, the Central Flying School, was founded at Upavon in Wiltshire. King George V granted the royal warrant. He also approved an inspiring motto, *Per Ardua ad Astra*.

Credit for the choice seems to lie with a young lieutenant of the Royal Engineers called J. S. Yule, who was attached to the new corps. He was strolling across Laffan's Plain one evening in May 1912 with another subaltern. They were discussing the proposal of the RFC's commanding officer Major Frederick Skyes that the new service should have a motto. Yule had just been reading *The People of the Mist* (1894) by H. Rider Haggard. The second paragraph of the book describes the hero entering the stone gates of a mansion on which are carved "coats of arms and banners inscribed with the device 'Per Ardua ad Astra'. Yule liked the sound of it and Sykes agreed." The Latin is generally translated as "Through struggle to the stars", though an authoritative translation has never been agreed.

The RFC also had its own, suitably innovative new uniform. Officers and men wore a slate-blue, high-collared, double-breasted tunic which fastened on the inside so that there were no buttons showing to snag on wires. It was considered unattractive and soon became disparaged as the "maternity jacket". Those who could took advantage of a rule that allowed officers to wear the uniform of their parent regiment.

The military wing aimed at an establishment of 160 officers and 1,000 men. The naval wing target was only 50 officers and 500 men. The technical demands of modern warships meant there was a pool of skilled other ranks. The army had to struggle to find technicians and an appeal went out inviting civilians working as blacksmiths, carpenters and joiners, clerks, coppersmiths, draughtsmen, electricians, fitters, harness-makers, instrument repairers, metal turners, painters, pattern makers, photographers and other trades to join up.

From the beginning the new service attracted adventurous men — and later women — from all levels of Britain's multilayered society. Wealthy and well-educated young men were both excited and enchanted by aviation. It seemed to offer another dimension in which the ethos of the playing field could expand and thrive. Sir Walter Raleigh, official historian of the 1914 air war, wrote in 1922 that Britain's scramble to catch up with her continental rivals was greatly helped by the presence of "a body of youth fitted by temperament for the work of the air, and educated, as if by design, to take risks with a light heart — the boys of the Public Schools of England".

Among them was Philip Joubert de la Ferté, who came from an upper-middle-class Anglo-French family. After Harrow and the Royal Military Academy at Woolwich he was commissioned into the Royal Field Artillery. On visits to his family home at Weybridge, he had been bewitched by the sight of the aeroplanes at nearby Brooklands aerodrome. The aviators he saw there, lurching into the skies aboard a "motley collection of stick and string kites", seemed to him to be "giants, supermen, whom no ordinary mortal could hope to follow". One day in 1912, while watching the flying near Farnborough with a colleague "one of the aircraft taxied close by and I recognized the pilot as someone who had been at the Military Academy with me. I turned to the Major and said, 'If that chap can fly, so can I!' " The next day he set about trying to join the newly formed RFC.

Before starting instruction at the Central Flying School, would-be pilots had to learn the basics and obtain a civilian certificate from the Royal Aero Club at their own expense, though the £75 outlay was refunded later. Only officers were likely to have the money to do so. To qualify, candidates were required to carry out two flights, making five figures of eight, landing each time within fifty yards of a specified point. They also had to climb to 150 feet, cut the engine, then drift down to a controlled landing.

29

Strong winds were potentially fatal. Joubert found that he had to get up at dawn or hang around until twilight when there was more chance that the breeze would be gentle enough to allow a few circuits of the aerodrome. Even so, "tragedy came from time to time to remind the enthusiasts that they were adventuring along a perilous path." Undeterred, Joubert joined the school in 1913.

The technical nature of aviation meant that it was not only the officer class who would be allowed into this magical new world. Cecil King, a wheelwright and coach builder by trade, was one who managed to penetrate it. In 1913 he was stuck in a dead-end job in a dreary, subterranean London workshop. He found it "very depressing ... I wanted to get into a more open-air life." One day he was strolling through Kingston-upon-Thames when he met two soldiers. "They had an unusual badge with the letters RFC on their shoulders. I got into conversation with them and they told me they were members of a new unit called the Royal Flying Corps, which had just started — and why didn't I join?"

King had never heard of the new outfit. However, he was keen on the idea of flying. Two years before he had been enthralled by the sight of Gustav Hamel performing at Hendon aerodrome. Despite his name, Hamel was British, educated at Westminster School. In 1910, at the age of twenty-one, he went to the Blériot aviation school at Pau in south-west France. A year afterwards he was performing pioneering feats, such as carrying out the first airmail delivery, flying a sack of letters and postcards the twenty-one miles from Hendon to Windsor. After his encounter with the airmen, Cecil King presented himself at Kingston barracks, where he volunteered for the RFC. A little later he found himself posted to Farnborough aerodrome and awoke each morning to the sound of trumpets and bugles. "I was delighted," he remembered. King was to serve as a rigger and never flew as a pilot.

Several tradesmen who entered the RFC in the early days went on to glorious careers in the air. James McCudden, a sergeant major's son from Kent, joined the Royal Engineers as a bugler in 1910, aged sixteen. Three years later he volunteered for the RFC and in 1914 he went with No. 3 Squadron to France as a mechanic. He was soon flying as an observer, then as a pilot. His exploits over the trenches shooting down German aircraft won him the Victoria Cross and he became, along with Major "Mick" Mannock and Captain Albert Ball, one of the best-known British aviators of the war.

From the beginning the air force was to act in part as a machine of social transformation, elevating likely young men from the lower classes and making them officers — if not, as army and navy snobs maintained, quite gentlemen. The novelty of the air force made the traditionalists, who were abundant in the ranks of the military, suspicious. Philip Joubert recalled how "the criticisms and contempt of brother officers" that he and his fellow volunteers for the RFC encountered "was another trial we had to bear". One officer, a few years ahead of him, "took pleasure in stating that it was only those officers for whom their Commanders had no use whatsoever who were allowed to go into the Flying Corps". Joubert had the satisfaction of finding himself, two years later, "considerably further advanced in seniority than the man who had stuck to the horse as a means of locomotion". Scorn for the "arrivistes" of the new service persisted until well into the Second World War, at least among the likes of the novelist Evelyn Waugh. In his *Sword of Honour* trilogy the RAF is personified by a pompous senior officer who takes cover under the billiard table of Bellamy's club during an air raid, while the army types display the correct *élan* by remaining upright with drinks in hand.

In reality the RFC was filling up with some of the most effective and interesting warriors of the new century, many of whom would rise to lead the air force through the two cataclysmic conflicts that lay ahead. It attracted the adventurous, the unconventional and a fair sprinkling of the frustrated, who turned to it in the hope it might provide satisfactions that had been denied to them elsewhere. Into this category fell Hugh Montague Trenchard, who combined nineteenth-century mores with a twentieth-century appreciation of the new. He was the son of a West Country soldier turned solicitor who went bankrupt, and Hugh's education had been dependent on the charity of relations. In his youth he displayed little sign of intelligence or charm. He eventually scraped into the army where he served in India and South and West Africa. In October 1900 he was badly wounded fighting the Boers and was lucky to survive. He went on to spend six years in the interior of Nigeria surveying, mapping and subduing the natives. His exertions brought little reward. In 1910 he was back with his old regiment, the Royal Scots Fusiliers, in the backwater of Ulster. He was nearly forty, a mere company commander, disliked by his CO and unpopular with his fellow officers who found his teetotalism and long silences, interspersed with awkward utterances in a booming voice, a trial.

Trenchard's great strength was his tenacity. When Captain Eustace Loraine, a comrade who had served under him in Nigeria, wrote from Larkhill, a military camp on Salisbury Plain which had become the site of the first army aerodrome, describing the excitements of his new life as an RFC pilot, Trenchard set about trying to join him. Like everything in his life so far, this was not easy. Forty was the upper age limit for pilots. He couldn't fly and his physique — six foot three and heavily built — counted strongly against him. He wangled three months' leave and set off for Tommy Sopwith's flying school at Brooklands in Surrey to obtain the certificate he needed to enrol as a pupil at the RFC's Central Flying School. He did so after one hour and four minutes flying time. He arrived at Upavon in August. His friend Loraine was dead, killed in a crash in a Nieuport monoplane. For once, Trenchard's enthusiasm and efficiency were fully appreciated by authority. He was soon second-in-command of the school, the start of a rapid ascent up the ladder of the RFC hierarchy.

He was nurtured by the man who oversaw the birth and first steps of the new force. Brigadier-General Sir David Henderson was an expert in reconnaissance when he was put in charge of the Directorate of Military Aeronautics, formed at the same time as the RFC. He was unusually intelligent and far-sighted, and was blessed with handsome, classical features that seemed to reflect his noble character. They contrasted with the ferrety demeanour of the first commander of the RFC's military (as opposed to naval) wing, who was to go to France as Henderson's deputy. Frederick Sykes was bright, sharp, ambitious and seemed to engender instant mistrust in all who encountered him. "He never really gained the confidence of his command," was Joubert's diplomatic verdict. Inevitably, scheming Sykes and trenchant Trenchard fell out.

The men they commanded, pilots, mechanics and administrators, on the whole seem more enterprising, more intelligent and more ambitious than their contemporaries. The thin ranks of the first few squadrons are stuffed with names that would be famous later on. Hugh Dowding, who led Fighter Command through the Battle of Britain, is there, along with Wilfred Freeman, the overseer of the re-equipment programme that provided the Hurricanes and Spitfires. The foundation force includes the Salmond brothers, John and Geoffrey, both of whom would command the Royal Air Force, Edgar Ludlow-Hewitt, a future leader of Bomber Command, and a host of others whose exploits would inspire the airmen that followed.

In the short time between coming into existence and going off to war, the RFC developed a robust *esprit de corps* that was felt at all levels. Cecil King noted that "everyone who joined the Royal Flying Corps in the other ranks held some trade or other, whereas the men in the general regiments — they might be anyone . . . therefore we considered ourselves a bit superior to the infantry and cavalry, who may have come from any walk of life. We also got more pay than they did, and when they found that out they were a little bit jealous."

Similarly, those who gravitated towards the naval air service were often the cream of the Fleet. What the other ranks shared with the officer volunteers was a modern outlook and a taste for the new. It is reflected in early photographs. Pictures of soldiers and civilians of the period tend to have a stiff, formal air. The subjects fix the camera with a suspicious stare, their faces set in an expressionless mask, guarding their dignity and affirming their status. The airmen look more confident and comfortable in their skins. Sometimes there is even a smile.

One photograph from 1913 shows pilots of "B" Flight, 3 Squadron in their mess at Larkhill aerodrome. The two in the foreground are hunched over a chess board. Behind them, another is placing a disc on a wind-up gramophone. Three more are reading magazines and someone is sitting cross-legged on a couch, smoking a pipe, a banjo propped against the wall next to him. The whole effect is relaxed, stylish and slightly bohemian.

To outsiders the air force gave the impression of being more free-and-easy than the army and navy. On joining, they found that this was something of an illusion. Flying was new, but traditional discipline was imposed on the new recruits arriving from Civvy Street to join the military wing. Sykes agreed to a transfer of some Guards drill officers, whose roars soon echoed around the Aldershot barracks where the recruits were housed. Joubert noted approvingly that "in the end the RFC became an extremely smart and highly efficient corps ... there is no doubt in my mind that the meticulous disciplinary training to which our mechanics were subjected made them more thorough and more reliable in their technical duties."

Nonetheless, fitting, rigging and repairing aircraft and maintaining the engines that powered them was an empirical process. Everything was new. Progress was largely achieved and problems solved by trial and error. It was found that the copper pipes that fed oil and petrol to the engines cracked easily. The constant vibration hastened metal fatigue and regular annealing was required to stop them splitting and catching fire. Eventually, rubber hoses were substituted, but the rubber had a tendency to perish and block the flow.

The principles of flying were still only barely understood. In 1912 very little was known of the science of aerodynamics. Biplanes were more stable than monoplanes, but they were still subject to erratic and inexplicable behaviour, and even relatively experienced pilots still worried about stalling, spinning and nose-diving.

Attempts were made to codify flying drills. Major Charles James Burke, a stout Irishman known behind his back as Pregnant Percy, was the commander of 2 Squadron, which with 3 Squadron formed the first two aeroplane units of the RFC (No. 1 was a balloon squadron). Burke had served in the ranks in the Boer War before joining the Royal Irish Regiment. According to Raleigh, he "was not a good pilot and was most famous for his crashes. He was not a popular officer. He was not what would be called a clever man. But he was single-minded, brave and determined, careless alike of danger and of ridicule."

Burke approached his work with missionary zeal, spreading the word through papers with titles like "Aeroplanes of Today and their Use in War" and recording his thoughts in a booklet of "Maxims". These included such musings as "nothing is ever as good or as bad as it seems," but also practical observations. "Waiting about on an aerodrome has spoilt more pilots than everything else put together," he noted. Thirty years later the pilots of the Battle of Britain would agree that it was waiting at dispersal for the ring of the telephone and the order to scramble that jangled their nerves almost as much as actual combat.

The most pressing task facing those in charge of the new service was to find aeroplanes that were tolerably safe, reasonably reliable and relatively easy to fly. At its birth the RFC had only eleven serviceable aircraft. They were primitive machines capable of climbing only a few hundred feet and travelling at no more than sixty miles an hour. In August 1912 trials were held on

Salisbury Plain to find a higher-quality machine with which to equip the service. The contestants were to demonstrate that their machines could carry out simple manoeuvres, including landing and taking off from a ploughed field. The prize was won by Sam Cody who seems to have benefited from being last in the order, so that by the time he had to perform, the field had been nicely flattened out. His machine, though, was never adopted: the "Cathedral" was neurotically sensitive, particularly on the forward and aft control, and needed its master's touch to stay airborne. After two pilots used to less unstable machines crashed, it was dropped and the RFC adopted instead the BE2, which was already in development at the Royal Aircraft Factory. The letters stood for "Blériot Experimental", in recognition of the fact that it was an adaption of a design by the French pioneer. The modifications were largely the work of Geoffrey de Havilland.

The BE2 certainly looked good. Its upper wing lay further forward on the fuselage than the lower wing, giving it a rakish angle in profile, and the slender tail swelled into a graceful, rounded tailplane. It was considerably more stable than Cody's machine, and would generally fly straight and level without constant adjustments by the pilot. In other respects it was less satisfactory. The Wolseley, then Renault, engines with which the BE2 was equipped were badly underpowered. Later, on the Western Front, if long flights were planned the observer and his gun had to be left behind. The observer's secondary job of defending his aircraft was hampered by his position, forward of the pilot's cockpit, where he was surrounded by struts and wires that cramped his field of fire. The aircraft's improved stability meant it was less prone to sudden involuntary actions. But it also made it less responsive when the pilot did want to change course swiftly, which meant it was slow to take evasive action against more manoeuvrable enemies.

At the time, though, the BE2 seemed like a sound and versatile machine, and 3,500 of them would be built in several variations by a number of manufacturers in the years to come. The Royal Aircraft Factory at Farnborough, nonetheless, continued to produce other types, and by the time hostilities began the RFC was equipped with a plethora of different designs acquired over the early years.

The navy's approach to aviation was more enterprising. In the search for good aircraft they did not restrict themselves to the products of the Farnborough factory and sought out the wares of the private manufacturers like Short, Sopwith and A. V. Roe, springing up around the country, as well as encouraging Rolls Royce production of aero engines. The army believed that the main function of aviation in time of war was reconnaissance. The navy took a more aggressive approach. Airships and aeroplanes could be used against enemy shipping. They were also aware that the enemy would come to the same conclusion. They fitted floats on existing aircraft to create seaplanes and ten bases were set up around the coast, stretching from Anglesey in the west to Dundee in the north, from where they could defend the island and launch attacks against the enemy. Experiments took place in flying aircraft off ships, dropping 100 lb bombs and even torpedoes.

This independent policy reflected the fact that the Admiralty had never accepted that the RFC should have control over affairs that it believed lay firmly within its own domain. In July 1914 this divergence of opinion was formalized with the establishment of the Royal Naval Air Service (RNAS). From now on the RFC would operate solely as the air force of the army, while the RNAS answered to the Admiralty. The two would carry on their separate paths through most of the coming war, complicating the lines of command and competing for resources.

By the time the split was made official Europe was floundering into war. Most of the young aviators welcomed the prospect of action and adventure. Their spirits were dampened, though, as they surveyed the motley array of aircraft they would have to fight in.

"I shall never forget the solemn meeting of No. 3 Squadron when our Squadron Commander, Major [Robert] Brooke-Popham, told us what was expected," wrote Philip Joubert. "Up until then it is unlikely any but the more seriously minded of us young ones . . . had thought very much about war with Germany, but here we were faced with it in the near future and we knew that although we had plenty of energy and confidence, our equipment was woefully bad. There were at least eight different types among the serviceable aircraft, and of those only three were British. The engines were largely of French origin. We had no transport of our own worth mentioning, spares were lamentably deficient and the reserve of pilots and mechanics were derisory."

However, with Lord Kitchener now in charge at the War Office, plans were already under way for a massive expansion. Over the next four years this ragged outfit was to transform itself into the greatest air force in the world.

CHAPTER
TWO

A Wing and a Prayer

As the British Expeditionary Force embarked for France in August 1914, the RFC ranked low among its concerns. The airmen were left to make their own way to the war. There were four formed squadrons: Nos. 2, 3, 4 and 5. Two more — 6 and 7 — were being assembled and No. 1 Squadron was in the process of switching from balloons to aeroplanes. Two squadrons — Nos. 2 and 4 — were equipped with BE2s. The rest flew with the ill-assorted array of machines acquired in the first rush of growth.

The first great test was to get to the battlefield. Between them and the plains of northern France, from where they would operate, lay the English Channel, still a formidable obstacle. When the order came to move to a temporary encampment at Swingate on the cliffs above Dover, the squadrons were scattered around the country. No. 2 Squadron under Burke was in Montrose on the east coast of Scotland and got there without mishap. The journey of No. 3 Squadron, based at the new Netheravon aerodrome on Salisbury Plain, began disastrously. On the morning of 12 August, James McCudden, the former boy bugler who had now joined the RFC's ground staff, swung the propeller of an 80 hp Blériot carrying Lieutenant Bob Skene, a renowned aerobat, and Air Mechanic Keith Barlow, and watched "the machine flying very tail-low until it was lost to view behind our hedge up at about eighty feet".

Then the engine stopped. There was silence, followed by the rending noise of a crash, "which once heard is never forgotten". McCudden "ran for half a mile and found the machine in a small copse of firs, so I got over the fence and pulled the wreckage away from the occupants and found them both dead." Despite all the carnage McCudden was to see in his short life, he wrote later that he would "never forget . . . kneeling by poor Keith Barlow and looking at the rising sun and then again at poor Barlow who had no superficial injury, and was killed purely by concussion, and wondering if war was going to be like this always." Barlow and he had shared a tent earlier that summer while Netheravon was being built and McCudden had found him "an awfully interesting fellow . . . a really genuine soul and moreover a philosopher". Despite the experience, McCudden's determination to move from ground duties to flying was undiminished.

Other mishaps complicated the departure. No. 4 Squadron suffered two non-fatal crashes on the way to Dover. No. 5 Squadron was held up in Gosport and would have to follow later. But at 6.25 on the morning of 13 August the aircraft that had made it began, on schedule, to take off. First away was Lieutenant Hubert Harvey-Kelly, of 2 Squadron, at the controls of a BE2a.

Like a number of the early aviators, "Bay" Harvey-Kelly was of Anglo-Irish stock, hailing from Roscommon in County Mayo, and radiating an insouciance that made him stand out even in the risk-loving company of his peers. He was followed by Burke, who led his men over the French coast, then turned south towards the mouth of the Somme, which pointed them towards their destination, Amiens aerodrome. Harvey-Kelly was determined to touch down first and broke formation to cut across country, arriving at 8.20. The pilots of 2 Squadron all landed safely and by nightfall there were forty-nine aircraft on the base. The local people — who had been in some doubt as to whether the British would come to their aid — gave them an ecstatic welcome.

Henderson was to command the RFC in the field and went to France by boat with his deputy Sykes and the stores and ground staff. They left behind Major William Sefton-Brancker to represent the RFC in the War Office and Trenchard, who, to his intense frustration, was ordered to take over the rear organization, charged with overseeing the planned great expansion and maintaining the flow of equipment and new squadrons to the front. When the headquarters group arrived at Boulogne they, too, received a warm welcome. James McCudden remembered crowds apparently chanting "Live Long and Tear!" He later realized they were shouting *"Vive l'Angleterre!"* On their way to Amiens, whenever they stopped, they were "piled up with fruit and flowers and kissed by pretty French girls".

On 16 August the fliers moved forward to Maubeuge, seventy miles to the north-west on the border with Belgium and about twenty miles south of Mons. They left behind the crocks, including an old Blériot, acquired from the *Daily Mail*, which had been flown around Britain for an advertising stunt and still carried the newspaper's name painted in large letters under the wings. Even so, some of the machines they retained were treacherous. Second Lieutenant Evelyn Copeland Perry of 2 Squadron, an experienced pilot who had taught Trenchard to fly, was climbing away after take-off when his aircraft stalled, appeared to catch fire and plunged to earth, killing him and his passenger, air mechanic Herbert Parfitt. The machine was a BE8, the last of the variations on the Blériot Experimental that emerged from the Aircraft Factory and regarded by those who flew it as a vicious contraption. Another "Bloater", as the pilots called them, belonging to the newly arrived 5 Squadron went down shortly afterwards on the way to Maubeuge, seriously injuring the pilot Lieutenant Bob Smith-Barry and killing Corporal Fred Geard.

Six men were already dead from the tiny force and they had yet to encounter the enemy. The Germans were only forty miles away and the soldiers of the BEF were flooding up the road to Mons to block their path. The airmen spent the next few days checking engines, tuning flying wires, adjusting struts and studying maps, while they waited for the chance to show their worth. Their job was observation and reconnaissance. They had practised it in training on the BE variants that de

Havilland had specifically designed to provide the stability to allow them to note enemy movements and strengths.

On 19 August the RFC received its first order to launch a reconnaissance. The British army had taken up positions along a twenty-five-mile sector around Mons, there to make a stand against the advancing Germans. Any information about enemy dispositions would have a high value. The mission was given to Philip Joubert of 3 Squadron and Lieutenant Gilbert Mapplebeck of 4 Squadron. Liverpool-born "Gibb" Mapplebeck, an unhelpful six-foot three inches tall and not quite twenty-one, was known for his crashes and stunting and had been disciplined for defying a ban on pilots risking their necks and their aircraft by "looping the loop".

They were operating with tiny scale maps and Joubert got lost almost immediately. He was forced to land close to some friendly troops to ask for directions. None of the aviators had been issued with identification documents and it took some time to persuade the soldiers that he was not a spy. He returned with no useful information to impart. Mapplebeck did better, carrying out a limited air search and spotting a small cavalry force at a place where a large concentration was thought to be assembled. It was an uninspiring start.

Flights over the next two days had more success and some German units moving westward towards Mons were located and reported. On Saturday 22 August the squadrons flew twelve missions and this time they were able to build up a clear picture of a large enemy movement which appeared to be attempting to outflank the British line at Mons. This information played an important part in the development of the battle and helped Sir John French in his deliberations as he moved to escape envelopment.

This was a memorable day in other respects. The RFC recorded its first enemy-inflicted loss when the Avro 504 flown by Lieutenant Vincent Waterfall of 5 Squadron, with Lieutenant Gordon Bayly as observer, was brought down by enemy fire just inside Belgium. Bayly was killed, though Waterfall survived to be taken prisoner. Later that day a German aircraft appeared, approaching Maubeuge aerodrome at about 5,000 feet. The sight of the enemy sent the crews racing to intercept. One of the pilots was Louis Arbon Strange, the son of a wealthy Dorset farmer who had shown an immediate natural aptitude for flying and, after obtaining his certificate, had been commissioned directly into the RFC in 1912. He had become convinced early on that aircraft would make viable gun platforms and had mounted a weapon on his machine as an experiment. Now the chance had come to put his theory to the test. He climbed into his Henri Farman with another pilot, Lieutenant Leslie da Costa Penn-Gaskell, whose job was to operate the Lewis gun. It was fixed in the nose, where, as the Farman was a "pusher", there would be a clear field of fire unobstructed by the propeller, which was mounted behind the pilot. The aeroplane was woefully underpowered with a top speed of under 60 mph. By the time it had struggled to 1,000 feet the German was on his way back to his lines. "Its occupants must have enjoyed a good laugh at our futile efforts," Strange recorded wryly. The commander of 5 Squadron, "Josh" Higgins, blamed the weight of the gun for the failure to close on the enemy and the pair were told to use rifles in future.

The British stand at Mons gave way to a long retreat and the RFC fell back with them, setting up makeshift camps at Le Cateau-Cambresis, then St Quentin, then Compiègne, sleeping wherever they stopped, sometimes in a hotel bed, more often in a hayloft or even in the open under the wings of their aircraft. Despite the chaos they managed to maintain a flow of reports to headquarters. The main hazards came from the vagaries of their machines and from ground fire, which rose to greet them indiscriminately no matter which side of the lines they were over. Joubert described later and without rancour "the playful habit of the British soldier of firing at everything that flew, regardless of its appearance and nationality". The French troops were no more fastidious and in the early days the crews were as much at risk from friend as they were from foe.

Their duties did not prevent them from trying whenever possible to take the war to the enemy. On 25 August Lieutenant Euan Rabagliati, the short, energetic Yorkshire-born son of a prominent nutritionist, was flying as observer at 3–4,000 feet with his pilot Lieutenant C. W. Wilson — known as "Daddy" on account of his venerable thirty-seven years — when they sighted a German Taube monoplane in the distance. They had already encountered several enemy aircraft, but the Germans appeared to be under orders to avoid combat and stick to their reconnaissance duties. Rabagliati recorded that "this chap stayed and we immediately joined in and manoeuvred around". Rabagliati was armed with a service rifle. The German appeared to have a Mauser pistol with a shoulder stock. Wilson manoeuvred their Avro "tractor" into a position where his observer could get in a shot.

"Sometimes we'd be extremely close, it seemed to be almost touching," Rabagliati remembered. "Other times we'd be out of range. We couldn't shoot through the propeller in front so we had to shoot sideways." He "knew nothing whatever about the question of lay-off" — the science of shooting ahead of your opponent so he flew into your fire. "Not only was the other aeroplane going fast, but our own aeroplane from which I was shooting was also going fast . . . it was a purely hit-and-miss effort."

They circled each other, blazing away, with Rabagliati firing a hundred rounds. Then, "suddenly, to my intense joy, I saw the pilot fall forward on his joy stick and the machine tipped up and went down. I knew that either I had hit him or something had happened. We were of course completely thrilled. We'd had our duel and we'd won! We watched him going down. We circled round and he finally crashed."

The pilot escaped with his life. Nonetheless, this probably counts as the first dogfight fought by British fliers. It would be repeated tens of thousands of times over the coming years, in this war and the next. It was a form of combat that had disappeared from the terrestrial battlefield. It seemed to herald a return to classical times with champions pitted against each other, but now relying on skill, mixed with luck, rather than strength to bring their opponent down. You feel in Rabagliati's account his mouth drying, his senses sharpening as he realizes he is engaged in what could be a duel to the death. In the conduct of this first engagement are many of the elements of all the dogfights that followed: the tightly circling, high-speed chase as each pilot tries to get a bead on the other, the jinking and manoeuvring, the shifting of advantage and then the moment of victory, as definitive as the slump of the bull's head as the torero's sword pierces his spinal nerve.

Even with the puny ordnance at their disposal, the crews were also determined to inflict any damage they could on the streams of field-grey uniforms pouring along the roads below. They carried improvised petrol bombs and bundles of fourteen-inch-long steel darts called flechettes to shower on any troops they encountered. During the retreat, Eric Conran, an Australian subaltern with 3 Squadron, had James McCudden fit his Blériot "Parasol" monoplane — an oddity among the biplanes — with wooden racks to carry hand grenades. While on reconnaissance he noticed two German columns converging on a main road. He dived down over the closely packed men and horses and showered them with bombs, then flew off leaving a chaotic scene filled with angry soldiers and plunging animals.

It was the routine business of observation and reconnaissance that gave the RFC its *raison d'être*, however, and when the retreat was over General French gave fulsome recognition to the role the Corps and its commander, Henderson, had played in enabling his forces to escape.

"Their skill, energy and perseverance have been beyond all praise," he wrote in his despatch. "They have furnished me with the most complete and accurate information which has been of incalculable value in the conduct of operations. Fired at constantly both by friend and foe, and not hesitating to fly in every kind of weather, they have remained undaunted throughout."

Within a few weeks the RFC had established a fighting posture that it would maintain through the long years of what soon felt like an interminable war. Whatever the odds, whatever the weather, it was committed to answering every call the army issued. Part of the airmen's determination stemmed from the desire of newcomers — still regarded as upstarts in some quarters — to prove their worth. But it also reflected their sympathy for their earthbound comrades whose plight they saw with bitter clarity from what seemed like the relative safety of the air. The aviators felt themselves privileged and, in the months ahead, even pampered as they settled down in comfortable bases, while the soldiers endured the squalor of the trenches. It was a perception they never lost sight of, even when the demands placed on them by the generals brought appalling casualties.

In early September the German breakthrough was halted at the Battle of the Marne. Again, the reconnaissance reports of the RFC helped the Allies analyse German movements and guide their reactions. But the Allied counter-attack launched immediately afterwards failed after a few days. The war of manoeuvre was over and the armies began digging in along a line that by the end of November stretched, with a few gaps, from Nieuport in the north to the Swiss border. The war had changed decisively. It was stuck in the mud of Flanders and henceforth would be a ghastly battle of attrition that would define the future function of the air force.

It was clear that the RFC had an important, possibly crucial, part to play in the land war. The same could not be said of the Royal Naval Air Service and the war at sea. In August 1914 the War Office had insisted on control of the country's air defences, even though almost all of its aircraft were already earmarked for France. At the Admiralty, the First Lord, Winston Churchill, took advantage of the army's predicament to move in. Soon the Royal Naval Air Service had taken over the responsibility and a rudimentary aerial defence system was put in place. The RNAS set up a string of seaplane bases in east coast ports, facing Germany. In early September the army grudgingly accepted the situation and — for the time being at least — ceded the air over Britain to the navy.

The admirals' conviction that the special needs of the navy made close co-operation with the army impossible had led them to ignore the amalgamation the creation of the RFC was supposed to bring about, and had carried on their own course, training their own pilots and buying their own aircraft. Such was their power and political prestige that their disobedience went unpunished and was accepted as a fait accompli with the official recognition of the RNAS in July 1914. The navy's headstrong attitude, however, was not easy to justify. Wresting control of the domestic air space from the army was an empty victory, as in the first months of the war the German air force stayed away. Effort concentrated instead on how to put the navy's aeroplanes to use at sea. Flight brought huge potential advantages to the prosecution of naval warfare. In theory, aircraft could carry out reconnaissance from ships at sea, launch offensive and defensive operations against hostile aircraft and bases, attack enemy weak points on the ground and patrol the seas in search of enemy forces, in particular submarines. Huge logistical and mechanical problems had to be overcome, however, before the simplest tasks could be attempted.

Navy aviators were nonetheless innovative and daring. It was the RNAS that carried out the first offensive action by British fliers, a bold if ineffective attack launched on 22 September 1914 from its base at Ostend against the Zeppelin sheds at Dusseldorf. On 8 October, having fallen back to Dunkirk, the navy tried again. This time Flight Lieutenant Reggie Marix, aboard a Sopwith Tabloid, succeeded in dropping a couple of bombs on a hangar. They were tiny, weighing only twenty pounds each, but the results were sensational. Inside the shed was a just-completed

Zeppelin and the explosions ignited the hydrogen, generating a fireball that leapt 500 feet.

Another big operation was in the planning. Four Avro 504s were dismantled, shipped to Le Havre, then driven to an airstrip at Belfort on the Swiss — French border. On the freezing morning of 20 November, three of them set off to bomb the Zeppelin factory, 120 miles away, at Friedrichshafen on Lake Constance in southern Germany. Once again the results were impressive. A hydrogen-generating plant erupted, workshops were blown up and an airship badly damaged, delighting Winston Churchill, who described it as "a fine feat of arms".

This was another land-based effort and the RNAS could be said to be encroaching on operational space that logically belonged to the RFC — although at this time the army had no interest in long-range bombing. Then, on Christmas Eve 1914, the RNAS launched another imaginative operation that pushed the boundaries of the new technology and provided a glimpse of where the combination of warplanes and warships could lead. At the heart of the operation were three ships — *Engadine*, *Riviera* and *Empress*. They were large, fast, cross-channel ferries that had been converted into seaplane carriers. They set sail from Harwich at 5p.m., escorted by two cruisers, ten destroyers and ten submarines. Their destination was a point forty miles off the Friesian island of Wangerooge. From there, the nine Short "Folders" on board the carriers were to set off to bomb the Zeppelin sheds at Cuxhaven. The airships were not the primary target, however. The main intention was to lure at least some of the German High Seas Fleet lying at Wilhelmshaven, just down the coast to the south, out into the North Sea where battle could be joined.

The mission began in the icy dawn of Christmas Day. In the freezing conditions, two aeroplanes failed to start and the others sputtered along on misfiring engines towards the target. The clear conditions quickly gave way to dense cloud and the pilots failed to see the objective, let alone bomb it. On the way back they dropped a few bombs on ships moored in the Schillig Roads off Wilhelmshaven, then tried to rejoin the fleet at a pick-up position off the island of Borkum. It was a hugely perilous exercise. Fuel was running low and four of the aeroplanes that had been hit by anti-aircraft fire had to ditch. By a stroke of luck three landed near a submarine, but the rescue was interrupted by the arrival of a Zeppelin, which proceeded to bomb. One of the raiders was picked up by a destroyer and two more by the carriers. Another put down near a Dutch merchantman. Astonishingly, no one was killed in the operation. Although the mission had failed in its aims it had nonetheless been an important event. The episode had demonstrated that ships could work with aircraft to project force in a way that land-based aeroplanes at that time could not. This development was in keeping with the underlying principle of British sea power, that by possession of a large navy, a small island was able to amass wealth and power, while enhancing its own security by its ability to hit its enemies at long range.

The significance of what had happened was clear to the man who planned the raid, Squadron Commander Cecil L'Estrange Malone. "I look upon the events which took place on 25 December as a visible proof of the probable line of developments of the principles of naval strategy," he wrote in his official report. "One can imagine what might have been done had our seaplanes, or those sent to attack us, carried torpedoes instead of light bombs. Several of the ships in Schillig Roads would have been torpedoed and some of our force might have been sunk as well." L'Estrange-Malone, a remarkable figure who would go on to become Britain's first Communist MP, had grasped that at some point, the success or failure, in fact the very survival of a naval force, would depend on the strength and efficiency of its air forces and air defences.

That time was still some way off. The Cuxhaven raid was not repeated. Instead the RNAS would soon be preoccupied with one of its consequences. The fright that the Germans had received produced a strengthening of the anti-aircraft batteries around ports and bases, but also persuaded them to press ahead with air attacks on England. Rather than wait for long-range aeroplanes capable of doing the job, it was decided to use Zeppelins, and when the raids began early in the New Year it was naval pilots who had the task of hunting them down.

The results of the attacks on the Zeppelin sheds did not justify the effort and expenditure of manpower and resources that went into them. It was accepted that there might be future benefits in developing what was essentially a doctrine of strategic air warfare, but for the time being they were theoretical. The army's needs were obvious and pressing. It was inevitable that in the battle for resources the RNAS would lose out.

With the Western Front frozen it was clear that the war would not be over by Christmas. Many more soldiers would be needed. The British Expeditionary Force began to swell, and at the end of December divided into First Army, under Haig, and Second Army, under Sir Horace Lockwood Dorrien-Smith, while in Britain the War Minister, Lord Kitchener, issued a call for volunteers that brought tens of thousands flooding in. If the RFC was to do its job it would have to match the expansion. Plans were made for fifty new squadrons — more than ten times the number that had gone to France in August. Its structure was reorganized to harmonize with the new army arrangements. The squadrons were now divided into wings, which were teamed with the First and Second armies, with the expectation that there would be many more to follow.

CHAPTER
THREE

Archie

By the spring of 1915 the life of a British aviator on the Western Front had settled into a steady, if hazardous, routine. The first squadrons operated mainly from the aerodrome at St Omer, just inland from Calais, where the RFC set up its headquarters and which would remain its home in France until the end of the war. The fliers lived surrounded by a much larger force of ground staff and administrators. Maurice Baring, in peacetime an urbane man of letters who served as Henderson's aide-decamp, remembered "a stuffy office, full of clerks and candles and a deafening noise of typewriters", with a "constant stream of pilots arriving in the evening in Burberries with maps, talking over reconnaissances". The two-man teams of pilot and observer could expect to make two trips a day over enemy lines, usually to carry out the photographic reconnaissances which were becoming the norm, or spotting for the artillery batteries whose bombardments made up the main business of war in between "pushes".

The day began with the crew, insulated against the extreme cold of high flying in an open cockpit by layers of leather, fur and wool, climbing into their aeroplane. A mechanic swung the big, double-bladed wooden propeller, the engine coughed, spurted a plume of dirty exhaust smoke and the machine trundled out onto the grass field to take off. The prevailing wind was westerly. On the outward journey it whisked the aeroplane rapidly towards the German lines. On the return, if blowing hard, it could slow progress to what felt like a standstill.

There was less to fear now from friendly fire on the way to no-man's-land. The Germans were the first to identify their aircraft with large black crosses on white grounds and the Allies soon followed suit.

"We tried to decide on some kind of mark for our own," remembered air mechanic Cecil King. "Well the first thing was, they painted Union Jacks on the underneath of the plane, but that just looked like a smudge. Then they tried painting a bar, but that didn't seem much. Then we painted the target, as we used to call it [and] there was no more firing at our own machines." The "target" of concentric blue-and-white rings with a red bullseye became known as the "roundel" and soon symbol of Britishness.

The main hazard now was anti-aircraft fire. The shells could reach 10,000 feet and burst in the air, rather than on impact, as did the much-derided British ordnance. The aviators called it "ack-ack" (from the phonetic alphabet for AA or anti-aircraft) or "Archie". The latter name seems to have been the invention of Lieutenant Amyas "Biffy" Borton of 5 Squadron. According to his account, on 19 September 1914 he was on a reconnaissance flight west of Soissons with his observer Lieutenant R. E. Small. They were aware that a four-gun anti-aircraft battery was located in a quarry just north of the town.

"Over the town I turned into the wind and at once saw four flashes from the quarry," Borton remembered. "I turned forty-five degrees and drifted to the left and in due course up came four bursts to my right front, where I should have been had I not altered course. The next time they fired I repeated the manoeuvre to the right and the shells burst harmlessly to my left front. There was a music-hall song at the time called, 'Archibald, Certainly Not!'[1] My observer and I sang it each time the ruse was successful."

"Archie" affected aviators in different ways. By early 1915 McCudden had been promoted to corporal and had begun accompanying pilots on missions. He was flying with Eric Conran at 8,000 feet over Violanes when he "heard a c-r-r-r-mp, then another then another, and looking above we saw several balls of white smoke floating away. The pilot turned to mislead Archie, of whom I was having my first bad experience. However, I can honestly say that I did not feel any more than a certain curiosity as to where the next one was going to burst."

---

[1] This song was a favourite of the singer and actor George Robey. It is about an errant husband who is stopped by his wife from leaping, unclothed, into the water to save his paramour "Miss Hewitt".

This seems a remarkably cool reaction. Trundling at a top speed of little over 70 mph it was easy for a battery, once it had found its range, to keep up with its prey. "Marsh and myself went on reconnaissance at dawn and were told to have a look right into Wervicq [just north of Lille]," recorded Captain Harold Wyllie of 4 Squadron. "Before we could say knife, a battery of guns opened on us from two sides. The shells were bursting under, over and on both sides . . . I never could have believed it possible to be under such fire and survive. The noise was deafening and the air full of smoke." The pair made for home after being hit six times by bullets and shell splinters.

Many did not mind admitting that the experience rattled them badly. Comparing the accounts of airmen in the First and Second World Wars one is struck by the greater willingness of the pioneers to acknowledge fear.

"I wonder how long my nerves will stand this almost daily bombardment by 'Archie'," wrote Lieutenant William Read of 3 Squadron. "I notice several people's nerves are not as strong as they used to be and I am sure 'Archie' is responsible for a good deal. I would not mind so much if I were in a machine that was fast and that would climb a little more willingly. Today we both had a good dressing down by 'Archibald' and some of the shells burst much too near and I could hear the pieces of shell whistling past — and they have to burst very close for one to be able to hear the shrieking of loose bits of shell above the noise of one's engine. Well, well, I suppose the end will be pretty sharp and quick if one of Archie's physic-balls catches one. I think I would rather it caught me than crumple up Henri [his Henri Farman aeroplane], because one would have too long to think when falling from 4,000 feet."

There were several ways to die in an aeroplane. All must have shared Read's view that death by bullet or shrapnel was the best. The alternatives, burning up or a long, conscious descent to collision with the earth, did not bear too much reflection. Grotesque accidents abounded. Captain George Pretyman of 3 Squadron was returning from a reconnaissance when his aeroplane was rocked by turbulence. He looked behind to check on his observer only to see that the seat was empty. When Pretyman looked down, his comrade was turning somersaults on his way earthwards.

Had the unfortunate man been equipped with a parachute he could simply have floated to safety, but although parachutes were issued to balloon observers (and German airmen) they were not given to British aviators. One explanation that gained credence among the fliers themselves was that the authorities decided against doing so as it was felt that air crew might be tempted to abandon their aircraft in an emergency before it was absolutely necessary. Another explanation is that the parachutes used in balloons were crude affairs, jerked open by a fixed line when the observer jumped. They would not have worked for anyone trying to leave a stricken aeroplane spinning earthwards out of control. It was not until 1919 that Leslie Irvin invented — and tested himself — a reliable free-fall parachute that a man could activate once clear of his aircraft.

Once over enemy lines the work began. Reconnaissance missions no longer relied on the observer making sketches of earthworks, new roads and railway lines or anything else that revealed the enemy's intentions. The value of aerial photography had been recognized early on and after some initial experiments a small photographic section unit was established in January 1915 under Lieutenant John Moore-Brabazon. They designed a camera for air use, a cumbersome wood-and-brass box. Initially it was operated by the observer, hanging over the side of the cockpit and holding onto the straps, but later it was fixed to the side of the fuselage or mounted over a hole cut in the floor. Despite the difficulties of operating it, by early February the German front line facing the First Army sector had been photographed in meticulous detail.

The other principal duty was spotting for the artillery — identifying enemy guns and correcting the fire of friendly batteries. Once again, new technology greatly improved efficiency. Klaxons blaring Morse-code messages from on high and coloured flares fired from a Very pistol gave way to wireless telegraphy. The rapid development of air to ground co-ordination was largely due to two Royal Engineer lieutenants, Donald Lewis and Bron James, who pioneered the technique, each flying solo to leave room for the wireless equipment that weighed as much as a small man. The apparatus could transmit but not receive, so signals were acknowledged by placing coloured strips of cloth on the ground next to the battery.

At first they tapped out terse instructions in Morse code with one hand, while flying with the other. "Fire ... fire ... fire again ... a little short ... range OK ... you have hit them" ran a typical sequence. It required considerable sangfroid to keep this up while Archie was bursting all around and both men were eventually killed while at work in the air. Before they died a more accurate means of directing fire had been invented, using a squared map and a "clock code" that told a battery commander with some precision where his shells were falling.

A specialist wireless squadron, No. 9, was created under the command of Captain Hugh Dowding, a gunner who had developed an interest in aviation and transferred to the RFC in August 1914. The bright plumage of so many early airmen has obscured the presence of a significant number of more sombre figures in their ranks. The public face of the air force was provided by the gallant, the dashing and the colourful, who seemed to belong in the pages of the historical adventure books that British lads were brought up on, filled with tales of knights and highwaymen. Behind them, however, stood a faceless cohort of thoroughly twentieth-century men, without whom the RFC would not have grown so rapidly in size and importance.

Dowding belonged firmly in this category. He was a schoolmaster's son, a solitary man who approached duties and difficulties with Wykehamist intellectual rigour and an unshakeable belief in the rightness of his views. He shared this trait with Trenchard — though this did not prevent them falling out and, indeed, probably encouraged it. Dowding's stubborn convictions, arrived at after great thought, would steer Britain safely through the preparations for and conduct of its existential struggle twenty-six years later.

For both, the RFC had provided a providential opportunity to display their worth and talents. The transformation in Trenchard's fortunes was astounding. Two years before he had been a no-hoper heading for the military scrap heap. Now he was a coming man, highly regarded by his shrewd superior, Henderson. In November he got his wish and left the vital but tedious task of overseeing the expansion to go to France to command No. 1 Wing, working alongside Haig and his First Army. Trenchard sensed his moment had come, his rendezvous with destiny. His guiding principle was that "no call from the army must ever find the RFC wanting" and he drove his men and machines to their limits to achieve it. An early test came in 1915 with the Battle of Neuve Chapelle, the first big British push of the spring, designed to drive the Germans out of the Neuve Chapelle salient, which was thought to be only lightly defended.

Haig summoned Trenchard and revealed how important he regarded the role that the air element would play in the forthcoming battle. According to Trenchard's account, Haig told him: "I shall expect you to tell me before the attack whether you can fly, because on your being able to observe for the artillery, and carry out reconnaissance, the battle will partly depend. If you can't fly because of the weather, I shall probably put off the attack."

The aeroplanes did fly and on 10 March 1915 the operation went ahead, but with little result for all the effort expended — a pattern that would soon become depressingly familiar. The episode, though, confirmed how far the RFC had come since its arrival. Then it had been little more than a curiosity which might or might not bring some advantage. Now, seven months later, it was unthinkable that any major operation would take place without aircraft being involved.

At the meeting the airmen had been given another task. They were detailed on the day of the attack to carry out a couple of bombing raids on targets behind the lines to disrupt any attempt to rush in reinforcements. Expectations of what attack from the air could achieve were ludicrously high. Only three aeroplanes were allotted to the first operation and two for the second. The first flight took off at dawn for a chateau, six miles east of Neuve Chapelle, that was thought to house the enemy headquarters. It was led by Eric Conran, the Australian who had pelted German troops with hand grenades in the first weeks of the war. James McCudden often flew with him, but this time he was left behind and sitting in the observer's seat was Major John Salmond who had just arrived to take command of 3 Squadron.

"They bombed the château with great success from a height of a few feet," McCudden recorded. "Captain Conran's description when he returned of some fat old Landsturmers [reservists] running up a road, firing rifles without taking aim, was very funny, but the Morane was badly shot about, and a bullet had passed exactly between the pilot and the passenger at right angles to the line of flight." It was, he reflected "hard to decide who was more lucky."

In fact, Salmond had the closer shave. He had felt a blow to his stomach and imagined himself shot. On landing he discovered the bullet had passed through his clothing. When Trenchard heard about the escapade he wrote to Salmond: "You are splendid, but don't do it again; I can't afford to lose you."

Conran was unperturbed by this or any other escapade. He seemed to be nerveless and to have an insatiable appetite for adventure. It could only end one way. McCudden remembered how, less than a week after the raid on the château, Conran and a Lieutenant Woodiwiss "went out to drop some bombs [just south-west of Lille] . . . they arrived back in forty minutes and as they were landing I noticed some flying wires dangling and a stream of petrol running from the machine. I ran to the Morane and found Captain Conran badly wounded in the back and the arm . . . one shrapnel ball had embedded itself in his right arm and the other had gone in at his side and come out very near his spine. The machine . . . was literally riddled with shrapnel and how the observer escaped unhurt I do not know." Conran survived, but it was the end of his combat flying career. The luck of Woodiwiss did not hold. In May, together with Lieutenant Denys Corbett Wilson, a prewar playboy who had been the first man to fly the Irish Sea, he was shot down in flames over Fournes.

The second raid was launched in the afternoon, by two veterans — Louis Strange of 6 Squadron and George Carmichael of 5 Squadron. Strange was in a BE2c loaded with three bombs weighing less than 25 lbs hanging under the wings on racks, which he was to drop on Courtrai railway station. Carmichael piloted a Martinsyde biplane, carrying a single 100 lb bomb and his target was a railway junction at Menin. Strange came in low, below 200 feet, and was peppered by ground fire as he closed on the station. A troop train was waiting at the platform and his stick of bombs landed around it, killing, an agent reported later, seventy-five soldiers. Carmichael also managed to land his bomb on target, but with less effect.

Strange's success perhaps reinforced exaggerated notions of what bombing could achieve, for six weeks later a single aeroplane was once again sent to bomb the Courtrai rail junction, to disrupt the movement of tens of thousands of troops who were believed to be about to arrive there prior to an offensive to drive the British out of the Ypres salient. The pilot was Will Rhodes-Moorhouse of 2 Squadron, who, on the afternoon of 24 April, set off from Merville aerodrome in a BE, flying solo to make room for the single 112 lb bomb he was carrying. He flew in and dropped his bomb at 300 feet, but was caught in a blizzard of small-arms fire. Although wounded badly, he nursed his bullet-riddled machine back to Merville to gasp out his report to Trenchard. A few hours later he died.

Rhodes-Moorhouse's heroism won him the Victoria Cross, the first of eleven won by RFC personnel during the war. He left behind a fifteen-month-old son, also William, who earned his pilot's licence while still at Eton, joined 601 Auxiliary Squadron, flew from Merville aerodrome during the Battle of France in 1940 and, like his father, died in combat, shot down over Kent during the Battle of Britain with eight "kills" to his credit.

Aviators reacted differently to the perpetual risk and danger. An airman could sink into introspection or assume a mask of manly indifference to death. Some of the greatest aces of the war, like Mick Mannock, did both. But collectively, the RFC developed an ethos of defiance that sought to draw the sting of death, cultivating a lively fatalism that mocked the thing we most fear in a manner that even at this distance in time is both exhilarating and profoundly moving.

The pre-war pioneers had already expressed this spirit in a song called "The Dying Airman". One of the verses runs:

> Who dreads to the dust returning?
> Who shrinks from the sable shore,
> Where the high and the lofty yearning
> Of the soul shall be no more?
> But stand by your glasses, steady!
> This world is a world of woe,
> Here's a toast to the dead already
> Three cheers for the next man to go.

69

The words would ring out defiantly at the end of boozy evenings in mess and estaminet for the duration of the war, a magnificent "Up yours!" to the Grim Reaper as he sharpened his scythe in preparation for the next day's harvest.

The offensives of the spring and summer of 1915 confirmed the paramount importance of artillery in the struggle. Guns pulverized the battlefield day and night, obliterating the woods and churning the fields into a cratered moonscape. To escape the bombardments the soldiers dug trenches and dugouts, ever deeper and more elaborate. There they hid until the guns stopped long enough for them to stagger forward to seize a few yards of territory. In this form of warfare, close knowledge of your enemy's fortifications and the ability to shell accurately were essential to any success. By the middle of 1915 the air forces of both sides were struggling to expand to meet the demand for information. Many of the surviving veterans were sent back to act as instructors at the flying schools now generating a stream of often poorly prepared greenhorns. They filled the ranks of the five new RFC wings created between March and November 1915.

The growing importance of aircraft led both sides to reconsider their strategies. They arrived at the same, inevitable, conclusion. If they could drive their opponents from the skies, they would deprive them of what had become a vital component of modern warfighting and the balance would tilt in their favour.

To do so, they could not rely on anti-aircraft artillery alone. What was needed was a means of destroying

70

hostile aircraft in the air. From 1915 onwards the Allies and the Germans competed in a fierce technological race to develop aeroplanes and weapons that would give them the edge in aerial combat. For the rest of the war the seesaw of advantage would tip one way, then the other, as each side absorbed and adapted to each new advance in the science of aerial violence.

Increased engine power and the development of lighter weaponry meant that during 1915 rifles and revolvers were abandoned in favour of machine guns. Firing them accurately, however, was extremely difficult and dangerous. In a two-seater "tractor" aircraft like the BE2, shooting in the direction the pilot was flying was severely restricted by the arc of the propeller. The observer had to take great care not to hit the struts and spars, and the buffeting wind constantly threatened to tear the weapon from his hands. Any success depended on an understanding of "deflection" shooting — the art of calculating where to aim the stream of bullets to take account of your enemy's speed and direction as well as your own.

The Martinsyde S3 single-seater biplane, which carried a forward-firing .303 Lewis gun mounted on the top wing, put in a brief appearance in 1915. It was faster than the BE2s, but also inherently unstable. When one arrived at 6 Squadron it was given to Louis Strange, the innovator who had already tried unsuccessfully to mount a machine gun in a Farman. One day, while off on a hunting expedition, he spotted an Aviatik reconnaissance machine. The two-seater was no greyhound, but the weight and drag of the Lewis gun meant the Martinsyde was even slower and as Strange climbed to attack, his quarry drew away. In his frustration he fired off an entire drum of ammunition and turned for home. He was now twenty miles over the German lines. He needed to reload to defend himself from attack. He put his hand up to unclip the magazine, but it was stuck fast and the wind made it hard to get a grip. He throttled back and lifted the nose to reduce speed. Still it would not budge. Strange stood up in the cockpit and began wrenching at the drum. As he did, the Martinsyde tilted to port and slid sideways, knocking Strange off his feet and onto the joystick. The machine flipped upside down. Strange was now hanging by both hands from the drum, and praying fervently that it remained jammed, while the Martinsyde trundled along upside down, 9,000 feet above the ground. Swaddled in thick flying gear and battered by the wind, he somehow managed to haul himself up and hook his legs over the inverted upper wing. The shift of weight sent the aircraft into a spin. As it tipped into a downward spiral Strange tumbled back into the cockpit. One nightmarish predicament was replaced by another. He was hurtling earthwards and there was no agreed technique for recovering from a spinning aeroplane. Whatever it was that Strange did to the controls it worked. Somewhere between 1,500 feet and the ground he pulled out and, trembling with exertion and nerves, flew home at tree-top level.

Strange's 6 Squadron comrade Lanoe Hawker demonstrated that, with the limited technology available, it was possible for a pilot to shoot down enemy aircraft. He was an outstandingly courageous flyer who was also equipped with an inventive technological brain. Present in Hawker's make-up were some of the complexities that would show up again and again in the personalities of the aces of this war and the next. He was exceptionally combative, relishing any opportunity to get to grips with the enemy, yet when he scored a victory his excitement was tempered with sympathy for his victim. He had transferred from the Royal Engineers to the RFC, arriving in France in October 1914, and flew numerous reconnaissance missions before being wounded in the foot by ground fire during the fighting around Ypres. He resumed duty just as a new fast type, the single-seater Bristol "Scout", started to arrive in France and one was assigned to each squadron. The Scout could reach 90 mph in straight and level flight, nearly twenty miles an hour faster than a BE2, and climb to 6,500 feet in ten minutes — twice as rapidly as most RFC machines. In addition it was nimbler than the stolid Air Factory products which had made a virtue of stability, sacrificing the manoeuvrability that increasingly would be the key to both success and survival.

Hawker got his hands on 6 Squadron's Bristol and together with Air Mechanic Ernest Elton devised a way of fitting a Lewis machine gun to the port side of the fuselage, so that it could fire forward obliquely at an angle that avoided the risk of smashing the propeller to pieces. He alternated routine reconnaissance and artillery shoots with hunting missions seeking out enemy aircraft. On his first outings he managed to see off some intruders without succeeding in shooting them down, though he was delighted with the Scout ("a little beauty") and it was "quite exciting, diving at 120 miles an hour and firing a machine gun". Then, on the early evening of 25 July, he was over Passchendaele when he ran into three German aircraft and shot them down in quick succession. The feat won him the Victoria Cross. By the time he was sent home for a rest in September 1915 he had been credited with seven confirmed "kills". This made him the first British air force "ace", though official distaste for publicizing the feats of one man over those of his comrades meant that his fame, for the time being, was confined to the RFC.

There were few pilots with Hawker's skill. The business of air fighting became easier, however, with the arrival of biplane "pusher" type aircraft, like the Vickers FB5, known as the "gunbus", with the propeller mounted in the rear. This enabled the observer to perch in the nose of the aircraft behind a pillar-mounted Lewis gun, with a clear field of fire. The Gunbus was supplemented by another pusher, the DH2, which bore the initials of its designer Geoffrey de Havilland. It was a single-seater and equipped a new squadron, No. 24, commanded by Hawker.

In the summer of 1915 the British air force seemed to be at least holding its own in the battle for the air. Improved machines were arriving at the front, as well as a supply of new airmen — though the training they received was a poor preparation for operational realities. The engine of expansion was turning, albeit rather slowly — there were still only twelve squadrons in France at the start of the autumn. Above all there was energy and purpose, emanating in pulsing waves from the inarticulate but passionate figure of Trenchard, who had taken command of the RFC in the field in August when Henderson went back to London to become Director General of Military Aeronautics. "Boom" Trenchard would remain in charge for most of the rest of the war, driving the new force forward, stretching and exposing his men and machines, with a fervour that impressed all, while at times seeming to border on the inhuman.

The life-and-death demands of war forced the pace of technological innovation. As the summer progressed, a new development emerged that was to alter the balance dramatically in the enemy's favour. It ushered in a period of the air war that became known as the "Fokker menace" and it began in an almost accidental fashion. Roland Garros was a French aerial trailblazer, the first man to fly the Mediterranean. In 1915 he and the designer Raymond Saulnier set about trying to solve the problem of how to fit a machine gun to an aeroplane that could be fired straight ahead without the gymnastics required to operate a wing-fixed weapon. The main difficulty seemed to be the obstacle presented by the whirring propeller, oscillating at 2,000 revolutions a minute. But the pair decided that, unlikely though it might seem, most of the bullets could pass through its arc without striking the twin blades. Those that did hit could be deflected without doing damage by fitting wedge-shaped metal plates.

On 1 April Garros tried out a prototype and promptly shot down a two-seater. In the next seventeen days he repeated the performance twice. The device was fitted to other aircraft and other pilots repeated his success. Then Garros was shot down. He was too late to set fire to his machine and the wonder gadget fell into German hands. The propeller was handed over to a Dutch aircraft designer, Anthony Fokker, who was working with the Germans. On examining it they were reminded of a pre-war patent — which almost incredibly had been overlooked — for a synchronized gun with an interrupter gear, which timed the stream of bullets so they passed through the spaces between the blades. They revived it and tested it. It worked. The deflector plates became instantly obsolete.

Fokker developed a new aeroplane, the Eindecker E1 monoplane, on which to mount the new weapon system. Now a pilot had only to point his machine in the direction of his enemy to threaten him. Fokker had developed what was, in effect, a flying gun — the first efficient fighter aeroplane. The first few Fokker Eindeckers or E1s began to appear in July 1915, operating in pairs as defensive escorts for patrol aircraft. It was a little while before the Germans realized their offensive capability. It was pilots, rather than commanders, who grasped their potential. They were led by Oswald Boelcke, who had worked with another soon-to-be famous airman Max Immelman, with Fokker on the development of the E1.

Historians later claimed that despite its reputation the Eindecker was nothing special. However, Ira Jones, a young Welsh mechanic who went on to fly with 56 ("Tiger") Squadron and was credited with shooting down forty enemy aircraft, saw it in action and had a due respect for its qualities. It was a "fast, good climbing, strong-structured, highly manoeuvrable aeroplane — all essential qualities of an efficient fighting machine. When flown by such masterly, determined pilots as Boelcke and Immelmann it was almost invincible." During the autumn British pilots came to fear these two names.

Max Immelman was born into a family of wealthy industrialists in Dresden. He perfected a manoeuvre of diving, climbing and flicking over, ready to attack again, which became known as the "Immelmann turn". Oswald Boelcke was the son of a militaristic schoolmaster. He overcame childhood asthma to become an excellent sportsman. He was as diligent in the classroom as on the playing field, and most enjoyed mathematics. According to Johnny Johnson, one of the great British aces of the next conflict, he was "a splendid fighter pilot, an outstanding leader and a tactician of rare quality . . . his foes held him in high regard." Boelcke brought a scientific coolness to air fighting, codifying tactics in a book called the *Dicta Boelcke*. He laid down four basic principles: (1) the higher your aeroplane, the greater your advantage; (2) attack with the sun behind you, so you are invisible to your opponent; (3) use cloud to hide in; and (4) get in as close as possible. They sound simple, but in the sudden chaos that characterized fights, these rules were easily forgotten.

For all his professionalism he enjoyed the kill, as is apparent from his description of the downing of an unsuspecting Vickers "Gunbus". Boelcke was flying at 3,500 feet when he saw the enemy aircraft fly over the lines at Arras and head for Cambrai. He crept in behind it unseen and followed for a while. His fingers were "itching to shoot", but he controlled himself.

"[I] withheld my fire until I was within 60 metres of him," he wrote afterwards. "I could plainly see the observer in the front seat peering out downward. Knack-knack-knack . . . went my gun. Fifty rounds, and then a long flame shot out of his engine. Another fifty rounds at the pilot. Now his fate was sealed. He went down in long spirals to land. Almost every bullet of my first series went home. Elevator, rudder, wings, engine, tank and control wires were shot up." Surprisingly, both the pilot, Captain Charles Darley, and the observer, Lieutenant R. J. Slade, survived.

As the war entered a new year, it was vital to come up with a means of countering the German challenge if the British and French air forces were not to be cleared from the skies. Trenchard was determined that patrols should continue despite the threat. His solution was to provide a cluster of escorts for each reconnaissance flight. The method soaked up resources. On one flight, on 7 February 1916, a single BE2C from 12 Squadron took off, accompanied by twelve other aircraft. The approach was unsustainable.

Eventually Allied technology came up with an antidote to the Fokker and the menace subsided. In the spring of 1916 the trim French Nieuport 11, nicknamed the "Bébé", began to arrive on British squadrons. Its Lewis gun was fixed on the top wing, but it was more agile than the E1 and good pilots could get the better of it. The "Bébé" was joined by another French type, produced by the French firm JPAD, which carried a synchronized Vickers gun. The second-generation pusher types — the DH2s and robust FE2 "Fees" also learned how to cope and even prevail, exploiting the fact that the gunner, perched in the front nacelle, had a wide field of fire and his weapon laid down a more rapid stream of bullets than the armament of the Fokker, which was slowed by the interrupter gear. It was a Fee that did for Max Immelmann, who was brought down by the fire of Corporal J. H. Waller, an observer with 25 Squadron, on 18 June 1916 over the village of Lentz, shortly after he had scored his seventeenth victory. The appearance of the excellent two-man Sopwith "1½ Strutter", which combined a synchronized Vickers for the pilot and a Lewis for the observer, helped to turn the tide.

But no advantage lasted for long. The respite was short. The RFC's ascendancy faded with the appearance of the Albatros, a sleek, fast biplane with twin, fuselage-mounted Spandaus, which in "Bloody April" of 1917 would generate a new crisis. Each season brought another frightening novelty. This fear was not confined to the combatants. Across the Channel, civilians were learning what the birth of military aviation meant for them.

CHAPTER
FOUR

The New Front Line

With the invention of aeroplanes a new anxiety entered the lives of European civilians. As the prospect of war grew, fear began to erode their initial enthusiasm for aviation. It seemed increasingly likely that far from benefiting mankind, freeing humans from the shackles of gravity, shrinking distances and drawing the world more closely together, powered flight carried almost limitless potential for destruction. Never before had attackers struck from the air. Popular literature played up the nightmare of bombers reaching across seas to shower death on non-combatants, who, in Britain, had been largely insulated from the violence of outsiders for hundreds of years.

Politicians and soldiers shared the alarm. An attempt was made at the 1907 Hague Disarmament Conference to prohibit the use of bombing aircraft. It failed. But when Britain went to war no practical system of aerial defence was in place. The absence was due to a conflict — of interests and perceptions — that would affect the development of British military aviation for the next three decades. The rapid conquest of the sky created a new dimension in which wars could be fought, one that stretched over the traditional battlegrounds of land and sea. This reality forced a reassessment of the historical responsibilities of the army and navy. Earth and water created a natural division of duties. The air overlapped everything, creating endless possibilities for confusion and duplication. Soldiers and sailors anyway viewed the advent of aviation through the lens of their own particular needs, which, often, were not easily reconciled. The traditional rivalry between the services ensured there would be no smooth solution to the resulting problems.

In August 1914 the army had conceded that it would not be able to both defend Britain and support the army in France and it had grudgingly allowed the navy to take over responsibility for domestic air space. The difficulties of protecting a huge target like London were overwhelming and Churchill, then First Lord of the Admiralty, accepted from the start that ground and air defences should concentrate on protecting vital military and war-industrial targets. He favoured a "forward" strategy, attacking enemy aircraft as close to their point of departure as possible from bases on the French and Belgian coast. It was for that reason that the RNAS had set up a string of seaplane bases in east coast ports, facing Germany. Secondary interception forces based in London and its approaches would deal with the aircraft that got through. At the same time, civil-defence precautions were imposed. In central London street lamps were partially extinguished, illuminated shop lights banned and householders were forced to draw their shades after dark. Dummy lights were strung across the big parks to deny German aviators a landmark. The cautious began filling buckets with sand and water. Bolder spirits were amused at first, but soon everyone was doing it.

Airships were the only German aircraft capable of reaching Britain. They became known by the generic name "Zeppelins". They were about 150 yards long, held aloft by gigantic hydrogen-filled gasbags sewn from cows' intestines. About 200,000 were needed for each craft. By the beginning of 1915 the German army and navy had fourteen of them. The raids began in December 1914, not on London but over Dover and Sheerness, and did little damage or harm.

The first attack on the capital came as midnight approached on 31 May 1915. A Zeppelin arrived over Stoke Newington in north-east London and dropped an assortment of grenades and incendiaries on the terraced houses below. The resulting fires and explosions killed seven people and injured thirty-five. Among the dead was a three-year-old girl, Elsie Leggat, who lived in Cowper Road. Her little body was found curled up under her bed where she had vainly sought protection from the German bombs. Her eleven-year-old sister May died later of her injuries.

Looked at coolly, the results were less awful than both officialdom and the public had imagined. The bombs were scattered haphazardly and hit nothing of strategic importance. The anonymous *New York Herald Tribune* correspondent felt it "fell short badly on the spectacular side". The raid had "caused excitement in a certain section of London, but the inhabitants of the rest of its 609 square miles came home from theatres and picture shows undisturbed, to learn nothing of the . . . raid until they opened their morning papers."

Public reaction, however, was out of all proportion to the scale of the event. Starved of real information until the Government issued an official bulletin at 5 p.m. the following day, rumour ran riot. The *Herald Tribune* reported that "as the story of the raid passed from man to man on the streets, in public houses and on street cars it grew amazingly. Several hundred had been killed, churches destroyed, a theatre audience massacred and hundreds of fires started."

It was this aspect of the raid, rather than the fact that bombs had dropped within a few miles of the Bank of England and Buckingham Palace, that most alarmed the authorities. To Londoners and city dwellers throughout Britain the attack seemed to be the beginning of the fulfilment of prophesies that had been uttered even before aeroplanes had been invented. The smashed-up houses and the dead girls were the tragic proof that henceforth civilians stood on a new front line. On 6 June Hull was hit. Twenty-four people were killed and forty injured and many homes destroyed. The following day there was some good news when, over Belgium, Lieutenant Reginald Warneford of 1 Squadron, RNAS, shot down a Zeppelin which crashed in flames onto a convent.

In British skies, however, the "Zepps" seemed to operate with near-impunity. Anti-aircraft fire forced them higher rather than bringing them down. Even with the help of searchlights the paltry fighter forces deployed around London had no luck finding their targets. "You had about as much chance of spotting a black cat in the Albert Hall in the dark," said one RNAS pilot, Flight Lieutenant Graham Donald. After a while only token efforts were made to intercept the attacks. Two raids on consecutive nights in September 1915 killed forty. The death tolls were tiny compared with what was to come in the Blitz. The anticipation, though, was unnerving, and the sense of violation deepened anxiety, which, in turn, stoked a hatred of the Germans. The Kaiser had asked his airmen to spare civilian areas and — in deference to his British relations — royal palaces, but this pious hope was soon forgotten. Everyone knew that precise targeting was impossible and the men in the airships had no idea where their bombs would fall.

It seemed to those on the receiving end that the attacks had no purpose except to sow fear. "Zeppelins are intended as weapons of moral suasion," said the *Evening Standard and Saint James Gazette*. The airship, it went on, "has been built with the idea of spreading panic over as wide an inhabitant area as possible. It has been devised as the terror of the air, the very quintessence of frightfulness." The Germans' motivations were mixed. They had always planned to launch operations on British soil against industrial targets of military significance, but lacked an aeroplane with the range and power to carry them out. Frustration at the impasse in the ground war hastened the decision to use Zeppelins, which continued even after it became clear they were incapable of causing significant material damage. Instead, the effect on civilian morale was used to justify the attacks. It was an argument that — despite its patent falseness — would be used by the British in the war to come.

Official propaganda tried to capitalize on the thirst for revenge. "It is far better to face the bullets than to be killed at home by a bomb" ran the message on one recruiting poster, below an image of a looming Zeppelin. "Join the army at once and help stop an air raid."

Going off to the trenches would not stop the attacks. What was needed was an effective air defence system at home. Public anger spurred official action. Early winter weather at the end of 1915 forced a suspension of Zeppelin activity. During the lull, the number of mobile anti-aircraft batteries, mounted on lorries and trailers and supplemented by searchlights, was expanded. Fixed batteries were also in place at important points around the capital.

The Germans returned in the new year to more dangerous skies, yet they were still able to create havoc, killing seventy in raids on the industrial Midlands on the night of 31 January 1916. Calls for action and revenge rose to a crescendo, led by the *Daily Mail* urging "Hit Back! Don't Wait and See!" The mood could not be ignored. This raw public sentiment pushed both politicians and military planners down a strategic path that was to stretch into the next world war. Among those who responded to it was Winston Churchill, now out of government since his sacking from the Admiralty following the Gallipoli debacle of 1915, and William Joynson-Hicks. The latter was chairman of a new Parliamentary Air Committee, which pressed for Britain to launch punitive air raids against Germany.

Demands for action added to the pressure for a reorganization of the air forces to overcome army and navy rivalries and rationalize equipment and organization. In February 1916 a committee was set up under Lord Derby, the Secretary of State for War. It had no executive powers and was merely asked to report on how best to develop and supply aircraft to meet the needs of the RFC and the RNAS. Within a few months Derby resigned, having concluded that the best way to improve matters was to amalgamate the two services — a bureaucratic challenge he judged to be too difficult for wartime.

In May 1916 the problem was handed to Lord Curzon, the former Viceroy of India, who was put in charge of the first Air Board. He, too, took the view that a separate air service, controlled by an air ministry, was the way forward. The idea was opposed by the older services — and with particular vehemence by the navy. The organizational wrangling would drag on for two more years under successive committees until an agreement was ground out.

By now the RFC's rapid expansion had put it in a position to reclaim its place as defender of the home airspace. On 10 February 1916, after much vacillation, the navy agreed to a reversion to the original division of duties. It would be responsible for enemy aircraft approaching Britain. Once they crossed over land it was the army's job to deal with them. The RFC set up ten home-defence squadrons around the country. No. 39 Squadron, based at Sutton's Farm airfield, just south of Hornchurch in Essex, was charged with defending London.

It is hard to believe now that a target the size of a Zeppelin should prove so difficult to locate, stalk and shoot down. As was to be demonstrated in the next war, it is almost impossible to find anything in a night sky with the naked eye when there is no moon shining. Even if an interception was achieved, airships were surprisingly nimble and not much slower than an aeroplane. In the event of a pilot getting an airship under his guns, the results were liable to be disappointing. The .303 bullets of the Lewis guns pierced easily the steel skin of the Zeppelins and passed through the gasbags, but failed to ignite the hydrogen, causing only minor leakages that were easily patched up.

However, with the introduction of the Brock incendiary round — invented by a naval reserve officer who belonged to the firework manufacturing family — flying in a Zeppelin became an extremely hazardous activity. A single shot could turn an airship into a gigantic torch, and the balance of advantage tilted sharply and irrevocably in the defenders' favour. The first demonstration of the Zeppelins' new vulnerability came on the night of 2–3 September. It took place in front of an appreciative audience: the Londoners who for the previous fifteen months had cowered in the shadow of these silent and sinister monsters. At 2.30

that morning Muriel Dayrell-Browning, a thirty-seven-year-old linguist whose skills in Matabele, Zulu and German were being put to use in the War Office, was awoken at her house in central London by "a terrific explosion and was at the window in one bound when another deafening one shook the house". Muriel, whose daughter Vivienne would go on to marry the novelist Graham Greene, looked out to see sailing above "a cigar of bright silver in the full glare of about 20 magnificent searchlights . . . the night was absolutely still with a few splendid stars. It was a magnificent sight and the whole of London was looking on, holding its breath."

As the ghostly shape slid overhead, Lieutenant William "Billy" Leefe Robinson of 39 Squadron was approaching in his BE2 C, having taken off from Sutton's Farm on anti-Zeppelin patrol just after 11 p.m. He was twenty-one, the son of a coffee planter, who had served as an observer in scout planes on the Western Front before becoming a pilot. Earlier that year he had intercepted an airship, but it had got away and in his eagerness to succeed he now pushed his luck to the limit. He had already sighted — then lost — the target once and was running low on fuel when he encountered it again, picked out in the searchlights. He swooped down, braving the anti-aircraft shells bursting all around and the accurate fire of the airship's gunners, climbed up underneath and, as he wrote in his combat report, "distributed one drum" of Brock and explosive Pomeroy bullets along its belly.

"It seemed to have no effect," he remembered. "I therefore moved to one side and gave it another drum distributed along its side." Again his bullets seemed wasted. He swung round for a rear attack and from 500 feet blasted the rear. "I had hardly finished the drum before I saw the part fired at glow," he wrote. "In a few seconds the whole rear part was blazing." He "quickly got out of the way of the falling, blazing airship and being very excited fired off a few red Very lights and dropped a parachute flare."

Leefe Robinson seems to have felt a sort of ecstasy at his achievement. Writing to his parents seven weeks later he was still high on the memory. "When the thing actually burst into flames of course it was a glorious sight — wonderful! It literally lit up the sky all around and me as well, of course . . . I hardly know how I felt. As I watched the huge mass gradually turn on end and . . . slowly sink, one glowing, blazing mass, I gradually realized what I had done and grew wild with excitement." As he admitted to his "darling old mother", he was "not what is popularly known as a religious person", but he found himself thanking "from the bottom of my heart that supreme power that rules and guides our destinies".

Muriel Dayrell-Browning watched the end from her bedroom window. "From the direction of Barnet a brilliant red light appeared . . . we saw it was the Zep diving head-first. That was a sight . . . the glare lit up all of London and was rose red. Those deaths must have been the most dramatic in the world's history. They fell — a cone of blazing wreckage — thousands of feet, watched by eight million of their enemies. It was magnificent, the most thrilling scene imaginable."

That morning, like hundreds of others, she made the trip to Cuffley in Hertfordshire where the airship — it was a wooden-framed Schutte-Lanz, not a Zeppelin — had hit the ground. By now her sentiments were more measured. "The wreck covers only thirty feet of ground and the dead are under a tarpaulin," she wrote. "I hope they will be buried with full military honours. They are brave men. RIP!"

A fifteen-year-old schoolboy, Patrick Blundstone, was staying with family friends only a few hundred yards from the site, having apparently been sent out of London to escape the raids. He saw the bodies before they were hidden from view. "I would rather not describe the condition of the crew," he wrote in a letter to "Dear Daddy" in London. "They were roasted, there is absolutely no other word for it. They were brown like the outside of roast beef." He collected "some relics, some wire and wood framework". Before souvenir hunters could strip the wreckage bare, the War Office carted it off and donated it to the Red Cross, who had the wires by which engines and gondolas were suspended beneath the envelope cut into inch-long lengths and sold at a shilling apiece with a certificate of authenticity "to help the wounded at the Front".

Leefe Robinson's victory generated a flood of relief and he became an instant hero. Within four days he was awarded the VC, pinned on him by King George V at Windsor in front of a large crowd. A fund was started for him which raised a colossal £3,500. He was obliged to have postcards bearing his photograph, smiling shyly as he emerges from a tent to respond to constant requests for autographs. Commemorative table napkins declared that "his greatest reward" was "the heartfelt thanks of every woman and child in England". Billy Leefe Robinson stands as the prototype for the barely formed young paladins who, twenty-four years later, would stand between British civilians and German bombers. Like them, he performed his feats in full sight of those he was seeking to protect. Half of London seems to have watched Airship SL11 sinking earthwards in a ball of fire, taking its commander Wilhelm Schramm and fifteen crew members to their deaths. Thus was formed a direct link between combatant and civilian that was to define the way the public regarded airmen in the years ahead. Even though their domain was the air, they were far more visible and accessible than the soldiers across the Channel or on the high seas, their daring, their prowess and their sacrifice on show for all to see.

Leefe Robinson was promoted and sent off to France eight months later as a flight commander with 48 Squadron. On his first patrol he ran into the Jasta 11 of Manfred von Richtofen, the Red Baron himself, and four of the six aircraft in his flight were shot down, including his own. Leefe Robinson survived, but spent the rest of the war in prison, including spells of solitary confinement as punishment for repeated escape attempts. He returned to England only to die in the great Spanish 'flu pandemic in December 1918.

His victory marked the end of the Zeppelins' employment as a bomber. Henceforth they were easy meat for the night-fighters. In the next month, three more were shot down. During the winter of 1916 there were no further attacks, but in the spring of 1917 a new menace appeared in the shape of twin-engined Gotha GIV bombers. With these the Germans had the means to pursue their initial ambition to mount a serious aerial assault on the British homeland. Gothas were not the first long-range heavy bombers — the Russian engineer Igor Sikorsky had already designed a four-engine aircraft, which had been used effectively on the Eastern Front. They were, though, superior to anything so far developed in Britain. They got their name from the town in Thuringia, where the Gothaer Waggonfabrik, a rolling-stock manufacturer before the war, developed them. They had a wingspan of nearly eighty feet, were pushed along at about 80 or 90 mph by twin 260 hp Mercedes engines and carried ordnance weighing up to 1,100 pounds. The payload was smaller than an airship's, but whereas Zeppelins scattered their bombs haphazardly, the Gothas were able to achieve some degree of concentration. The results were apparent on their first raid, on the early evening of 25 May 1917, when twenty-one bombers crossed the Channel from Ostend and made for London. They found the capital covered in low cloud, so they headed back, bombarding the army camp at Shorncliffe in Kent and neighbouring Folkstone on the way, killing ninety-five people, the largest death toll yet.

On 13 June, a hot hazy day, the Gothas returned to London. This time the conditions were ideal and fourteen aircraft bombed the City and East End of London. Another record was set, with 162 dead and 432 injured, some of them as they stood in the street, gawping at the machines overhead. The raid produced one of the emblematic events of the civilians' war. One bomb landed on a primary school in Upper North Street, Poplar, an area of densely packed terraced houses. There had been some warning of the raid, but not enough to evacuate the children. The teachers tried to keep the pupils calm by getting them to sing, but soon their voices were drowned out by the sound of anti-aircraft guns and bombs. Eighteen children were killed, almost all of them infants between four and six years old, the sons and daughters of dock-workers.

With the fading of the Zeppelin threat, vigilance against air raids had slipped and aircraft were switched back to France, where they were wanted for the big pushes of 1917. The need to arm merchant ships against attacks by German commerce raiders meant they got priority in artillery production. Even so, ninety-odd fighters took off to intercept the Gothas over Britain, but they were too late and too dispersed to punish them. If they did manage to catch up, they were forced away by the bombers' three Parabellum machine guns.

In the aftermath of the raid, the calls for civilian protection resumed. Against the opposition of the military, squadrons were shifted from the Western Front, weakening the balance of airpower over the trenches as both sides prepared for their summer offensives. Pressure also mounted once again for reprisals, which would also divert resources away from a struggle which, in the view of Douglas Haig, the commander of British forces, would be "the most severe we have yet had".

It was essential, though, for the air raids over Britain to be halted or at least for the perpetrators to be punished if civilian morale and support for the war were to be maintained. The problem was that there were not enough aircraft to meet the demands of soldiers, sailors, politicians and civilians. The development of an efficient system of producing them had been held back by the haphazard development of airframes and engines, as well as the competing ambitions of the army and the navy. This began to be rectified when two forceful industrialists were given the job of boosting production. First Lord Cowdray, then Sir William Weir, promised dramatic increases in airframes and engines, but these came too late to stop another Gotha raid on 7 July, again on the East End, which killed another 54 and injured 190. A surge of public outrage generated yet another burst of bureaucratic energy. The Prime Minister, David Lloyd George, instructed Jan Christian Smuts to examine the whole question of the organization of the war in the air. Smuts, who fifteen years before had commanded a Boer army fighting the British in South Africa, set to work producing a report which was to shape Britain's air forces for the rest of the century. In the meantime, improved anti-aircraft defences, barrage balloons and searchlights and faster and better organized fighter units gradually reduced the threat from the air. On 19 May 1918 seven out of an attacking force of nineteen bombers were shot down and, with mounting pressures on other fronts, the air raids petered out.

In three years the Zeppelins and Gothas had launched 103 attacks on Britain, killing 1,414 civilians and wounding 3,866. This was a fraction of the death toll among soldiers on the Western Front, and fewer than the 1,480 who would be killed in a single night in London in the worst attack of the Blitz (1940–41). It was the air raids of Zeppelins and Gothas, however, rather than any other experience of the First World War, that would change the nature of Britain's air forces when it went to war with Germany again.

CHAPTER
FIVE

Death, Drink, Luck

Despite the great expansion of the Allied and German air forces from 1916, the struggle in the skies retained a human scale. Aeroplanes were small and flimsy and the numbers involved in the fighting were small. It was possible for the participants to make some sense of it — unlike the nightmarish clash of steel and high explosive shaking the ground below them.

The combatants fought at close quarters. At the end of an aerial duel the protagonists might be only a few yards apart. Writing to his parents shortly after his arrival in France in February 1916, Albert Ball described an encounter with an Albatros, one of the sleek and powerful machines that were now consistently out-performing their enemies: "The interesting point about it was that we could see the Huns' faces and they could see ours, we were so near."

Aviators could identify an opponent by his flying style. Later the German aces advertised themselves by painting their aircraft gaudy colours: blood-red for Manfred von Richtofen, a disciple of Oswald Boelcke, who had witnessed Boelcke's banal death in a mid-air collision with a friendly aircraft, and inherited his crown as Germany's top ace. Another flamboyant flier, Lieutenant Friedrich Kempf, had his name painted in giant letters on the top wing of his Fokker triplane, and the words *Kennscht mi'noch? (Remember Me?)* on the middle one.

German and Allied propagandists portrayed the war in the air as a chivalrous affair. It was an easier task than trying to prettify the swarming carnage on the ground. The public swallowed the line and, to some extent, the aviators themselves went along with it.

"To be alone," wrote Cecil Lewis, who had lied about his age to join the RFC in time to take part in the battle of the Somme, "to have your life in your own hands, to use your own skill, single-handed against the enemy. It was like the lists in the Middle Ages, the only sphere in modern warfare where a man saw his adversary and faced him in mortal combat."

The airmen were grateful to be at one remove from the dirt and stink of the front lines, returning at the end of each day to an aerodrome where they could get a bed, a bath, a drink and decent food. They looked down on the men toiling in the churned and polluted earth below and blessed their luck. One day in July 1917 Captain Edward "Mick" Mannock went to scavenge a souvenir from a two-seater he had shot down (a habit he shared with von Richtofen).

"The journey to the trenches was rather nauseating," he wrote afterwards. "Dead men's legs sticking through the sides with putties and boots still on — bits of bones and skulls with the hair peeling off, and tons of equipment and clothing lying about. This sort of thing, together with the strong graveyard stench and the dead and mangled body of the pilot . . . combined to upset me for a few days."

The airmen were in a unique position to comprehend the futility of what was happening on the ground. From their vantage point they saw all too clearly how miniscule were the gains that resulted from all the enormous effort.

"The war below us was a spectacle," wrote Cecil Lewis. "We aided and abetted it, admiring the tenacity of men who fought in verminous filth to take the next trench thirty yards away. But such objectives could not thrill us, who, raising our eyes, could see objective after objective receding, fifty, sixty, seventy miles beyond."

This perspective encouraged feelings of detachment. Many airmen on both sides clung to the idea that what they were engaged in was somehow "clean" in comparison to the vileness of trench warfare. British pilots used public-school lingo to describe what they were doing. "Have just been up to test my new machine [one of the newly arrived Nieuports]," Albert Ball wrote to his parents in May 1916. "Well, I have never had so much sport. I fooled about and banked it, having such a topping test ride." He finished: "Huns, look out!"

The exuberance in Ball's early letters home is the last sparkle of schoolboy innocence. He was nineteen years old when he arrived in France in February 1916, but in photographs his taut, uncreased skin makes him look even younger. He stares straight at the camera, giving nothing away. The letters, however, reveal his inner confusion as the values of the playing field jostle uncomfortably with the neurosis of the battlefield.

Ball was the first British pilot to become famous. He was brought up in a middle-class home in Nottingham, where his father had become Lord Mayor after starting his working life as a plumber. He went to a local public school organized along Christian lines with plenty of cold baths and exercise. When the war broke out he hurried to join up and was posted to the infantry. Bored with waiting to be sent to France he took flying lessons with a view to joining the RFC. He fell instantly in love with flying, despite the dangers. "It is rotten to see the smashes," he wrote in a letter. "Yesterday a ripping boy had a smash and when we got up to him he was nearly dead. He had a two-inch piece of wood right through his head and died this morning." He informed his parents — without apparent irony — that he "would be pleased to take you up any time you wish".

Ball reached France in time for the big Somme offensive of the summer of 1916 and soon made his mark by his extraordinarily aggressive approach. By now airmen were developing new tactics. The more skilful pilots disliked the close escort duties that Trenchard had demanded, which restricted their tactical options and made life more dangerous both for the aircraft they were supposed to be protecting and themselves. They preferred to operate solo, going off on hunting missions to seek out the enemy before they arrived over no-man's-land. It was a singularly British approach and RFC fliers spent more time to the east of the front lines than the Germans did over British territory.

Ball was the embodiment of this approach. He would set off alone, having first tuned his aeroplane to his liking. Odds meant nothing to him and he would fly straight into swarms of opponents, closing to almost point-blank range and opening up with his Lewis gun. If he failed to down his victim with the first drum of ammunition he would break off, change the magazine and try again. Frequently, on his return from combats, his machine was found to be riddled with bullet holes.

The RFC was tolerant of unconventionality, but Ball still struck his fellow airmen as odd. At his first base at Savy Aubigny, north-west of Arras, he didn't like the look of the billet allotted to him in the village and instead had a bell tent erected at the edge of the airfield, which as well as suiting him better also meant that "if ever a Hun comes I shall always be on the good work at once". Later the tent was replaced by a hut. Ball had the ground next to it dug up and turned into a kitchen garden and asked his family to send seeds for marrows, lettuce, carrots, mustard cress and cucumber, as well as some flowers. It was an inconvenient two miles from the mess, but that did not bother Ball.

He preferred to spend his evenings with his violin, which he sometimes played after dinner, walking round and round a flaming red magnesium flare. A fellow pilot, Roderic Hill, described Ball sitting brooding outside his hut, listening to his gramophone. "He had but one idea: that was to kill as many Huns as possible, and he gave effect to it with a swiftness and certainty that seemed to most of us uncanny. He nearly always went out alone, in fact he would not let anyone else fly with him and was intolerant of proffered assistance."

For all his oddness Ball was respected. A young pilot from New Zealand, Keith Caldwell, saw him as "a hero . . . and he looked the part, too: young, alert, ruddy complexion, dark hair and eyes. He was supposed to be a 'loner', but we found him friendly . . . we felt that it could only be a matter of time before he 'bought it', as he was shot about so often."

In his first eleven weeks in France Ball flew at least forty-three operational sorties and witnessed daily the deaths of friends and enemies. It is hardly surprising that the adolescent optimism soon fades from his correspondence and darkness creeps in. Only nine days after describing his test flight he admitted in a letter to his sister Lois and brother Cyril that his mind was "full of poo-poo thoughts. I have just lost such a dear old pal, Captain Lucas. He was brought down by a Fokker last night about 5p.m." By the middle of July, after a frantic few days of combats, Ball could take no more: "The day before yesterday we had a big day," he wrote to his father. "At night I was feeling very rotten, and my nerves were poo-poo. Naturally I cannot keep on for ever, so at night I went to see the CO and asked him if I could have a short rest." The request was granted, but after a short respite Ball was back again and by the end of August he was yearning for home. "I do so want to leave all this beastly killing for a time," he sighed in a letter.

In October he was sent back to England to rest before moving on to a new post as an instructor. He was already a public name, with thirty-one victories to his name, the MC, DSO and bar. In the search for positive propaganda about the war, the ban on promoting aces was abandoned and Prime Minister Lloyd George invited Ball to breakfast. However, the peace Ball had yearned for in France soon bored him. He agitated to go back and in February 1917 he was posted to 56 Squadron, which was being formed as an elite unit equipped with the new Hispano-Suiza-powered SE5 fighters which could fly at 130 mph and climb to 10,000 feet in ten minutes. During the wait Ball got engaged to an eighteen-year-old florist called Flora Young, who he met when a friend brought her to the aerodrome. Ball had suggested a flip in his plane and she gamely agreed.

In April 1917 the squadron went to France. It numbered eighteen aircraft, arranged in three flights, and Ball was given command of one of them. This new responsibility meant that his lone-wolf tactics would be restricted. They were arriving at a time when the RFC was in trouble. It was "Bloody April". The German Albatroses had gained a deadly advantage and Manfred von Richtofen lorded it over the skies. He had already achieved a dark celebrity — as the Red Baron to the British, Le Diable Rouge to the French and Der Rote Kampfflieger (The Red War Flier) to his applauding countrymen, who read his own accounts of his exploits in a vainglorious but remarkably revealing autobiography.

Fundamental changes were in progress on the Western Front. Faced with the stalemate on the ground, the Germans had switched strategy. They were now putting their faith in starving the Allies into submission by using unrestricted submarine warfare — declared as policy in 1 February 1917 — to cut the enemy's Atlantic trade routes. The land forces, meanwhile, fell back to a line of formidable natural and man-made defences, between Arras and the Aisne, onto which they hoped to draw the British and French armies and bleed them white.

In the spring of 1917 the Allies moved into the ceded ground and prepared for what they hoped was a final break-through. The Spring Offensive bore the name of the man who planned it, the French general Robert Nivelle, and the RFC was expected to support it to the utmost. It would be a costly undertaking, as everyone from Trenchard downwards knew. They had aircraft in quantity — more than the German squadrons could muster — but this advantage was more than cancelled out by their poor overall quality. The Germans had a new improved Albatros — the D.III. They were also better organized. In October 1916 their air force was given institutional coherence with the foundation of the Deutschen Luftstreitkräfte ("German Air Force"), with its own commander and staff. At a tactical level, fighter units were now formed into Jagdstaffeln or "Jastas", fourteen aircraft units which operated with devastating efficiency. The most feared was Jasta 11, commanded by Richtofen.

103

As preparations for the latest big push warmed up, Trenchard's policy of aggression no matter what the odds ensured that the RFC was flung forcefully into battle. He accepted that losses would be high, and so it turned out. Ten squadrons, with 365 aircraft, took part in the Battle of Arras, which began on 9 April 1917. By the end, 245 aeroplanes had been destroyed, 211 aircrew were dead or missing, and another 108 were prisoners of war. This massacre went down in history as "Bloody April". The Germans had suffered too, with 119 machines shot down. But even when set against the routine carnage of the conflict, these losses seemed unacceptable. The war in the air appeared to be matching the attritional slog on the ground and many wondered whether the sacrifices were worth it.

It was in this period that the RFC came closest to defeat on the Western Front. It was saved by another shift in technological advantage. In the following months Bristol Fighters and Sopwith Camels — difficult to handle but superbly manoeuvrable — began to arrive on the squadrons. Here at last were aeroplanes that could outfly and outshoot the Albatroses. The crisis of April passed and the tide turned towards increasing Allied dominance of the air.

The bigger picture was of little concern to Ball. In his letters to Flora he revealed that he had set himself a target: he wanted to pass the record set by Boelcke, who had knocked down forty planes by the time he died. Ball did indeed beat that tally, but he never made it back to his fiancée. At 5.30p.m. on Monday, 7 May 1917 he set off with ten other SE5s from 56 Squadron, heading for the skies over Arras in an effort to tempt Richtofen and his men into action. Cecil Lewis, who was with him, described the chocolate-coloured fighters flying into "threatening masses of cumulus cloud, majestic skyscapes, solid-looking as snow mountains, fraught with caves and valleys, rifts and ravines".

Then the Germans they were looking for appeared, led not by the Red Baron but by his brother Lothar von Richtofen. A swirling dogfight developed. Lewis saw Ball disappear into a cloud. A little later German officers on the ground saw Ball's aeroplane emerge from the cloud, upside down, trailing black smoke. It smashed into a low sloping field. When the officers reached the wreckage a young woman from the village had already pulled Ball clear. There were no marks on his fresh features, but he was dead. Lothar seized the credit for downing him, but the claim was never accepted. Like many aces of this and the following war, the precise details of how Ball met his end have never been conclusively established.

After the carnage of Bloody April, Ball's death further depressed morale. "The mess was very quiet that night," wrote Cecil Lewis. They held a sing-song in a barn to try and cheer themselves up. A band played the hits of the time — "There's a Long, Long Trail", "Way Down Upon the Swanee River", "Pack Up Your Troubles". Then Lewis performed Robert Louis Stevenson's "Requiem", which ends: "Glad did I live and gladly die, / and I laid me down with a will."

Ball's brief existence had been strange and disconnected, warped by an appalling routine of daily risk and death, reaching his end before he had time to form mature feelings and thoughts. At least it was clean. Despite the chivalric pretentions, death in the air was no less gruesome than the ends met by the ground troops whom the airmen pitied. Oswald Boelcke accepted that his life would terminate violently and he only wondered whether it would be "*feucht oder getrocknet*": "wet or dry". Wet meant a crash. Dry meant being consumed by flames.

The appalling reality was spelled out by a German airman, Hans Schroder, describing an incident that took place in July 1917. As a counter to the notion that air fighting was somehow less gruesome than the terrestrial struggle it is worth recounting in full. Schroder was driving past the wreck of a British aeroplane that had just been shot down when "it exploded in front of my window and burst into flames. The burning petrol greedily consumed the unlucky pilot, whose face was charred; his breeches were burnt away at the thighs, and the roasting flesh sizzled in the heat. From all sides came men with buckets intending to throw water on the blaze."

Just then a car drew up full of airmen, including Schroder's friend Klein, who had scored the victory. He was exultant. In the fight that had just finished he had bested his opponent, who had signalled that he was going to land, then at the last moment had "pulled his nose up and put at least twenty bullets into my machine". Klein hardened his heart. After that "there was no mercy for him. We buzzed round and round . . . at a height of fifty metres, like two dogs chasing one another. He had no notion where he was, but he pulled his machine up, and I zoomed after him." After putting a burst into him, Klein watched his opponent "go down by one wing and crash by Wevelghem". There were no regrets. Klein judged him "a bad lot. That sort spoils the chivalry one expects in flying. He deserved his fate."

And what a fate it was. Schroder watched in horrified fascination as the blaze died down gradually. There was "a hiss from the burnt thighs when the spectators emptied their buckets of water on the body. There was a ghastly smell of grilled ham, but the legs below the knees were hardly touched by the fire. The fine new laced boots reaching almost to the knees proclaimed that this was the body of a human being who only a little while ago had been full of the warm life that pulsated in all our bodies."

When he returned to his quarters that night he found the splendid boots awaiting him and two bottles of Bols liqueur in his overcoat pockets, gifts from his batman, who had scavenged them from the wreck. The boots carried "an odour of smoked bacon" and he shoved them quickly outside. The Bols he drank. Its presence in the aircraft gives us an idea of how airmen dealt with the constant, hovering attendance of death.

It was a fate like this that haunted all pilots and none more so than Mick Mannock. Mannock had been inspired to transfer from the Royal Engineers to the RFC after hearing and reading of the exploits of Albert Ball. Both men shared the same dedication and ruthlessness, both enjoyed playing the violin. Otherwise their characters and backgrounds were strongly contrasted. Mannock was already twenty-seven by the time he arrived at the main RFC depot in St Omer. He had a rough upbringing. His father was a violent, hard-drinking NCO in the Inniskilling Dragoons, who abandoned his family when Mick was twelve, leaving his wife Julie to bring up two sons and two daughters in poverty in Canterbury.

Mannock left school at fourteen to become a clerk in the local office of the National Telephone Company, but soon graduated to a technical job checking the lines. His experiences made him a socialist and an admirer of Keir Hardie, and Mannock would later enjoy alarming his middle-class brother officers with his views on class and privilege. When the war came he was working as a foreman for a cable-laying company in Turkey and had to be freed from internment by the Red Cross before he could join up.

Mannock arrived on 40 Squadron in the late spring of 1917 at the height of the Albatros ascendancy. He survived the first, desperately dangerous weeks, learning his craft quickly and on 7 June, while flying as an escort on a bombing mission to Lille, he shot down his first aeroplane.

"My man gave me an easy mark," he wrote in his diary. "I was only ten yards away from him — on top, so I couldn't miss! A beautifully coloured insect he was — red, green, blue and yellow. I let him have sixty rounds . . . there wasn't much left of him. I saw him go spinning and slipping down from fourteen thousand. Rough luck, but it's war, and they're Huns." It was the start of a sequence that would end with an astounding seventy-three victories.

If Ball was a lone wolf, Mannock was a pack leader. As a flight commander with 74 Squadron and as CO of 84 Squadron, he instilled in his men the need for teamwork and training as well as constant caution and vigilance. "Always above, seldom on the same level and never underneath" was his motto.

But he was also almost manically determined, persisting with his attacks until he was certain his man had gone down. When it came to a kill, Mannock suffered the same emotional confusion that Hawker had experienced. After downing an Albatros whose pilot put up a good fight, he wrote in his diary that he was "very pleased that I did not kill him". On 5 September 1917 he attacked a DFW biplane over Avion, which "went down in flames, pieces of wing and tail, etc., dropping away from the wreck. It was a horrible sight and made me feel sick." On another occasion, after destroying four enemy aircraft in the space of twenty-four hours, he "bounced into the mess shouting: 'All tickets please! Please pass right down the car. Flamerinoes — four! Sizzle-sizzle wonk!' "

It seemed to be a case of making light of what he most feared, and he carried a pistol with which to shoot himself if he ever became a "flamerino". On leave in London in June 1918 Mannock went down with influenza and spent several days in bed at the RFC club, unable to sleep because of the nightmares of burning aircraft that filled his head when he closed his eyes. He visited friends in Northamptonshire, who were shocked by his appearance and manner. When he talked about his experiences he subsided into tears and said he wanted to die.

Mannock went back to France as commander of 85 Squadron. On 25 July he spent much of the day with his friend Ira Jones, who wrote in his diary: "Had lunch, tea and dinner with Mick. I can't make out whether he has got nerves or not. One minute he's full out. The next, he gives the impression of being morbid and keeps bringing up his pet subject of being shot down in flames. I told him I had got a two-seater in flames on patrol this morning before breakfast. 'Could you hear the sod scream?' he asked with a sour smile. 'One day they'll get you like that, my lad. You are getting careless. Don't forget to blow your brains out.' Everyone roared with laughter."

The following day he took off at dawn with a greenhorn pilot, Lieutenant Donald Inglis, who had yet to shoot anything down, to show him how it was done. They ran into a two-seater over the German lines. Mannock began shooting, apparently killing the observer, and left the *coup de grâce* to his pupil, who set the aeroplane on fire. Instead of following his own rules, which advised climbing away immediately after a kill, Mannock then swooped to examine their victim.

Inglis followed his leader as he "made a couple of circles around the burning wreckage and then made for home. I saw Mick start to kick his rudder, then I saw a flame come out of his machine; it got bigger and bigger. Mick was no longer kicking his rudder. His nose dropped slightly and he went into a slow right-hand turn and he hit the ground in a burst of flame. I circled at about twenty feet, but could not see him and as things were getting hot made for home . . . Poor Mick . . . the bloody bastards had shot my Major down in flames." Once again the exact cause of an ace's death was a mystery. It is not known where the shots that downed him came from and his body was never recovered.

So even great skill was no protection from the attentions of the Grim Reaper. It was no wonder that the fliers believed so much in the power of luck. Superstition was rife and rational men followed obsessive lucky routines and reverenced lucky charms. Authority recognized their importance and made generous accommodations. Hubert Griffith, a twenty-year-old aspiring writer who joined 15 Squadron from his yeomanry regiment, told a story of how "one evening, in some mess skirmish or other, I had broken a ring that I used to wear. It was a Russian-silver peasant ring of no negotiable value whatsoever; but I had had it throughout the war, it had seen me through a winter in the trenches, I had flown with it and had survived a disastrous flying crash and other eventualities and I had come, rightly or wrongly, to regard it as an omen of good luck. I had gone straight to the Squadron Commander and had said that I didn't want to be on the flying programme next day till after the ring had been mended by the squadron workshops. He had agreed in full seriousness to this grotesque proposition."

111

It would never have happened in the army. As Griffith pointed out, "if an infantry subaltern had gone to his Colonel and said, 'Colonel, Colonel, I don't want to go up the line today because one of the eyes of my teddy bear mascot has fallen out,' he would not necessarily have been charged with cowardice, but would merely have been certified as a lunatic."

The RFC's accommodating attitude reflected the fact that flying was new and different. The old rules and attitudes did not always fit the new circumstances and realities. It was also, perhaps, a recognition of the fact that the men now fighting the air war were not as conformist — or naturally obedient — as their terrestrial counterparts. By the time Griffith arrived on his squadron the social composition of the RFC had changed. At the start it had been composed of adventurous young soldiers drawn from the usual social strata that supplied the ranks of the officer class. When Griffith joined 15 Squadron on attachment in 1917 he was struck by the "infinite individuality and variety, the cosmopolitanism of the Flying Corps". He found that the "average types of young English public-school boy . . . were on the whole in the minority". The rich social mixture included "types who had been promoted from the ranks . . . Canadians, Australians, South Africans, New Zealanders, and pilots and observers from every other part of the Empire". Among them were "a man who had been a cow-puncher in the Argentine, and a Maltese-born pilot, a cross-country jockey who was later to win the Grand National,[1] a man who had had half an ear shot off in some American brawl and a little New Zealand observer who used to read Homer in the original Greek."

The RFC in general radiated an air of raffishness, which pervades the pages of *Sagittarius Rising* (1936), the classic memoir of Cecil Lewis, who, while more representative of the run of RFC officers than Ball or Mannock, was very far from being a stock product of his class. Lewis describes one evening in the mess when the CO of A Flight returned from Amiens with a case of whisky, a case of champagne, and a large bath sponge, and announced his intention to "throw a drunk" for the other two flights. After dinner a tin basin was placed on the mess table and filled with whisky and champagne. The Major then dunked the sponge in the mixture and squeezed it over the heads of his pilots. The evening ended in a drunken melee as the flights pitched into each other, squirting soda siphons.

Other evenings involved a trip to the local town in search of women, despite the high risk of a dose of clap. A 1915 drinking song describes the finale to a particularly trying day:

But safely at the 'drome once more, we feel quite
    gay and bright.
We'll take a car to Amiens and have dinner there
    tonight.

---

[1] Fred Rees on Shaun Spadah in 1921.

We'll swank along the boulevards and meet the
  girls of France.
To hell with the Army Medical! We'll take our
  ruddy chance!

The raffishness and insouciance were part of the
RFC's rapidly forming identity. When Lewis joined in
1915 it was only three years old, but it was already
brimming with confidence. "The RFC attracted the
adventurous spirits," he wrote. "The devil-may-care
young bloods of England, the fast-livers, the furious
drivers — men who were not happy unless they were
taking risks. This invested the Corps with a certain style
(not always admirable). We had the sense of being the
last word in warfare, the advance guard of wars to come
and felt, I suppose, that we could afford to be a little
extravagant."

The swagger was largely justified. But beneath the
dash, the lines of an efficient organization were forming
and for every brilliant maverick like Ball and Mannock
there were many more who combined courage with
high intelligence and vision, and many of those who
survived would form a cadre that would come to the
fore of the air force in the 1930s and lead it through the
war years. Names that will crop up in the pages to
come, such as Charles Portal, Arthur Harris, John
Slessor and Arthur Tedder, were all RFC pilots.

CHAPTER
SIX

The Third Service

By the time the final year of the First World War began, air power had penetrated the lives of everyone involved in the conflict — soldiers, seamen and civilians. On the Western Front the RFC had become an extra limb for the army, and one on which it leaned heavily. Airmen and aircraft played an essential part in almost all operations. Unlike their comrades on the ground, they had established a clear ascendancy over the enemy. Huge numbers of aircraft were pouring out of the factories. In 1917 there were 14,832 deliveries to the Front. The following year that number more than doubled. The RFC and the French air force ruled the skies and the arrival of the Americans in the early summer sealed Allied air superiority. Flying was still a bloody business. The outnumbered Luftstreitkräfte shifted Jastas up and down the line to try and win some temporary and limited dominance, and the Germans were able to inflict considerable damage. More than a third of the total aggregate of casualties suffered by the air force occurred in the last seven and a half months of the war.

Many were sustained in the spring of 1918, when the Germans launched their last great effort. After the October Revolution of 1917, the Russians were out of the war and Germany could switch its resources to a single front. This respite was the signal for the 1918 Spring Offensive, a huge outpouring of desperate energy that took the Allies by surprise, pushing them back — forty miles on some sectors of the Front. The air forces were thrown in to try and stem the flood. The squadrons found themselves caught up in massed, swirling air battles as spotters called down fire on the advancing formations — protected by fighters who buzzed above them, trying to keep the Germans at bay — while underneath, at dangerously low altitudes, others swooped on and raked the enemy on the roads, lanes and rail tracks. The effect they had could be devastating, as nineteen-year-old Ewan Stock of 54 Squadron observed when out on a strafing mission in his Sopwith Camel on the afternoon of 22 March. "I saw what seemed to be a long wall of sandbags," he wrote. "I could not understand why I had not seen it before, until diving at the enemy behind it, I noticed that it was a wall of dead bodies heaped one upon the other. The enemy were on the east side of it, so I was able to sweep this wall with machine-gun fire until there must have been a hundred or so German soldiers to add to this human wall." On 12 April the air force carried out more operations than on any other day of the war. It was the crescendo of the German effort. Exhaustion set in and the offensive faltered.

The air force had taken a mauling. Nearly a thousand aircraft and 400 men had been lost. As spring turned to summer, life in the air became less dangerous for the squadrons engaged in the routine activities of flying in support of the army corps, and on the ground things were rather pleasant. In his memoirs Hubert Griffith, the London literary gent who flew with 15 Squadron, describes some encounters with "Archie" and near misses with friendly aircraft. But his memory was "equally insistent on the other side of life — the bathing, the fishing in the lake . . . of riding through green French fields when we could get hold of some horses, and of many, many hours of sheer idling, lying on the grass." It was, he confessed, "in many senses an idyllic situation. Almost for the first and last time in one's life one had as much money as one needed. A flying officer's pay was good; mess bills, drinks and minor luxuries (silk shirts and nice French soaps) were cheap. Merely by being in France one was saving more than enough money to see one through one's home leaves."

As the Allies pressed forward again they increasingly used air power to reach behind the lines and hit the German homeland. The possibility of using aeroplanes as airborne artillery had been seen early on and the Germans had almost from the beginning tried to carry the war deep into their enemies' territory. Britain had made periodic attempts to retaliate. This process was formalized in October 1917 when a specialist wing, No. 41, was used to launch "strategic attacks" against factories, railways and the like, using twin-engined

Handley Page heavy bombers and lighter DH4s. In June the wing was expanded into what was called the Independent Force. It was made up of nine squadrons, including a detachment of Sopwith Camels to provide a fighter escort. By the end of the war they had dropped 550 tons of bombs, most of them by night.

The operations had little effect on the course of events. The Independent Force nonetheless gave a powerful indication of the direction in which military aviation was heading. From the start of the conflict politicians had struggled to make sense of air power, and organizational confusion and inter-service jealousies had further confused the picture. It was clear that aeroplanes were of immense value to land forces. Their usefulness to the navy had taken longer to establish. Part of the problem was physical and practical. On land soldiers and airmen could operate side by side with ease. At sea, huge logistical and mechanical problems had to be overcome before the simplest tasks could be attempted.

Flight brought huge potential advantages to the prosecution of naval warfare. Aircraft could carry out reconnaissance from ships at sea, launch offensive and defensive operations against hostile aircraft and bases, attack enemy weak points on the ground and patrol the seas in search of enemy forces, in particular submarines. As yet, with the big-gun ship the supreme symbol of naval potency, few were prepared to endorse Glenn Curtiss's view (see chapter 1) that in time aircraft would mean the death of battleships, although there were notable far-sighted exceptions.

The innovatory path taken by the Admiralty in the early days soon petered out. Much of naval aviation in the middle years of the war was carried out using airships to exercise traditional military functions. Attempts were made to use observer-carrying balloons tethered to ships to improve reconnaissance, but they found it hard to keep up with the fleet. The danger posed to British shipping by German submarines created a new use for airships, one that fell naturally into the domain of the navy's activities. Under the encouragement of the First Sea Lord, Jacky Fisher, large-scale production began of "Submarine Scouts" that could pin-point marauding U-boats when they surfaced to recharge their batteries, and then direct destroyers and corvettes to them. The craft were crude — a flabby sausage-shaped envelope, with the wingless fuselage of an old BE2 C slung underneath — but surprisingly effective. They were manned by young volunteers, lured by the promise of a ten-shilling-a-day bonus and undeterred by Fisher's prediction that those who answered the call were liable to have been killed or awarded a Victoria Cross within a year.

The airships attracted the nickname "blimps", apparently on account of the noise that resulted if the inflated envelope was flicked with a finger. Soon it was attached to all lighter-weight airships. They would stay in service patrolling coastal waters for the rest of the war, but their uses were limited. Having spotted an enemy vessel they lacked the means to attack it effectively. They carried a small quantity of bombs, which, in the absence of racks, hung on strings over the side, ready to be cut with a sheath knife if needed.

Seaplanes and the flying boats that were now beginning to appear seemed to offer more possibilities for aggressive action. Adapting aeroplanes to water was a slow process and seaplanes took longer than land-based aircraft to prove their practical and enduring worth. A great chance to demonstrate their value arose at the Battle of Jutland, the full-scale naval showdown for which Britain and Germany had been preparing since the 1890s. It began in the North Sea on 31 May 1916. As the Grand Fleet under Admiral Sir John Jellicoe, with the Battlecruiser Fleet under Vice Admiral Sir David Beatty in advance, moved towards the German High Seas Fleet, early knowledge of the enemy dispositions could decide the battle. *Engadine*, one of the seaplane carriers which had taken part in the Cuxhaven operation, was with Beatty's force and had two Short and two Sopwith seaplanes on board. Early in the afternoon smoke was spotted to the north north-east and an air reconnaissance was ordered. However, only one aircraft was sent off. It managed to locate German cruisers, but on the way back was forced down with engine trouble. The pilot, Lieutenant F.J. Rutland, radioed back his sighting, but it was never received. Having repaired his engine and returned to the fleet his information was out of date.

The Germans fared better. The commander, Vizeadmiral Reinhard von Scheer, had the use of a Zeppelin whose reports helped him to plot a course for home, which enabled him to avoid the route that

Jellicoe had guessed he would take and evade the waiting trap.

As aircraft and complementary technologies improved, so did the performance and standing of the RNAS. Seaplanes and flying boats operating out of east-coast ports and Dunkirk played a large part in countering the submarine menace, just as aircraft would in the Battle of the Atlantic twenty-five years later. They were used not only to locate U-boats but to destroy them. The first successful sinking took place on 25 May 1917, when UC-36 was hit by two bombs while she lay on the surface.

The patrols were limited by the aircraft's endurance and the fact that they had to return to dry land to put down. Work resumed on the original notion of launching aircraft from ships — and landing back on them again. The perilous trial-and-error work that was an inescapable part of all early aviation experimentation was even more acute when it came to the business of manoeuvring a light machine onto the heaving deck of a warship, butting through the waves of a northern sea.

The impetus for change came when Beatty, who had learned a hard lesson at Jutland about the value of naval aviation, replaced Jellicoe as commander-in-chief of the Home Fleet in November 1916, and two months later ordered a reorganization of the RNAS. A Fifth Sea Lord was added to the Board of Admiralty with responsibility for naval aviation, and a Grand Fleet Aeronautical Committee was set up to devise a strategic direction for the navy's ships. Its findings prescribed a new approach which concentrated on the navy's needs. Naval aircraft and pilots operating from land bases would no longer act as a reserve for the operations of the RFC. Henceforth the emphasis would be on using ships and aircraft in a more coherent way. Beatty envisioned swarms of aircraft carrying torpedoes, launching cheap and devastating attacks on German warships. For this to be realized, vessels would have to be developed that fulfilled efficiently the function of a floating airbase.

In March 1917 further work was carried out on HMS *Furious* to try and improve her ability to handle aircraft. The forward eighteen-inch gun was removed and a 228 foot take-off deck fitted in its place. At this point the ship carried three Short "Folder" seaplanes and five Sopwith Pups — light, fast fighters. The seaplanes were launched and retrieved. The Pups were launched and then ditched, being deemed cheap enough to be dispensable. Their pilots naturally disliked the idea of risking their lives every time they returned from a sortie and struggled to solve the problem of landing back on board.

They were led by twenty-five-year-old Squadron Commander Edwin Harris Dunning, who had won a Distinguished Flying Cross after being wounded in a fight with German seaplanes. In his efforts to find a solution, Dunning showed a staggering disregard for his own safety. Light though it was, the Pup still had insufficient deck room to put down safely. Dunning and his colleagues discussed the possibility of landing into wind while *Furious* was steaming straight ahead, thus cutting down drastically the aircraft's approach speed. On 2 August 1917 Dunning put the theory to the test.

The experiment took place off Scapa Flow in front of an audience of admirals and generals. *Furious* worked up to a speed of twenty-six knots (30 mph) and headed into an oncoming twenty-one knot wind. That meant that Dunning's pup was approaching at only three knots when it side-slipped in over the deck. Waiting below, seven or eight airmen reached up to grab rope toggles attached to the wings and wrestled the aircraft down, taking care to avoid being minced in the still-whirring propeller.

Dunning thus became the first pilot to land an aircraft on a moving ship and his feat produced a flurry of congratulations. He was not satisfied. He had failed to touch down unaided and five days later he tried again. This time he succeeded, but his machine was blown backwards and damaged. He climbed out, commandeered another Pup and set off yet again. When he came in to land the engine stalled and the aeroplane careered off the deck and over the side. It was twenty minutes before a rescue boat got to him and by then Dunning was dead, drowned after apparently being knocked unconscious. His sacrifice was acknowledged by the Admiralty, who wrote to his father that the data obtained from the experiments that cost him his life was "of the utmost value. It will make aircraft indispensable to the Fleet and possibly revolutionize naval warfare."

Further attempts at alighting on the take-off deck were abandoned after this tragedy, but other approaches were examined. *Furious* was fitted with a landing-on deck at the stern, equipped with an arrester system based on the same principle as the one that Eugene Ely had used when he first alighted on the *Pennsylvania*. Crucially, the ship had been at anchor at the time. When the new deck on *Furious* was tested at Scapa in March 1918 the results were disastrous. Out of thirteen landings, only three aircraft got down undamaged and the rest, in the words of an onlooking pilot, Lieutenant W. G. Moore, "just dropped on the deck like shot partridges". All efforts had to deal with two fundamental problems: the turbulence created by the ship's upperworks, and the hot gases blasting from her funnels, which rocked the light and fragile biplanes. These difficulties would only be overcome with the development of purpose-built aircraft carriers. They required a long and broad landing deck with the superstructure arranged on the starboard side.

Despite these difficulties, in the closing months of the war aircraft operating off *Furious* launched an attack that realized the potential revealed in the Christmas Day raid on Cuxhaven at the start of the conflict. Once again the targets were Zeppelin sheds, this time at the German naval base at Tondern on the border with Denmark. The aeroplanes that took part were Sopwith Camels, which, over the Western Front, were establishing themselves as the outstanding British fighters of the war. They had been modified for marine service with a fuselage that detached behind the cockpit, enabling them to be stowed more easily. They had also been fitted with racks under the wings carrying two fifty-pound bombs. Seven Camels, arranged in two flights, took part in the operation.

Furious sailed from Rosyth on the night of 16–17 July 1918, escorted by a squadron of cruisers and eight destroyers, and arrived at the flying-off position, ninety miles east of the target, early on the eighteenth. The aircraft started to take off at 3.14a.m., formed up into two flights and set off for Tondern. On the way one developed engine trouble, crash-landed and was picked up by an escort. Even though German fighters were based nearby, surprise was complete and the Allies arrived unhindered in clear skies. The three Camels in the first flight swooped down on the biggest of the three sheds, scoring direct hits and setting ablaze the two Zeppelins inside. Despite heavy ground fire from the now thoroughly alert defenders, the second flight managed to drop their bombs on a second shed, destroying a captive balloon.

Pursued by exploding flak, the attackers set off to rejoin the fleet. It had been decided that ditching in the sea would be less dangerous than attempting a landing on the afterdeck. Most of them had been hit, and two crash-landed in Denmark after running out of petrol. Another failed to find the ships and returned to put down on land. Two flopped into the sea near the destroyers and were hauled on board. A sixth plane crashed into the sea and its pilot, Lieutenant Walter ("Toby") Yeullet, was killed. He had just turned nineteen. He was one of the tens of thousands of young men whose boyhood love of flying had led him into the ranks of the wartime aviators and set him on the path to death. Yeullet was born in Walton-on-Thames, Surrey, in June 1899 and by the age of twelve he was designing and flying his own model aircraft. After leaving school he worked for a while as a trainee engineer for an aeroengine manufacturer in Weybridge, before joining the RNAS in July 1917. The action at Tondern seems to have been his first operation.

The novelty of launching bombing missions from vessels appealed to the press. When King George V went aboard *Furious* during a visit to the Grand Fleet a week after the raid, it was described by the *New York Times*'s London correspondent as a "mystery ship", which was "a great puzzle to the foe".

As the war drew to a close something resembling a modern aircraft carrier had emerged, from which aeroplanes could take off and land in relative safety. A requisitioned Italian liner, the 15,750-ton *Conte Rosso*, was refitted to carry a continuous flight deck, 567 feet long, which stretched from bow to stern. Unlike later fleet carriers there was no island from which the captain conned his ship. Instead there was a small structure that was raised and lowered hydraulically, and two bridge wings extending on either side of the flight deck. She was renamed HMS *Argus*, and in October 1918 Commander Richard Bell Davies flew his Sopwith 1½ Strutter off the long deck and landed it again without mishap.

By the time the war finished another purpose-built carrier, HMS *Hermes*, was on the stocks. *Furious* underwent yet another conversion to combine her fore and aft landing decks into a flush entity and another battleship (purchased from Chile) was converted for air use as HMS *Eagle*. The Royal Navy thus led the world in its possession of the ships that it was now clear would play a vital part in any future war at sea. Their effectiveness, however, was dependent on the aircraft that flew from them — although by now an organizational revolution had occurred which meant that the choice no longer lay in the hands of sailors.

Since the start of the war a bureaucratic conflict had been raging that paralleled the one being fought in the air. Bureaucrats, industrialists and politicians struggled with soldiers and sailors to rationalize the supply of equipment to the respective air forces and put aircraft and men to their most efficient use. It was hard work. A major obstacle in the search for harmony was the attitude of the War Office and the Admiralty, which both maintained they were the best judges of how their air services should be equipped and used. Their political chiefs — Lord Curzon and Harold Balfour — fought their corners in the War Committee with as much ferocity as if they had been in uniform.

Several bodies had been set up to solve the problems. The first, under the War Minister Lord Derby, was triggered by the "Fokker Menace" and convened in February 1916. It had no real powers and Derby soon resigned. He believed that the solution lay in the amalgamation of the two air services, but reckoned this too difficult a bureaucratic feat in wartime. In reality, it was the atmosphere of accelerated — not to say hasty — decision-making that the war engendered that made the union possible. Derby was succeeded by Lord

Curzon, who shared his predecessor's views. Any attempt to implement a merger was scuppered by the vehement opposition of the navy, however.

On 3 January 1917 a new committee, the Second Air Board, was set up under the presidency of Lord Cowdray, a Yorkshireman who had built his fortune constructing railways, docks, dams and harbours around the world. The board took on responsibility for designing aircraft and engines (actually making them was now the province of the Munitions Ministry) and for allocating them to the army and navy. Representatives of all the departments concerned, including the naval and military air executives, were gathered under one roof in offices at the Cecil Hotel in the Strand, London. Production was overseen by another powerful figure from the industrial world, a Scotsman, Sir William Weir. By the end of the year production of new types (which, on the whole, had the advantage over their German opponents) was in full swing and there was no shortage of pilots to fly them.

By then the move to create a single, independent air force was building up powerful momentum. It was the air war over Britain — rather than events in France or at sea — that made it unstoppable. Compared with the bloodletting in other theatres, the casualties caused by the German air raids of 1915–17 were miniscule. Nor was the material damage great — about £3 million worth of property was destroyed. The *moral* effect, however, was huge. The panic that gripped the streets of London when the Germans appeared overhead was not confined to the masses. The alarm felt by their masters was just as intense, as was demonstrated on the day of the great Gotha raid of 7 July 1917, when three tons of explosives dropped on the capital killed fifty-seven people. It was a Saturday and as ministers made their way to Downing Street for an emergency cabinet session, they witnessed the alarm of citizens in the streets. The mood was catching. The demeanour of the politicians was noted disapprovingly by the Chief of the Imperial General Staff, Sir William Robertson, who was at the meeting and wrote in a letter to Haig that "one would have thought the whole world was coming to an end . . . I could not get a word in edgeways."

The raid crystallized the feeling that arrangements were hopelessly inadequate to fight the air war. There was no doubt in the public mind as to where the responsibility for protecting civilians lay. Ira Jones had finished his flying training at Northolt, Middlesex, and had just returned to the Regent Palace Hotel in London after a night out when he "heard the air raid buzzers for the first time . . . I have never seen the mood of a happy throng change so quickly," he recorded afterwards. "One moment, all was gaiety, the next there was a stampede of shrieking creatures who had been transformed from apparent fairies into wild women. I followed the mob from the grill room into the foyer, where most of the hotel's customers had assembled. One 'lady', pointing at me, angrily screeched: 'You're in the Flying Corps! Why aren't you up there, chasing those devils away?'"

Something had to be done. Four days after the July raid General Smuts was instructed by the Cabinet to examine "the air organization generally and the direction of aerial operations". Jan Christian Smuts was a brilliant all-rounder who had succeeded at everything he had tried. He had turned from the law to politics and then to warfare, fighting the British in the Boer War, then negotiating a peace that unified South Africa and established Boer dominance. His former enemies became his friends and supporters. He led the British military campaign against the Germans in East Africa before being sent to London. There, in the summer of 1917, the Prime Minister David Lloyd George invited him to join the War Policy Committee.

Smuts took less than a month to produce his first report. It ran to only a few thousand words and its recommendations were straightforward and commonsensical, restricted to the sphere of improving London's dismal anti-aircraft defences. There were to be more guns and searchlights, and three new RFC fighter squadrons, controlled by a central organization, the London Area Defence.

His second report, which came out in August, was a far more significant document. Smuts employed an apocalyptic tone, which echoed the panicky mood of July. For him, the crucial factor was how to prepare for a dreadful new era of warfare, of which the Gotha raids had provided only a glimpse.

"As far as can be foreseen," he wrote, "there is absolutely no limit to the scale of its future independent war use, and the day may not be far off when aerial operations with their devastation of enemy lands and destruction of industrial and populous centres on a vast scale may become the principal operations of war, to which the older forms of military and naval operations may become secondary and subordinate."

Like his predecessors, Smuts came to the conclusion that to produce an air force capable of meeting the challenge, the RFC and the RNAS would have to amalgamate. The efficiencies created and the extra aircraft production generated by the reforms of Cowdray and Weir would allow the establishment of a bombing force that was capable of reaching out to German cities and factories.

Thus, the principal rationale for an independent air force was to produce a bombing fleet that could punish Germany for attacking the British homeland and deter it from doing so in the future. As it was, the Independent Force that resulted was stillborn and its "strategic" bombing campaign against the war economy of the enemy never amounted to more than a series of incoherent and patchy raids. In the judgement of Arthur Harris, a young RFC pilot at the time, who would go on to preside over the effort to reduce German cities to rubble a generation later, "the bomber was in no way an important weapon of the 1914–18 war".

At the core of the report was Smuts's recommendation that the separate existences of the RFC and the RNAS should cease and that they should be reborn as a single entity: the Royal Air Force (RAF). As was appropriate for what was the world's first independent air service, it would have its own government department: the Air Ministry. However, this amalgamation

131

was no more popular at the top of the army and navy now than it had been when it was first mooted. The man who might be expected to give it a warm welcome — Hugh Trenchard — was initially opposed to it, believing that the structural, buttressing relationship that had grown up between the RFC and the ground forces would be weakened if the air force stood alone. He would nonetheless agree to be the RAF's first Chief of the Air Staff, a post he held for only a few months before falling out with scheming air minister Lord Rothermere.

In peacetime it is unlikely that such an institutional evolution would have taken place at such speed — or indeed at all, given the strength and vehemence of opposing institutional interests. But the decision had been taken at a time of emergency in the middle of a war that seemed likely to continue for years. The likelihood of — and domestic terror of — air attack was almost certain to grow. In the eyes of politicians and the public, a joint air force seemed to offer a rational response to the threat. Wrested from Admiralty control, the navy's aircraft would now be free for land operations. The new bombing force offered the illusion of retaliation against the Germans for their air assault on the homeland, as well as the possibility that the Germans might be deterred from continuing with it. The process had gone too far to be deflected by sophisticated military arguments. The decision was made, the official birthday set, and, on 1 April 1918, the Royal Air Force came into the world.

This historic moment was barely noticed by those it most affected. In France the Germans were about to launch the second phase of their Spring Offensive and the airmen were locked in an exhausting series of mass battles over the Somme plains. However, one event seemed to offer hope that events were going the Allies' way. On the morning of 21 April Manfred von Richtofen was on the ground at Cappy airfield, about ten miles south-east of Albert on the banks of the Somme, waiting for the ground mist to lift. At 10.20 a.m. it began to clear and, in his Fokker triplane, he led a flight off to intercept some British aircraft reported to be well over the German lines and heading their way.

He was in a sombre mood. A few days before he had been reflecting on the tone of his boastful autobiography. "When I read [my] book I smile at my own insolence," he wrote. "I am no longer so insolent in spirit." Flying alongside him was Leutnant Hans Joachim Wolff who recorded that they saw seven Sopwith Camels flying in their direction, and above them, seven more. Battle was joined. There was the initial, inevitable confusion, then Wolff looked over at Richtofen and saw that he was "at extremely low altitude, over the Somme near Corbie, right behind an Englishman".

The intended victim was in fact a Canadian, twenty-three-year-old Second Lieutenant Wilfred "Wop" May, who was on his first mission and had been told to stay out of the fighting, watch carefully and try and learn something. When a German fighter approached, the temptation was too great and he had gone for him,

133

only for his guns to jam. As he headed for home he looked round to see a blood-red triplane on his tail. He "kept on dodging and spinning . . . until I ran out of sky and had to hedge-hop over the ground. Richtofen was firing at me continually."

As they crossed the German front line, ground troops opened up and the firing continued as they flew over the British trenches. When he reached the Somme, May flattened down close to the water, but as he rounded a bend in the river Richtofen "came over the hill. At that point I was a sitting duck. I felt he had me cold." Then, seemingly miraculously, Richtofen stopped firing. He too was under attack, from another Canadian, Captain Roy Brown of 209 Squadron, whose report later stated that he "dived on a pure red triplane . . . got a long burst into him and he went down vertical." Australian machine gunners on the ground also claimed the credit. Either way, Richtofen was dead. His body was retrieved from the wreckage and taken to Poulainville airfield ten miles away. Richtofen was laid out in a hangar on a strip of corrugated metal, staring upwards, in unconscious imitation of the knights that he and his fellow aces were said to resemble.

The following day — ten days before his twenty-sixth birthday — Richtofen was buried with full military honours. Among the mourners was Major Sholto Douglas, who would rise high in the new RAF. He recorded that "it was impossible not to feel a little emotional about it". He nonetheless repeated the general view that the Red Baron was a calculating sort of warrior who used "the utmost caution" and "never hesitated to avoid a fight or pull out of one if he thought the odds against him were too great".

Mick Mannock, who employed the same scientific approach, shed no tears for his rival. "I hope he roasted all the way down," he was reported to have said on learning of his death. It would soon be his turn. On 26 July Mannock had been out with a novice pilot, showing him the ropes, and had just attacked an enemy two-seater, leaving his pupil to finish it off. Mannock was flying low, breaking one of his own cardinal rules, when a German machine-gun post got his range. The flames he so dreaded sprang from the engine and he spiralled down to his death. Mannock's demise had a profound effect on his comrades. Ira Jones, by now a veteran pilot and a devoted admirer of "the greatest air fighter of all time", usually recorded the deaths of colleagues with a resigned "poor old so-and-so bought it today", but this was different. "Mick is dead," he wrote. "Everyone is stunned. No one can believe it . . . I have a deep aching void in my breast. I keep on repeating to myself: 'It can't be true. Mick cannot be dead.' "

Of the great aces of the war, very few on any side survived. The British stars, Hawker, Ball, Mannock and McCudden had all gone. The Germans had lost Boelcke, Immelmann and Richtofen, and the French Georges Guynemer and Roland Garros. Aces would reappear in the next war, but they were fewer and their celebrity was more artificial as their personalities were moulded by the official publicity machines to fit the demands of propaganda. The heroic age of air fighting was at an end. From its amateur, makeshift origins military aviation had, in the space of a decade, come to rival the existing services in size and importance. The numbers involved would have seemed incredible to the pilots of the first handful of squadrons as they prepared for that first hair-raising hop across the Channel.

By November 1918 the RAF had swollen to a force of nearly a million. Its 280 squadrons roamed the skies not only of France but of Macedonia, Mesopotamia, Palestine and East Africa. In the course of the First World War they had destroyed 7,054 German aircraft and lost 9,378 aircrew. The airmen's exploits had won eleven VCs. Soon the life of this vast organization was to be imperilled, however, not by any foreign enemy, but by the politicians who had built it up and by its brothers-in-arms.

CHAPTER
SEVEN

Jonah's Gourd

On Armistice Day 1918 the Royal Air Force was the largest air force in the world. That did not mean that its future was assured. Despite its size it stood on shaky political and bureaucratic foundations. It was understaffed, ill-equipped and operated in a poisonous atmosphere of suspicion and intrigue. It soon emerged that the older services regarded the consent they had given to its creation as temporary. It had, they believed, been obtained under coercion, wrung out of them by the exigencies of war. Now peace had arrived, it was null and void. The Prime Minister, Lloyd George, seemed to agree with them. Returning to office at the head of a Liberal-Tory coalition in the "Coupon" election of December 1918, he decided not to keep the newly formed Air Ministry as a separate department and passed it to Winston Churchill, who became joint Secretary of State for both war and air. The implication was that the Prime Minister cared little about the fate of the new service. His Conservative successor, Andrew Bonar Law, who took over as Prime Minister in the autumn of 1922, showed even less concern.

Churchill supported the notion of an autonomous air force and he was reluctant to see it die. However, he was fighting a wave of anti-military revulsion that swamped politicians and public alike in the aftermath of the War to End All Wars, and the RAF with its vast array of aircraft and squadrons was an affront to this new mood. Demobilization was swift and devastating. The wartime strength of 280 squadrons was run down to fewer than thirty, and men who had been princes of the air found themselves struggling to find work as chauffeurs and policemen.

The RAF had been as strong as a lion when the war ended. A year later it was as weak as a kitten and the predatory eyes of the army and navy were fixed upon it. They were soon agitating respectively for the return of the RFC and the RNAS and for the RAF and the Air Ministry to be wound up. The campaign would persist through much of the decade — and the struggle against traditional services to strangle the infant at birth would become part of the foundation myth of the RAF. There were, as an Air Ministry mandarin Sir Maurice Dean pointed out, "distinct elements of truth" in the story. "In the early Twenties, the Royal Air Force was indeed actively disliked by the other services," he wrote. "They considered it an upstart and its officers for the most part socially impossible . . . [it] was an innovation and the way of innovators in Britain is hard. The first instinct is to ignore, the second is to despise, the third is to attack."

Credit for the survival of the Royal Air Force in these treacherous years is usually awarded to Boom

Trenchard. In RAF circles, wrote Dean, "the story is often told in pantomime terms with the Royal Air Force as the beleaguered maiden, the army and navy as the dragon and its mate, and Trenchard as St George." Again, though oversimplified, this tale is true in its essentials.

In January 1919 Trenchard, fresh from putting down a mutiny of disaffected soldiers, was asked by Churchill to take over again as Chief of the Air Staff, the job he had held briefly before falling out with Rothermere. Before he did so Trenchard was asked to produce a paper on how the air force should be reorganized in the light of the mood of austerity. He came up with a plan that made the most of the limited resources available and Churchill confirmed his appointment.

Despite his previously expressed convictions that air forces should serve the objectives of parent services, Trenchard now became the most ardent defender of an autonomous RAF. Some saw this as evidence of his malleability, bordering on hypocrisy. Those who knew him well, like John Slessor who served under him on the Western Front and ended up Marshal of the Royal Air Force, discerned something else. "Whatever Trenchard's faults may have been," he wrote, "I class him with Churchill and Smuts as one of the three greatest men I have been privileged to know."

Slessor defined Trenchard's qualities as "self-confidence without a trace of arrogance; a contemptuous yet not intolerant disregard for anything mean or petty; the capacity to shuffle aside the non-essentials and put an unerring finger on the real core of a problem or the

139

true quality of a man, a sort of instinct for the really important point; a selfless devotion to the cause of what he believed to be true and right. Trenchard [had] all those qualities, and above all a shining sincerity."

Trenchard was philosophical about the difficult task he had set himself. In a memorandum setting out the post-war organization of the RAF he compared the force to "the prophet Jonah's gourd. The necessities of war created it in a night, but the economies of peace have to a large extent caused it to wither in a day, and now we are faced with the necessity of replacing it with a plant of deeper root." Always mindful of the scarcity of resources, he set about providing the vital essentials of a skeleton force, while giving way on every possible detail where he felt expense could be spared. What was needed were institutions that would provide the foundations of the new force and establish it as an independent reality, and to arrange the limited manpower at his disposal in the most efficient and flexible way.

In the paper he had written for Churchill, Trenchard had set out two choices. One was "to use the air simply as a means of conveyance, captained by chauffeurs, weighted by the navy and army personnel, drop bombs at places specified by them . . . or observe for their artillery." The other was "to really make an air service which will encourage and develop airmanship, or better still the air spirit, like the naval spirit, and to make it a force that will profoundly alter the strategy of the future." Throughout the war the vehement partisan of the first approach, Trenchard was now the equally

140

forceful champion of the second. Lloyd George accepted Trenchard's case and the document was expanded into a White Paper. Its adoption guaranteed the survival of the RAF, although its service rivals made periodic raids to try and reclaim lost territory.

The fact was that the argument for an autonomous air force was by no means unanswerable. Britain's allies in the Great War did not rush to establish third services and the United States and France continued to tie aircraft to the requirements of their armies and navies. In the years before the next war broke out, the RAF's struggle to establish its identity took precedence over the needs of the other services. As it was, the fact that most of the work done between 1914 and 1918 was in conjunction with the army meant that, after the RAF's conception, it was military genes that predominated. The result was that naval aviation was badly neglected. This error was only corrected when the Fleet Air Arm (FAA) was belatedly handed to the Admiralty in May 1939, leaving it pitifully unprepared for the new realities of war at sea.

In the early 1920s, when the thought of another major war was too unbearable to contemplate, the natural reaction was to flinch from consideration of long-term strategic possibilities. Trenchard busied himself with stretching the limited bricks and mortar in his barrow to build something that would last.

He was concerned initially with humans rather than machines, concentrating on training officers and men to provide a wealth of expertise, that could be drawn on to instruct others and to be brought into play when a

141

crisis arose. Flying was a young man's game — a fact which posed an immediate problem. It meant that at any time there would be a large number of junior officers and comparatively few senior ranks. Trenchard invented a new system. Only half the officers at any time would hold permanent commissions. Of the rest, 40 per cent would be short service officers, serving for four or six years with another four in the reserve. The other 10 per cent would be seconded from the army and navy. The permanent officers would come from an RAF cadet college, the air-force equivalent of Dartmouth or Sandhurst, and also from universities and the ranks. Once commissioned, they would be posted to a squadron. After five years they were required to adopt a specialist area like engineering, navigation or wireless.

Flying was also highly technical. The new air force would need a steady supply of skilled riggers and fitters. Like the pilots, the mechanics who had kept the aeroplanes in the air had returned to civilian life. Trenchard's solution was to bring in "boys and train them ourselves". They would start off with a three-year apprenticeship, before entering the ranks. To carry out the research and development necessary to keep abreast of rapidly changing technologies there would be specialist centres for aeronautics, armaments, wireless and photography.

The army and navy had offered the use of their facilities to train up volunteers. Trenchard spurned them. The RAF would have its own colleges in which to inculcate the "air spirit": Cranwell in Lincolnshire for the officer cadets; Halton in Buckinghamshire for the apprentices. Cranwell had been an RNAS station during the war and it was plonked on flat, wind-scoured lands in the middle of nowhere. This, in Trenchard's eyes, was one of its main attractions. He told his biographer that he hoped that "marooned in the wilderness, cut off from pastimes they could not organize for themselves, they would find life cheaper, healthier and more wholesome". This, he hoped, would give them "less cause to envy their contemporaries at Sandhurst or Dartmouth and acquire any kind of inferiority complex".

Halton, on the other hand, was chosen for its proximity to London. "Trenchard brats" — as the apprentices became known — were thought to be more prone to homesickness and boredom. Halton Hall and the surrounding estate, bought from Lionel de Rothschild for £112,000, was within easy reach of dance halls and cinemas and the railway stations of the metropolis for parental visits.

In February 1920 RAF Cranwell was transformed into the Royal Air Force College. It was a grand name for a dismal, utilitarian cantonment. One of the first intake of fifty-two cadets described a "scene of grey corrugated iron and large open spaces whose immensity seemed limitless in the sea of damp fog which surrounded the camp". They lived in single-storey huts, scattered on either side of the Sleaford Road, connected by covered walkways to keep out the rain and snow borne in on the east wind. It was not until 1929 that a proper edifice was in place. The design was inspired by Sir Christopher Wren's Royal Hospital in Chelsea, and the brick and stone and classical proportions helped create an instant sense of tradition.

The likes of Hawker, Ball, Mannock and McCudden had provided a cohort of paladins around whom a glorious narrative could be constructed. Churchill set the tone in the first issue of the college magazine.

"Nothing that has ever happened in the world before has offered to man such an opportunity for individual personal prowess as the air fighting of the Great War," he wrote. "Fiction has never portrayed such extraordinary combats, such hairbreadth escapes, such an absolute superiority to risk, such dazzling personal triumphs. It is to rival, and no doubt to excel these feats of your forerunners in the Service that you are training and I . . . look forward with confidence to the day when you will make the name of the Royal Air Force feared and respected throughout the world."

The likes of Mannock and McCudden, though, would have been out of place socially at Cranwell. The overwhelming ethos and atmosphere was muscular and public school, and fun was boisterous and painful. First-termers were forced to sing a song for the other cadets and failure to perform well earned a punishment called "creeping to Jesus". The victim was stripped almost naked, blindfolded and forced to sniff his way along a pepper trail that ended at an open window, where he was tipped outside and drenched in cold water.

144

Trenchard set the tone in a typically interfering letter to the first Commandant, Air Commodore Charles Longcroft. "Who have you got up there who can train the boys in Rugby Football?" he wanted to know. "After all, this is the best game for making an officer and a gentleman out of any material. If we want to do well in the Air Force, I believe that rugby is the best game to help us."

Longcroft himself was ex-Charterhouse, an early aviator who had transferred from the Welch Regiment and commanded No 4 Squadron on the Western Front. He rode to hounds and followed beagles. Cranwell had its own pack and its first master was Charles Portal, another RFC veteran, who commanded the flying training wing and would be Chief of the Air Staff for most of the Second World War.

But as Trenchard's missive suggests, Cranwell existed not just to acquire gentlemen but to manufacture them. From the outset it had been understood that a modern force could not rely exclusively on the traditional recruiting grounds of the military class. In 1919 a committee was set up under Lord Hugh Cecil — a Tory MP from the Salisbury dynasty who had served as a ground officer with the RFC — to try and define the educational and human qualities needed for the officer corps. It was accepted that, in theory at least, it should be open to all talents. Cecil decided that all officers must be able to fly, though this qualification was not so rigid as to exclude good technicians who were poor aviators. The RAF wanted boys who exhibited "the quality of a gentleman". It was careful, though, to emphasize that by this it meant "not a particular degree of wealth or a particular social position but a certain character".

Ordinary boys from ordinary families were nonetheless unlikely to find the gates of Cranwell flung open to them. Air Ministry officials set out to recruit people like themselves, writing to the headmasters of their old schools, selling the college's virtues, playing down the perils of air-force life and seeking candidates. Eton had a dedicated liaison officer.

Unlike the public schools, few state schools had the resources to provide coaching for the entrance exam. Fees were steep. Parents were expected to pay up to £75 a year, plus £35 before entry and £30 at the start of the second year towards uniform and books. This was at a time when a bank manager earned £500 a year.

So, despite the pious utterances of the Cecil committee, the young men who passed through Cranwell in the interwar years were drawn largely from the middle and upper middle classes. The stuffier army and navy may have regarded them as arriviste, but to the less sophisticated air-force officers seemed rather polished and aloof. Their style was caught by the beady eye of Richmal Crompton, creator of the Just William series of boys' books and a reliable social observer. In one story William's sister Ethel is taken to a dance by a stuck-up airman from the local base, somewhere in the Home Counties.

"It's a rotten floor, of course," drawled Wing Commander Glover, adjusting his monocle.

"Absolutely rotten," agreed Ethel languidly, as she leant back in her chair and sipped her tea elegantly.

"But interesting to watch the natives."

"Frightfully interesting," said Ethel, trying to look as little like a native as possible.

"Some pretty frightful dancing, isn't there?"

"Frightful," said Ethel with an air of aloof disgust.

"An awful crowd, too."

"Awful," agreed Ethel with a world-weary smile.

"Well," said the Wing Commander, "shall we tread another measure or are you tired?"

"Oh no," said Ethel, trying to strike the happy mean between readiness to tread another measure and lofty amusement of the whole affair.

The Wingco's snooty demeanour does not sit easily with the notion of the flier as being intimately connected with the society he was defending, which would be promoted during the Battle of Britain.

There was a backdoor route to Cranwell. It led from Halton, where every year the three best apprentices were offered a cadetship to the college with the expectation, frequently fulfilled, that this would lead them to the highest reaches of the service. The first appeal for apprentices had received an overwhelming response. Five thousand boys applied for the first intake of 300 places. They were mostly drawn from the lower-middle and upper-working classes, who saw the RAF as a way into the intoxicating world of aviation.

The entrance exam tested them on mathematics, science and English. The candidates were expected to be at school certificate standard, a tough exam taken at sixteen, which was the threshold to higher education (it was a requirement for Cranwell), so most of the boys had parents who were prepared to keep them on after the normal school leaving age of fourteen. The sacrifices this must have entailed in some cases are evident in a 1924 magazine photograph of proto-apprentices as they set off from a London railway station to their new life. They are all cheering. Many wear shabby suits and flat caps. The caption noted that "the variety of class of boys was very striking, many of them having quite an imposing kit, whilst not the least pleased with the whole proceedings were those whose belongings were kept within bounds in brown paper parcels".

The apprentices were divided into trades. They were to become fitters, working on engines, and riggers, responsible for the airframes. The third, smaller, category of wireless technicians was trained at a sub-unit of Cranwell. Many — maybe most — of these eager lads harboured an ambition to fly aeroplanes, rather than merely to service them. In 1921 a new class of airman pilot was announced that offered flying training to outstanding candidates from the ranks. They served for five years before returning to their own trades, but retained the sergeant's stripes they gained for being in the air. This policy meant that by the time the next war started about a quarter of the pilots in RAF squadrons were NCOs — a tough, skilful, hard-to-impress elite within an elite. Trenchard was as proud of Halton as he was of Cranwell. He understood that he was engineering a new class of educated other ranks — something that had never happened in British military history.

Cranwell and Halton did not produce enough men to staff the new service — skeletal though it was. To create the manpower needed Trenchard brought in a system of short-service commissions. In 1924 the Air Ministry advertised for 400 officers for flying duties. They had to be British born and of pure European descent. Once in, their contracts ran for six years with a further four on the reserve. The system was a godsend for many ex-wartime pilots who had caught the flying bug but were unable to find work in the restricted world of commercial aviation.

In his search for a cheap supply of trained fliers available in case of emergency Trenchard had come up with the idea of an aerial equivalent to the territorial units that supplemented the army. In 1925 the Auxiliary Air Force (AAF) was formed. The first four squadrons were No. 600 (City of London), No. 601 (County of London), No. 602 (City of Glasgow) and No. 603 (City of Edinburgh). The pilots were amateurs who flew in their spare time. The machines and the mechanics who maintained them were supplied by the RAF. As with the territorial yeomanry regiments, the idea was that these forces would have a strong local character. Trenchard also wanted them to have social cachet. They would succeed, he said, "if it was looked

149

upon as as much of an honour to belong to one as it is to belong to a good club or a good university."

The AAF provided an institutional framework in which the attraction that "sportsmen" had felt towards aeroplanes since the pioneering years could be formalized. Some of the units gloried in their snobbery. No. 601, the "Millionaires' Squadron", was formed by Lord Edward Grosvenor who, after Eton and a stint in the Foreign Legion, had served as an RNAS pilot in the war. He recruited from his own circle. According to the squadron historian, he "chose his officers from among gentlemen of sufficient presence not to be overawed by him, and sufficient means not to be excluded from his favourite pastimes — eating, drinking and White's [the exclusive St James's Club]".

The squadron had its headquarters at a townhouse at 54 Kensington Park Road in Notting Hill. Their gatherings echoed to the sound of broken glass. One after-dinner game involved trying to circumnavigate the room without touching the floor, another ended with unsuspecting visitors having tankards of beer poured down their trousers. It was all good, high-spirited fun, but the auxiliary squadrons took their flying seriously and the japes were mixed with a conscientious approach to training that would serve the RAF well later. Initially they were equipped with bombers, but from 1934 gradually switched to fighters. During the Battle of Britain the AAF provided nearly a quarter of Fighter Command's strength.

They were supplemented by the University Air Squadrons, which fulfilled a similar function. The inspiration for them came from RFC veterans who went to Cambridge to study engineering. With Trenchard's encouragement, others were set up at Oxford and London.

One section of the population from which cheap and diligent labour could be drawn was no longer available. Women had begun to infiltrate the British military organization in France in the latter years of the First World War, when it was officially decided that they were fitted to do clerking and support staff jobs that had previously been the province of males. In January 1918 a Womens' Auxiliary Air Force Corps was formed to work with the nascent RAF, which was then renamed the Women's Royal Air Force (WRAF). By the end of the war it was about 25,000 strong. As well as clerical work they also did domestic duties: cleaning, cooking and laundering. But there was also a growing technical section engaged in working as welders, riggers, electricians and mechanics, as well as drivers.

The path into the world of men was not easy. In a letter to the *Daily Telegraph* in January 1919 a WRAF told how she "joined up as a carpenter", but instead of getting the month's training she had been promised she received "only a few drills". She was eventually drafted to an aerodrome and put to work in the carpenter's shop. She found she was "tolerated by the men as another military nuisance. There I have been six weeks, spending eight hours a day (most days) in that shop, and have never yet done one single day's work. I should go on like the rest, enjoying my drills, physical and otherwise and my hockey and dances, but I have a conscience."

In the post-war budget-slashing the WRAF was marked down for the chop. Throughout 1919 women who had operated wireless sets, ridden motorbikes and painted liquid cellulose "dope" on the fabric of wings and fuselages were laid off, leaving only a handful kept on to help run a hospital and the records department. Women would have to wait nearly twenty years before the demands of war made them employable once again.

Even in its reduced state the RAF managed to keep its place in the popular imagination. It showed itself off at the annual air display at Hendon in north London, where enormous crowds gathered to watch aerobatics.

The reluctance to entertain the dreadful thought of another world war hung over all decision-making. It was enshrined in the "ten-year rule" covering all service planning — the idea, based on little more than wishful thinking, that there would be no major conflict for a decade. The effect of this rule was felt most heavily in the quality of the equipment available to the reduced RAF. Between 1919 and 1934 the squadrons flew aeroplanes that were little different from those they had flown in the First World War. The names of the types have a forlorn and redundant air. For bombers they had Handley Page Hyderabads, Fairey Fawns, Vickers Virginias and Victorias, and Westland Wapitis. For fighters, Armstrong Whitley Siskins and Gloster Gamecocks. At a time when monoplanes were starting to appear in the fleets of the civil airlines linking the great cities of Europe all the RAF's models were biplanes. Little attempt was made to develop the science of navigation — a disastrous omission that was to render the British bombing effort almost completely ineffective in the first years of the next war.

As it was, these primitive machines were more than capable of carrying out the tasks that fell to them in the years before German rearmament galvanized governments into action. For much of the time they were engaged in police actions, quelling unrest in remote parts of the Empire. In January 1920 a dissident who became known as "The Mad Mullah" rose up against British rule in Somaliland. After the army failed to deal with him, Trenchard sent a squadron of De Havilland DH-9s to bomb the rebel forts and camps. The Mad Mullah surrendered and British control was reestablished. By dropping a few bombs and loosing off their machine guns the RAF had shown it could achieve results for very little cost. A pattern was established. Thereafter the air force was used to impose order in Palestine, Mesopotamia, Aden and the North-West Frontier. This activity resulted in an exotic and adventurous existence for service airmen, some of whom would go on to the commanding heights of the RAF in the next big war. They included John Slessor who, in the spring of 1921, was sent to command a flight of 20 Squadron then stationed at Parachinar, "a delightful place" just over the border with Afghanistan.

In many respects life was pleasant. "We enjoyed ourselves in India," he wrote. "In those days officers and airmen went overseas on a five-year tour and often remained with the same squadron throughout.

153

Squadrons changed stations as units. The aircraft, of course, flew to their new station, while the personnel, wives and children followed in slow, dusty troop trains — with two or three trucks of polo ponies tacked on behind. We played a lot of not very high-class polo. We went on leave to Kashmir or down into Central India and shot or fished. We played a bit of cricket."

In other ways life could be trying. The remoteness of the location meant that the RAF squadrons on the North-West Frontier were under army control and funded from the Government of India budget. Many of those in authority had spent the war years in India and had only the dimmest idea of the developments in the air. According to Slessor, "it was inevitable that among the senior advisers of the Viceroy the combination of ignorance about air matters, ingrained tradition and the Englishman's natural suspicion of anything new, should have had the result that when cuts in military expenditure were required, they should fall upon this new service which no one understood." At one point a blunder in the accounting department meant that there was an embargo on stores and spare parts being shipped out from Britain. The result was that while the RAF had a theoretical strength of six squadrons in India, each with an establishment of twelve aircraft, "I doubt whether we could have put a dozen aircraft into the air on any one day."

Arthur Harris, who in January took command of 31 Squadron, equipped with Bristol Fighters, felt keenly the consequences of the neglect. "We lacked everything in the way of necessary accommodation and spares and materials for keeping our aircraft serviceable," he wrote. "The only thing there was never any shortage of was demands for our services when the trouble blew up on the frontier." That autumn the squadron was based at Peshawar and busy with bombing and strafing raids against tribesmen, who launched periodic attacks on border posts. "It was not unknown for aircraft to take off on operations on wheels with naked rims, because there were no tyres, and with axles lashed on with doubtful, country-made rope, because there was no rubber shock-absorber rope. We flew on single-ignition engines which the Air Force at home had long discarded as un-airworthy." It was, he concluded, "no joke to fly over the mountains on the frontier with worn-out and out-of-date equipment, where a forced landing meant probably being killed outright in the crash, or if you survived this, a still less pleasant death on the ground."

Harris felt angry enough about the situation to offer his resignation, though he was persuaded to withdraw it and moved on to Iraq for a further stint of showing the natives who was boss. Anger at Britain's failure to grant the independence the tribes had been promised when inveigled onto the allied side during the First World War had boiled over into sporadic rebellions. In Iraq the RAF was free of army control. Indeed the senior RAF officer in the country, Sir John Salmond, commanded not just the air force but also the small number of ground forces. In March 1921 Winston Churchill, whose clutch of portfolios included the Colonial Office, had called a conference to sort out how Britain would

155

administer Iraq and Transjordan, which, thanks to a League of Nations mandate, it now governed. Trenchard had persuaded Churchill that control could be imposed from the air and the Air Ministry was given responsibility for maintaining law and order.

Harris was to command 45 Squadron, with which he had flown over the Western Front. His flight commanders were Flight Lieutenants the Hon. Ralph Cochrane and Robert Saundby, both of whom became trusted lieutenants in Bomber Command, twenty years later. The squadron was equipped with Vickers Vernons and engaged in transport duties. The aeroplanes lumbered rather than flew — they could manage only 68 mph. But they were strong, capable of carrying one ton of freight and staying airborne for seven hours. Harris soon persuaded Salmond to allow him to convert them for bombing. Rather than consult London and get bogged down in a bureaucratic process, they would do the job themselves. "By sawing a sighting hole in the nose of our troop carriers and making our own bomb racks we converted them into what were really the first of the post-war, long-range heavy bombers," he wrote.

He then set about devising an accurate means of dropping 20, 50 and 100 lb bombs, and incendiaries using a home-made bomb-sight made of a length of shock absorber and a trigger-release mechanism. If Harris is to be believed, in practice sorties it was able to achieve an average accuracy of 26 yards from 2,000 to 3,000 feet — a far better result than would be achieved in the early years of the coming war. They first went into action against the Turkish army, which had crossed the border and was threatening Kirkuk. The appearance of the bombers forced the Turks to withdraw. Salmond was delighted. Much of the work amounted to aerial intimidation of tribes that rejected the rulers imposed on them by the British.

Harris recalled the period with characteristic rough candour. "When a tribe started open revolt we gave warning to all its most important villages by loud speaker from low-flying aircraft and by dropping messages that air action would be taken after forty-eight hours. Then, if the rebellion continued, we destroyed the villages and by air patrols kept the insurgents away from their homes for as long as necessary until they decided to give up, which they invariably did." It was, he claimed, "a far less costly method of controlling rebellion than by military action and the casualties on both sides were infinitely less than they would have been in the pitched battles on the ground which would otherwise have been the only alternative." Dropping bombs on mud huts and cowing primitive warriors was effective and, for Harris at least, fun. It was no preparation for the confrontation that was looming against a modern enemy armed with more than just rifles.

CHAPTER EIGHT

Arming for Armageddon

At the end of January 1932 Japanese naval aircraft bombed the Chapei district of Shanghai, a thickly populated area on the north bank of the Suchow river. A few days later film of the event appeared in newsreels in cinemas all over the world. The images were shocking. They showed mushrooming explosions, rolling clouds of black smoke and tottering buildings. More sinister to the men and women watching were the scenes of folk like themselves, trundling barrows loaded with their household goods, rushing in a blind panic for the open countryside, leaving pavements littered with bodies. "The marksmanship of the fliers is uncanny!" raved the American commentator on the Universal Newspaper Newsreel report. "Streets that were once a hive of activity are clammy with the shadow of death, and things that were once human beings lying where they fell."

In London the Prime Minister Stanley Baldwin watched and was sickened. "Shanghai is a nightmare," he declared. The attack took place a few days before the opening of the World Disarmament Conference in Geneva. The vast outflow of pious declarations about world peace did nothing to allay a general feeling that another cataclysm might be on the way, one in which civilians — like the poor, fear-maddened flocks of Shanghai — would be the principal victims.

In Britain the Government admitted as much. In November, during a disarmament debate in the House of Commons, Baldwin made a prediction that would haunt the years to come. "I think it is as well for the man in the street to realize that there is no power on earth that prevents him from being bombed. Whatever people may tell him, the bomber will always get through." He went on to spell out the logical consequences of that reality. "The only defence is offence, which means that you will have to kill more women and children more quickly than the enemy if you want to save yourselves."

Baldwin was stating — with appalling eloquence and clarity — the essential strategic thinking of the RAF at that time. It stemmed — inevitably — from Trenchard and was the result of the second of his great about-turns. Once, he had set his face against the idea of an autonomous air service. He had retired as Chief of the Air Staff in 1929, applauded as the "Father of the RAF". He had vigorously asserted that bombing should only be carried out in alliance with the objectives of the ground forces. Now he was an equally energetic proponent of "strategic" bombing, based on the theory that air power could deliver a "knockout blow" against

159

the enemy, and that aeroplanes rather than armies could decide the outcome of a conflict.

In the 1920s it was unclear who Britain's enemy was likely to be. Germany was crippled by reparations payments and neutered militarily by the punitive restrictions forced on her by the Versailles Treaty (1919). The absence of an obvious foe and the peaceable, often pacifist mood pervading European electorates allowed a sort of relieved complacency to settle upon decision-making whenever military spending was considered. However, when Hitler became Chancellor in January 1933 everything changed. Within a few months Germany had withdrawn from the Disarmament Conference and then from the League of Nations. The only recently defeated enemy was stirring once again. Despite periodic bouts of appeasement, only the suicidally naive could kid themselves that while grovellingly pursuing peace there was no need to prepare for war.

It was going to cost. The RAF's reliance on struts and wires and canvas had inured it to the price of the modern, metal-skinned monoplanes that were now skimming the skies of the world as civil aviation took aircraft on their next great evolutionary step. It was with horror that the Air Ministry learned that a new generation of fighters might cost £20,000 each, and a bomber five times that sum. New aircraft would require proper runways, not the 1,000 × 800 yard grass strips that sufficed for the lightly loaded likes of the Gloucester Gladiator; a fine, lively aeroplane much loved by those who flew it, but as a war machine

160

hopelessly anachronistic. In 1934 this biplane, which had the antique lines of a bygone era, was billed as the RAF's new generation front-line fighter. The bombers were no better. The Handley Page Heyford, which came into service in late 1933, was another biplane. It looked like an airborne lorry, slab-sided and trailing enormous underslung wheels.

This mood of parsimony penetrated all aspects of procurement. The Air Staff were reluctant to test the patience of the politicians and officials holding the purse strings. Junior officers pointed out that the existing warning system of sound locators and observer posts was inadequate to deal with modern bombers zooming in at 200 mph and more. Perhaps a better telephone system would help communications between the headquarters and the squadrons. Reluctantly, a grant of £2,000 was made. "So," wrote Philip Joubert, then commandant of the RAF Staff College that Trenchard had established at Andover, "the administrative machine creaked and groaned and its slaves winced under the fear of the Treasury lash."

At least the young officers had aeroplanes to fly and anterooms to repair to for a drink before a good dinner. The NCOs and skilled tradesmen also lived in decent comfort. At the lower levels, however, existence was grim, as T. E. Lawrence, enlisted as an aircraftman under the pseudonym "John Hume Ross", discovered. Describing life in the Uxbridge Depot in the early 1920s, he wrote: "Our hut is a fair microcosm of unemployed England, not of unemployable England, for the strict RAF standards refuse the last levels of the

161

social structure." The standard of living seems to have been little better than that endured by men in the dole queues. The food was horrible, the uniform misshapen and scratchy, and the haircut he was given would have embarrassed a convict. Lawrence of Arabia, upon whose words princes and prime ministers had once hung, was put to work in the kitchen of the officers' mess. The gap between those with commissions and those who served them was oceanic. "Through the swing doors came an officer's head . . . sherry and bitters, gin and bitters, martinis, vergins, vermouths. Three whisky sodas *quickly* . . . the bartender splashed full his glasses and hurried to and fro."

With much energy and persistence it was possible to cross the great divide. George Unwin was a clever Yorkshire miner's son who had passed the Northern Universities Matriculation exam aged sixteen. But there was no money to put him through college and the only job available was to follow his father down the pit. Just before he was due to leave school his headmaster showed him an RAF recruiting poster. Unwin joined as an administrative apprentice at the training centre at Ruislip and in 1931 passed out as a leading aircraftman. The sights and sounds of the aerodrome excited his ambition to join the aviators. He soon discovered flying was regarded very much as the preserve of officers and of those who applied from the ranks "only 1 per cent per six months was taken".

Unwin persisted. "I was getting a bit fed up at not being accepted," he remembered. "I had everything else. I was playing for the RAF at soccer and that was one of the things you had to be, to be very good at sport. I couldn't understand why I wasn't being selected." Eventually he reached the final stage of the interviewing process and, determined to succeed, mugged up on the interests of the senior officer who would decide his fate. He discovered that he "loved polo and kept his own polo ponies". At the interview, the inevitable question was raised about Unwin's hobbies. "I said 'horse riding'. He pricked up his ears and said, 'Really?' I said 'Of course I can't afford it down here, but the local farmer at home has a pony and lets me ride it.' The only time I'd ridden a pony or anything on four legs was in the General Strike when the pit ponies were brought up and put in the fields." It worked. Unwin was in and in 1936 would be posted to 19 Squadron at Duxford as a sergeant pilot.

Hitler's arrival in power and the acceleration of German rearmament forced a decision to scramble to make up the ground lost in the 1920s. In July 1934 Expansion Scheme A was announced. It was the first of thirteen such schemes unveiled over the next four years, most of which never got beyond the proposal stage. The aim was to achieve some rough parity with Germany, though the target would keep shifting. The initial intention was to signal to Hitler that Britain was prepared to compete in an aerial arms race. The plan laid the foundations for a training programme and a framework for wider expansion, should the warning be ignored. The programme increased the targets for RAF growth laid down in 1923 — though not by much. The planned number of Britain-based home defence

163

squadrons would rise from fifty-two to sixty-four. Of these, twenty-five would be fighter squadrons — eight more than in the earlier plan.

This shift towards fighters was a concession to politicians who, despite having warned that the bomber would always get through, were anxious to show the public that the raiders' job would be made as difficult as possible. The air staff — and in particular their chief, Sir Edward Ellington — maintained their view that a big bomber fleet was central to Britain's security. This would remain the prevailing wisdom at the top of the RAF for several more years.

Nonetheless, the rapid changes in the performance of small aircraft could not be ignored. The age of the biplane was clearly at an end. It was fortunate that in 1933 the Operational Requirements Section of the Air Ministry was commanded by a bold, intelligent and far-sighted officer. Squadron Leader Ralph Sorley was thirty-six years old, a former RNAS pilot who had won a Distinguished Service Cross (DSC) for daring attacks on the German warships *Goeben* and *Breslau* in 1918. He was also keenly aware of technological innovation and its implications for future warfare. The Air Ministry had no designers of its own and relied on private firms to meet its requirements for new aircraft. Sorley came up with a wish list of specifications for a world-class fighter, which he believed to be achievable, and it went out to the manufacturers. The new aeroplane should have eight machine guns, mounted in the wings, an enclosed cockpit and an engine that would take it to at least 300 mph and 33,000 feet.

In August 1933 Sydney Camm, the chief designer at Hawker Aircraft Limited in Kingston upon Thames, had produced a new model, the Fury, which came in both biplane and monoplane versions. They were offered to the Air Ministry, but rejected as "too orthodox" — a welcome indication that the need for radical new designs had been recognized. The board at Hawker nonetheless allowed Camm to continue work on his monoplane. What he came up with was a hybrid, halfway between the pioneering and the modern ages of aviation. The frame was of metal tubes and wooden formers and stringers. The skin was fabric, coated with dope to reduce drag and stressed metal wings were only added at a fairly late stage. But it definitely looked modern, and it carried an inspiring name, the Hurricane, which conveyed a note of confidence and aggression that was absent from the placid Harts, Flycatchers and Grebes of the previous generation.

The question was: would it fly as well as it looked and sounded? On 6 November 1935 it made its first flight at Brooklands. The test pilot was George Bulman, a short, bald, ginger-moustached extrovert who had flown with the RFC in the war and won a Military Cross. The prototype Hurricane had been developed in great secrecy and when the tarpaulins were stripped away and the hangar doors opened there were murmurs of surprise.

The new machine had been painted a futuristic silver, which emphasized its smooth, aerodynamically efficient lines and the way the wings fitted flush to the fuselage below the neat narrow cockpit. It was big —

bigger than any existing fighter — and very heavy at more than 6,000 lbs. It seemed unlikely that a single engine could get it airborne. Bulman strode to the aeroplane, clambered up onto the wing root and hopped into the cockpit, watched by Camm and a clutch of Hawker executives from the edge of the field.

The Hurricane bumped away into the distance, then turned into the wind. The rumble of the Rolls Royce engine deepened into a growl. The aeroplane moved forward, but slowly, so that it seemed to some that Bulman would run out of field before he got airborne. At the last moment the Hurricane left the ground in an abrupt bounding movement and climbed steeply. Neatly, the undercarriage folded inwards and disappeared into the underside of the wings. The muscular shape dwindled, then disappeared and the engine note faded to nothing. Then, half an hour later, it was heard again. Bulman touched down in a perfect three-point landing and rolled over to where Camm was waiting to report that the flight had been a "piece of cake". It was clear to all that in the Hurricane a star had been born.

It would soon be eclipsed by another. Sorley's call had also produced a response from Supermarine, makers of high-performance aeroplanes that had several times carried off the Schneider seaplane speed trophy, and now owned by the armament giant Vickers. They offered the Spitfire, the first prototype of which flew in March 1936. It was a more modern design, all metal with a monocoque fuselage and thin, elliptical wings. It had the same Rolls Royce Merlin engine as the Hurricane and carried the same guns, but weighed

1,000 lbs less and so went 30 mph faster. No one has ever established where the name came from. Its designer, Reginald Mitchell, was said to have thought it "bloody stupid". In the propaganda film of his life, *The First of the Few*, which came out in 1942, he is portrayed as coining it himself: "A curious sort of bird . . . a bird that spits out death and destruction . . . a Spitfire bird." Mitchell was worth a biopic. He really did give his life's blood for his creation, as "Johnnie" Johnson, whose flying skill was perfectly and devastatingly married to the Spitfire, acknowledged. Mitchell knew that he was dying of cancer, yet "convinced of Germany's evil intentions he did not spare himself, and as his beautiful machine took shape, so his life wasted away . . . every day he could be seen in the workshops, contemplating the progress of his machine, walking round and examining its graceful lines, rejecting this, approving that, talking with the mechanics, and then going back to his office where he would sit for hours, face cupped in hands, elbows on the drawing board, pondering the latest problem." Mitchell lived long enough to see the first Spitfire fly. Another 20,000 would be built and it was a further tribute to his engineering powers that the basic design could bear endless improvements, so that by the end of the Second World War it had gone through twelve incarnations.

The quality of the two types was apparent. The Air Ministry did not hesitate and ordered 600 Hurricanes and 310 Spitfires. They began arriving on the squadrons in 1938. Pilots enjoyed flying the latest generation of biplanes. The Hawker Hart, for example,

167

was fast, handled beautifully and could be thrown about in the air in whatever fashion a skilled flier fancied. But when an aviator took the controls of a Spitfire for the first time he felt he was undergoing the sensation of flying anew. Like birth and death, it was an experience that could only be undergone solo. There were no dual-seater trainers and after a certain point the instructor pointed you at the cockpit and you were on your own. No one ever forgot their first flight in a Spitfire and when they remembered it these modern men, practical men, reached for the language of poetry to describe it. The first squadron to receive it was No. 19, and George Unwin, the former Ruislip apprentice, was one of the five pilots selected to put it through a 500-hour series of tests.

It was love at first flight. "There was no heaving or pulling and pushing and kicking. You just breathed on it. She really was the perfect flying machine. She hadn't got a vice at all. She would only spin if you made her and she'd come straight out of it as soon as you applied opposite rudder and pushed the stick forward . . . I've never flown anything sweeter."

The Spitfire's engine note was instantly recognizable to those who had flown it, somehow distinct from that of the Hurricane, even though they were both powered by Merlins. Many years later, Unwin was coming out of Boots the chemist in Bournemouth with his wife when he heard "that peculiar throaty roar . . . I said to her, 'There's a Spitfire somewhere.' A taxi driver was standing there and said, 'There she is, mate.' It's a noise you will never forget."

168

In the Spitfire and the Hurricane, Britain made a crucial technological leap. She now had two aircraft that were as good as — and in the case of the Spitfire perhaps better than — anything around. With them they could face the perils ahead with some confidence.

The modernization of the bomber fleet was slower and the results were far less satisfying. The requirements of an effective bomber were more complex and often hard to reconcile. It was argued that as aircraft speeds increased, the performance gap between fighters and bombers was likely to narrow. Why not aim at building a bomber that could outstrip interceptors and therefore have no need of on-board guns? Something like this would eventually emerge in the shape of the Mosquito. But in the meantime the thought was too radical. The confidence of the crews in the machines they flew had to be considered and they demanded some degree of protection, particularly from attack from the rear. The result was a compromise, which produced the twin-engined bombers of the early years of the war — the Blenheims, Whitleys, Wellingtons and Hampdens, which, while respectable machines, were not adequate for the strategic task they were supposed to perform.

The RAF's real work, as conceived from the 1920s onwards, was to launch a bombing offensive which would at least deter attack and possibly — in the minds of dedicated bombing enthusiasts at least — deal the enemy a "knockout blow". To achieve this they needed big aeroplanes, carrying big payloads and travelling long distances. Four-engined aircraft were needed and

169

here, in accepting this fact, Britain was ahead of the game. Long before the war began, Britain alone among the belligerents in the European theatre was preparing a super bomber intended to prove the theory that aerial bombardment could decide wars.

In July 1935 the Air Ministry issued a set of specifications, coded P12/36, seeking an aircraft with a crew of six, a bomb load of not less than 12,000 lbs and a normal cruising speed of not less than 180 mph at 12,000 feet. This initiative produced the first four-engined RAF monoplane bomber, the Short Stirling. It was followed by a second specification, the P13/36. This was the genesis for the Halifax and the Avro Manchester, which evolved into the Lancaster — the greatest bomber of the war. Its designer, Roy Chadwick, was the third in the triumvirate of British aeronautical engineers whose efforts made a huge contribution to victory. Roy, Reginald and Sydney, homely names, now long fallen into disuse, were heroes of the drawing board and the test bed.

The bigger the aeroplane the more problems there were to resolve and it was not until August 1940 that Stirlings began arriving on squadrons, Halifaxes began flying operations in the spring of 1941, and Lancasters a year later. Even the most urgent development was a lengthy process, and had the work only begun after the outbreak of war the new types might not have emerged in time to have any effect. As the government scientist Sir Henry Tizard pointed out when asked by Philip Joubert in the spring of 1940 for his opinion on some promising ideas offered by inventors: "My dear fellow!

You must realize that any project that is going to have some influence on the course of the war must have been examined, tested and put into effect already."

The most dazzling example of foresight was the development of radar in which Tizard — himself a former RFC pilot — played a crucial role. It was he who sought the advice of Robert Watson-Watt, Superintendent of the Radio Department of the National Physical Laboratory at Teddington. When Watson-Watt suggested that it might be possible to detect aeroplanes by reflected radio waves, which could be seen and measured on a cathode-ray tube, there was none of the self-interested scepticism that often greets revolutionary innovation. Though other scientists in America, France and Germany were on the same scent, it was Britain that seized on the possibilities and took the lead, so that by the time the war began the coast was protected by a chain of stations that allowed squadrons to be controlled with maximum efficiency, multiplying the effective fighter strength and improving the odds against the Luftwaffe.

The growing number of machines had to have men to fly in them. The snobbery that had held back George Unwin was relaxed, allowing more ground staff to take to the air and the number of short service commissions on offer was boosted. But who would fill the gaps left by the casualties when the fighting began? In another demonstration of imaginative planning, the Director of Training at the Air Ministry, Air Commodore Arthur Tedder, had conceived the idea of a "Citizen Air Force". This, in August 1936, would become the RAF

171

Volunteer Reserve (RAFVR). Tedder's idea was that it should be "open . . . to the whole middle class in the widest sense of that term, namely the complete range of the output of the public and secondary schools". Given its nature it was felt "inappropriate to grade the members on entry as officers or airmen according to their social class". Everyone therefore started out as airmen under training, before being given the rank of sergeant pilot once they had qualified.

The RAFVR cleared away social and economic obstacles to open up the air force to young men from families of moderate means. Advertisements appeared in newspapers and flying magazines, offering males between the ages of eighteen and twenty-five the opportunity to learn to fly, for free, in their spare time. They would receive £25 a year and after an *ab initio*, fifteen-day course at a local flying school, attend weekday classroom sessions with training flights at the weekends. The recruitment offices were swamped with volunteers.

Charlton Haw would never have become an RAF pilot under normal circumstances. He left school at fourteen to become an apprentice in a lithographic works in York. As soon as he was eighteen he applied to join the RAFVR. "I'd always wanted to fly, from when I was a small boy. I never wanted to do anything else, really, but I just didn't think there would ever be a chance for me. Until the RAFVR was formed, for a normal schoolboy it was almost impossible." Haw went solo after four hours and forty minutes instruction, when the average time was eight hours, and ended up commanding two squadrons during a long, brave and distinguished wartime career.

By the spring of 1939 there were 2,500 RAFVR pilots in training. When the war broke out, 310 had already entered Fighter Command. It was there that, at the start of the war, they would be needed most. By the end of 1938 the rearmament effort had swung behind fighters. Though the doctrine that ultimately it was the bomber force that mattered persisted, the speed at which war was looming made it clear that defence, for the time being at least, was more important than attack. It was the Government not the air force that forced the change. At the time the Air Ministry was still pressing for parity with the German bomber force. The minister in charge of defence co-operation, the dry, lawyerly Sir Thomas Inskip, stated crisply the new thinking. "I cannot . . . persuade myself that the dictum of the Chief of the Air Staff that we must give the enemy as much as he gives us is a sound principle. I do not think it is a proper measure of our strength. The German Air Force must be designed to deliver a knockout blow within a few weeks of the outbreak of war. The role of our Air Force is not an early knockout blow — no one has suggested we can accomplish that — but to prevent the Germans from knocking us out."

It was true that the bomber force was in no condition to launch a serious air offensive. But at least the process of building an air fleet capable of doing so was under way. Britain's ability to wage an air war at sea, on the other hand, was severely restricted, and there was no training or building programme in place to make good the deficit. RAF pilots had flown the Fleet Air Arm's carrier-borne aircraft and RAF technicians had kept them flying. When the service was finally handed back to the Admiralty in April 1939 these vital personnel went too, leaving the navy with a desperate shortage of skilled men, both pilots and tradesmen. The aircraft were no compensation. The FAA went to war five months later equipped with 232 machines, of which only eighteen were modern Skua monoplanes.

By then, however, it was fighters that mattered most. On the warm sunny Sunday morning of 3 September 1939, the long-expected announcement finally came. Most of the pilots heard Chamberlain's address in the mess or clustered around portable radios rigged up at the dispersal areas, where already their aircraft stood at readiness. At Tangmere in Sussex, Peter Townsend, a flight commander with 85 Squadron, was lounging on the grass with his pilots next to their Hurricanes when they were told that "the balloon goes up at 11.45". They walked over to the elegant mess, covered in pink creeper, and listened, drinks in hand, to the broadcast. When it ended, "the tension suddenly broke. The fatal step had been taken. We were at war." That night they raced to the Old Ship at nearby Bosham. "What a party we had; at closing time, we went out into the street and fired our revolvers into the air. Windows were flung open, people rushed from their houses, thinking the invasion had started."

At Cranwell Tim Vigors and his fellow cadets were ordered to the anteroom to hear the broadcast. When the declaration of war came "a shout of excitement rose from all our throats. As one man we rose to our feet, cheering. There was not one amongst us who would not have been bitterly disappointed if the declaration . . . had not been made."

There was the same reaction in the Hull classroom where Charlton Haw and thirty other RAFVR pilots were gathered after being called up the week before. "A tremendous cheer went out from all of us. We were very pleased about the whole thing. We didn't think about the danger. We all had visions of sitting in a Spitfire the following day. And then the disappointing thing was we were all sent home."

Not everyone was so carefree. Brian Kingcome of 92 Squadron noted Chamberlain's gloomy tone, devoid of drama or tension, "just this sorrowful, defeated voice going on". He looked around at his comrades in the Hornchurch hangar office, "thinking to myself, probably the whole lot of us will be dead in three weeks". As soon as the broadcast was over, the air-raid sirens in London sounded, the first of many false alarms that would add to the confusion and uncertainty of the coming days ahead.

CHAPTER
NINE

Into Battle

It would be some months before Fighter Command felt its way into the conflict. The blaring sirens did not signal the onset of an all-out aerial assault. The Luftwaffe had other targets. Hitler was anyway reluctant to antagonize an enemy whom he hoped to neutralize by negotiation. At the fighter stations dotted among the fields and villages of south-east England the squadrons watched and waited. Some flew off to join the small British Expeditionary Force (BEF) in France, operating from the same Pas de Calais airfields as their RFC forbears twenty-five years before. The excitement of the move soon dissipated and they settled down into the routine of false alarms and inactivity that was the *drôle de guerre*.

For Bomber Command there was no Phoney War. It went into action on the day war was declared and on many days thereafter. The experience of battle was a painful one: there were virtually no successes. Instead, the crews received a succession of bruising lessons on how little they knew and how inadequate their aircraft were to the gigantic task that had been imagined for them.

The first raid set a pattern that was to become dismally familiar. Barely had Chamberlain's voice faded than the men of "A" Flight, 89 Squadron, based at Scampton in Lincolnshire, were told to prepare for a raid on the North Sea port of Wilhelmshaven. The flurry of initial activity subsided as the take-off time was delayed. The men stood by their Hampden bombers, smoking and fretting. One pilot, with a reputation for cockiness, found his "hands were shaking so much that I could not hold them still. All the time we wanted to rush off to the lavatory. Most of us went four times an hour."

Eventually, just after 6p.m., six aircraft took off, climbed over the towers of Lincoln Cathedral, then headed out over the ridged, grey monotony of the North Sea. Their instructions were to attack pocket battleships believed to be lying in Wilhelmshaven Harbour. If they couldn't locate the target they had permission to bomb an ammunition dump on the shore. Under no circumstances were they to risk hitting civilian housing or even dockyard buildings and there would be "serious repercussions" if they did. Like Hitler, the British government was extremely wary of provoking reprisals if non-combatants were killed.

As they approached what they thought was the target, the cloud clamped down to a hundred feet. They had nothing to aim at apart from the muzzle flashes from anti-aircraft batteries firing blindly towards them through the murk. Squadron Leader Leonard Snaith, who was leading the attack, ordered them to turn back. They jettisoned their bombs in the sea and headed for home. The initial disappointment of the pilot whose earlier nerves had initiated so many trips to the loo gave way to the realization that this was the right decision. "For all we knew," he wrote, "we were miles off our course. The gun flashes ahead might have been the Dutch Islands or they might have been Heligoland." They reached the Lincolnshire coast in darkness and touched down, tired and dispirited, at 10.30p.m. "What a complete mess-up," recorded the pilot. "For all the danger we went through it couldn't be called a raid, but we went through all the feelings." The remarks were made by twenty-year-old Guy Gibson who led the Dams Raid to become one of the most famous air warriors of the age. The experience of that initial, fruitless raid would be repeated thousands of times before Bomber Command approached anything like the efficiency that the oracles of air power had prophesied.

At least Gibson and his comrades had survived. The following day twenty-nine Blenheims and Wellingtons set off for Wilhelmshaven and nearby Brunsbüttel. Some of the force managed to find the pocket battleship *Admiral Scheer* and the cruiser *Emden* and to drop bombs. By extraordinary determination and some luck, a few bombs hit the *Scheer*. They bounced off. Seven of the attacking aircraft were destroyed by anti-aircraft fire from fighters. Ten aircraft failed to locate their targets and one unloaded its bombs on the Danish town of Esbjerg, 110 miles to the north, resulting in the death of two civilians. Twenty-four airmen were killed — the first of the 55,573 men from

Bomber Command who would lose their lives in the next six years.

Thus were laid bare Bomber Command's fundamental weaknesses: the primitive navigational aids available meant that aircraft faced huge problems finding their targets; when they did locate them, they lacked the technology to deliver their bombs accurately; and if they did score a lucky strike, there was a sizeable chance the bombs would not explode. On the plus side, this and the raids that followed demonstrated that whatever the crews lacked in equipment they were superbly endowed with courage. There was no shortage of the "press-on" spirit that would sustain the Strategic Air Offensive through the dark years that lay ahead.

The Wilhelmshaven disaster gave the planners pause. For the next few months activity was confined to "Nickel" leaflet-dropping operations, reconnaissance and shipping sweeps over the North Sea. Then on 14 December 1939 the RAF launched the biggest raid of the war so far: forty-three assorted aircraft were sent off to search for ships to bomb. A squadron of Wellingtons found a convoy in the Schillig Roads off Wilhemshaven and spent half an hour battling with low cloud trying to get into a favourable position to attack. They were intercepted by fighters and hit by flak, and five were shot down. Then, four days later, another biggish raid was mounted against shipping at Wilhelmshaven. Twenty-four Wellingtons were despatched. Mindful of the effectiveness of enemy anti-aircraft fire, they were told not to stray below 10,000 feet. But flak was not the problem. The radar station on the Friesian island of

Wangerooge picked up the raiders. Messerschmitt 110 fighters were waiting in the cloudless skies when they arrived. Half the force — twelve aircraft — were shot down and forty-two men killed. Five escaped from stricken aircraft to be made prisoners of war, an early indication of the meagre survival rates once a bomber went down. The Wellington had twin machine guns in the nose and tail turrets, firing .303 rifle-calibre bullets. They managed to shoot down two fighters. It was clear, however, that formations of bombers flying in daylight could not fend off fighter attacks. Before long almost all operations would take place under cover of darkness.

Flying in a bomber was a very dangerous business and would be the most hazardous wartime activity open to British servicemen. Non-operational flying could be almost as lethal as facing the enemy. Of the 202 airmen killed in bombers between the start of the war and the two disastrous Wilhelmshaven missions, ninety-nine were killed while on training or ferry flights.

By the end of the year nothing like the scenario envisaged in the RAF's pre-war strategic blueprint had emerged. The Western Air Plans, drawn up in 1936, had as their target the factories, oil installations, roads, railways and utilities on which the enemy's war effort depended. Political considerations meant that the moment to execute them had not yet arrived. Thirty months before the war Britain had moved to occupy the moral high ground in the debate over the ethics of aerial warfare. Chamberlain told the Commons that the air force would bomb only military objectives and take every measure to avoid civilian casualties. A few days after the war started, John Slessor, by now the RAF's Director of Plans, had promised that "indiscriminate attacks on civilian populations as such will never form part of our policy". Within a few years, the bombing effort would be organized to do just that.

For the moment, though, the desire to avoid killing non-combatants was sincere and attacks on land-based targets were banned. It was only when spring came and the German armies were on the move again that the restraint crumbled, then collapsed.

The winter stasis came to an end with the occupations of Denmark and Norway in April 1940. Both Fighter and Bomber Command were thrown into Allied attempts to prevent the invasions, to no effect and painful losses. The Hampdens could just about reach southern Norway from Britain, but as Arthur Harris noted the bomber was "cold meat for any determined enemy fighter in daylight" and six were shot down in a single operation against Kristiansand on 12 April.

Then the Germans began their great surge westwards. This had been long expected. Bomber Command's job was to attack advancing troops and to disrupt supply lines by destroying railways, roads and bridges. A number of bomber squadrons had been based in France since the start of the war. Eight of them were equipped with Fairey Battles. In their first, occasional encounters with the enemy it was clear that these were bad aeroplanes. They carried a three-man crew and were protected by two small-calibre machine guns, one mounted in a wing and the other in the rear. They were slow, a hundred miles an hour slower than the Luftwaffe fighters they would face. Nonetheless, the men who flew them continued to cling to hope. According to one of the fighter pilots waiting alongside them for the fighting to start, they were "pathetically confident in their tight formation with their fire-concentration tactics. We admired their flying and guts, but although we gave them as much practice and encouragement as we could, we privately didn't give much for their chances."

So it turned out. On the morning of 10 May the German forces began to flow into the Lowlands like a river of molten lava. From midday, Battles, arranged in small formations of eight, set off to try and stop them. Ranged against them were great swarms of Luftwaffe fighters and bombers, sometimes hundreds strong. Of the thirty-two British bombers deployed, thirteen were shot down. The others returned riddled with flak, cannon rounds and bullets. There was nothing to show for the losses. The columns they had been sent to attack had usually moved on by the time the Battles arrived.

The battering continued. On 12 May Battles of the Belgian air force had been attempting to bomb the bridges over the Albert canal to the west of Maastricht to deny passage to the advancing Germans. They failed, losing ten of the fifteen aircraft that took part. Then it was the turn of Bomber Command's 12 Squadron, also equipped with Battles. There was an appeal for six crews. The entire squadron stepped forward, so the first six on the duty roster were selected. One was unable to take off when its hydraulics failed, but the rest swooped down on the bridges at Vroenhoeven and Veldwezelt. Only one aircraft made it back, sieved with shot and shell. There were devastating losses elsewhere on the Front. In two days of fighting, the entire RAF force in France had been halved from 135 to 72.

With the blitzkrieg rippling towards France there was no longer any virtue in restraint. Any remaining hopes that the Germans might choose a more scrupulous approach against Western targets than they had shown against Polish ones were shattered with the mass bombing of Rotterdam. After some dithering, permission was given for an attack on road and rail junctions at Mönchengladbach. This was the first of thousands of raids directed at German towns. The results were negligible, but four civilians were killed by the tumbling bombs. Three were Germans: Carl Lichtschlag, sixty-two, Erika Mullers, twenty-two, and a two-year-old girl called Ingeborg Schey. The fourth was a British citizen. Ella Ida Clegg had been born fifty-three years before to a British father, who left Oldham to work as a factory foreman in the Rhine. Nothing else is known about her. She was listed in official records only as a "volunteer". The first corpses had names, but that did not last long. Soon these losses became commonplace and names gave way to numbers.

Four days later Bomber Command at last set out to implement its grand design, laid out in the pre-war Western Air Plans: to paralyse the enemy by attacks on its oil supply and transport nexus. Ninety-nine aircraft — thirty-nine Wellingtons, thirty-six Hampdens and twenty-four Whitleys — flew off to attack sixteen targets in Germany's industrial heartland in the Ruhr.

Nothing much happened. Most of the aircraft dropped their bombs, but to little effect. The standard of accuracy was abysmal. One bomb apparently aimed at a factory in Dormagen landed instead on a large farm, killing a dairyman, Franz Romeike, who was on his way to the lavatory. Some bombs fell on Münster — even though it was not on the list of towns to be hit. This black farce was the opening scene of one of the war's great dark dramas.

"Thus began the Bomber Command strategic air offensive against Germany," wrote Noble Frankland, himself a bomber navigator and the author with Sir Charles Webster of the official history of the campaign. "For many years it was the sole means at Britain's disposal for attacking the heart of the enemy, and, more than any other form of armed attack upon the enemy, it never ceased until almost exactly five years later Germany, with many of her cities in ruins, her communications cut, her oil supplies drained dry and her industry reduced to chaos, capitulated . . . It was probably the most continuous and gruelling operation of war ever carried out."

The fighter squadrons based in France, and those sent over from England to join them, were swept up and tossed around by the tempest blowing across the flatlands of Flanders. Flying Officer Maurice Stephens, a Cranwell graduate, had flown off from Kenley with the rest of 3 Squadron just after midday on the day of the German attack. He bumped down on the grass at

Merville, an old RFC base, to see that, despite all the time the defenders had had to prepare, confusion reigned. "On the far side of the airfield another Hurricane squadron had just arrived," he wrote. "There was feverish activity as pilots and ground crew sorted the mass of equipment which had been hastily unloaded from the transport aircraft." They "snatched a hasty lunch of bully beef and biscuits, with the inevitable mug of strong, over-sweet tea". Then, over the field telephone came an order for a flight of six aircraft to patrol a line between Maastricht and Bree in Belgium, where the German forces were expected to attempt the breakthrough into France. There was only one map available, which was given to the flight commander; the other pilots were expected to follow him. They saw nothing "except roads packed solid with the pathetic stream of refugees. It was to become a depressingly familiar sight."

Back at Merville they were refuelling when a formation of Heinkel 111s appeared and began dropping bombs. "We took off in whatever direction we happened to be pointing, hoping to catch the Heinkels," Stephens wrote. "It was hopeless. There was no radar, no fighter control at all. We were just wasting aircraft and hazarding aircraft in the hopes of finding our quarry in the gathering darkness."

They kipped in a Nissen hut at the airfield and awoke at dawn to take to the skies, pitting themselves against an enemy that swept forward with all the inexorability of a force of nature. This time events were more satisfactory. Stephens was patrolling with five other 3 Squadron Hurricanes between Saint-Trond and Diest in Belgium. They realized now that the absence of radar and ground control made little difference, as "the scale of enemy air activity was so great that the odds were very much in favour of making contact". Sure enough, "suddenly we spotted about sixty tiny black dots . . . flying west like a swarm of midges. The next moment we were among them — Stukas, with an escort of about twenty Me 109s."

Stephens manoeuvred his Hurricane behind one of the dive-bombers until it was framed in his reflector sight, then "opened fire from about fifty yards". The range could hardly have been closer and the approach would have won the approval of Mannock and Ball. The effect was spectacular. "After a short burst he blew up in an orange ball of flame, followed by a terrifying clatter as my Hurricane flew through the debris." Stephens went on to shoot down a Dornier 17 before his fuel warning light glowed red and he looked for somewhere to put down.

The British fighters put up a terrific fight against the Luftwaffe, inflicting more casualties than they suffered. But the numbers were overwhelmingly against them and the impressive paper strength of their allies in the Armée de l'Air was illusory. The French Air Force were unreliable allies and co-operation was ragged and sometimes only grudgingly given, and, by the end, often not at all. The squadrons were soon reeling. Every aircraft shot down or abandoned in the headlong retreat (which mirrored the experience of the RFC in the opening weeks of the First World War) was one less machine to defend Britain.

On 13 May the first German tanks crossed the Meuse. The following day, seventeen British fighter pilots were killed or mortally wounded. Twenty-seven Hurricanes had been shot down. These attrition rates could not be sustained, yet the French were still clamouring for more aircraft. Churchill was inclined to oblige them, but Hugh Dowding, Fighter Command's austere chief, resisted further sacrifice.. As it was, the hopeless defence had thinned the ranks of men and aircraft alarmingly. The fighters had knocked down about 300 enemy aircraft, but they had lost just over 200 in the process. Altogether, fifty-six pilots were killed in the twelve days between 10 and 21 May, with another thirty-six badly wounded. Most of them had been extensively and expensively trained, and had far more theoretical preparation for aerial war fighting than those who were going through the flying schools at home. Some units had been eviscerated by the fighting. When Stephens and 3 Squadron returned to England after ten days, just before the arrival of the Germans, they left behind nine dead pilots.

There was no time to lick wounds, for another battle was already looming. At Dunkirk, some half a million British and French troops were penned in with the sea at their backs, awaiting the Germans' final onslaught. The honour of finishing them off had been given to the Luftwaffe. Their leader, Hermann Goering, had promised Hitler it would be an easy task. The RAF now had the duty of defending the exhausted lines of soldiers, waiting stoically on the beaches for salvation. Like the airmen of the last war, the RAF pilots had a detached view of the battlefield, one that was unlikely to make them want to swap their role, whatever its dangers, for the life of a foot-soldier. Brian Kingcome of 92 Squadron looked down from the cockpit of his Spitfire and saw "beaches [that] were a shambles, littered with the smoking wreckage of engines and equipment . . . The sands erupted into huge geysers from exploding bombs and shells, while a backdrop to the scene of carnage and destruction was provided by the palls of oily black smoke rising from the burning harbour and houses." He marvelled at how the "orderly lines of our troops stood, chaos and Armageddon at their backs, patiently waiting their turn to wade into the sea".

The task meant not only mounting continuous patrols above the port and beaches, but roaming behind the lines to intercept the attackers before they could reach their victims. These sorties took place out of sight of the troops, leading to many a shouted accusation of "Where was the RAF?" in the weeks after the Dunkirk evacuation, and many a brawl. The charge was unjust. Awful as the experience of the evacuation was, it would have been immeasurably worse were it not for the efforts of Fighter Command. Churchill acknowledged this in his speech in the House of Commons on 4 June 1940, when he spoke of the "victory" that had been won by the air force. For the pilots of Fighter Command the satisfaction of having tested themselves against the Luftwaffe and not been found wanting could not be savoured for long. It was clear at the beginning of June that the real showdown awaited them and it would not be long in coming.

CHAPTER
TEN

Apotheosis

In July 1940 the greatest air battle ever fought began. Nothing like it had happened before. Nothing like it would happen again. The military and political consequences of it were colossal, shaping the way we live and think today. As well as being one of the great events of history, the Battle of Britain was also the moment when the RAF came of age. Fighter Command's victory embedded the air force in the minds and hearts of the nation, and validated, resoundingly, the existence of the third service.

One of the unique characteristics of the battle was its visibility. Civilians were able to watch their defenders in action. Men, women and children could look up from city streets, suburban avenues and country lanes, and see tiny machines twisting and swooping, streams of glittering tracer, ragged banners of oily smoke, the blossoming of a parachute and afterwards, the fading chalk marks scribbled in the cornflower blue of an English summer sky by the condensation trails.

A sophisticated seventeen-year-old, Colin Walker Downes, was staying with his mother in Hampstead and watched as "the RAF fighters weaved their white vapour trails through the lace pattern of the Luftwaffe bombers and fighters against a background of deep azure". Downes's reaction was similar to that of every young male who witnessed these sights. He "longed to join the gallant Few". Unlike most, his wish was granted and he ended the war as a fighter pilot.

The spectators' fates and those of the young men fighting in their name were vitally intertwined. The Government seized on this fact to cement social cohesion, and propaganda moved fast to associate the airmen with those they were fighting to protect.

Britain's greatest propagandist was Winston Churchill. Even before the contest began he was at work creating the myth. In his speech to the House of Commons on 18 June he gave the battle its name, set out the stakes — no less than "the survival of Christian civilization" — and identified the heroes on whom deliverance depended. "I look forward confidently to the exploits of our fighter pilots, who will have the glory of saving their native land, their island home, and all they love from the most deadly of attacks," he told the packed benches of parliamentarians and galleries stuffed with VIPs. On 20 August, before the battle had reached its climax, he struck another indelible image when he created the legend of "The Few": the "fighter pilots whose brilliant actions we see with our own eyes, day after day".

To build the notion of commonality, of shared endeavour and sacrifice, the egalitarian characteristics of the air force were given the maximum emphasis. It was the boy-next-door aspect of The Few that artist (and former RFC pilot) Cuthbert Orde stressed in the

Foreword to the collection of portraits of Fighter Command pilots he was commissioned to draw by the Air Ministry in September 1940. "I have often been asked if I have found a definite type of Fighter Pilot," he wrote. "I have thought about this a lot, but I feel sure the answer is 'No' . . . The most striking thing about the Fighter Pilots . . . is their ordinariness, just 'You, I, Us and Co.', ordinary sons of ordinary parents from ordinary homes. So when you wonder where they come from, dear reader, whoever you may be, contemplate your own home, your profession and your background, and you have the answer."

By the end of the battle, Orde's claim was to a large extent true. Fighter Command was the most motley elite the British armed forces had ever seen. In the summer of 1942 the range of pilots in 32 Squadron — based at Biggin Hill, the quintessential fighter station, set in the bucolic Kent countryside — was a propagandist's dream. It included Sergeant John Proctor, who left school at fourteen to become an RAF apprentice, before graduating to flying duties; Ollie Houghton, a Coventry-born ex-aero fitter, who joined the squadron via the RAFVR; Bill Higgins, another RAFVR man and former village schoolteacher; Alan Eckford, from solidly middle-class Thame in Oxfordshire, who joined the RAF on a short-service commission in 1938; and Michael Crossley, the squadron commander and an old Etonian.

It was no wonder that when an American newspaperman was seeking a story, the Air Ministry steered him in their direction. The reporter spent the evening of Thursday 15 August 1940 with 32 Squadron in their local, the White Hart at Brasted. It was the end of one of the hardest days of the battle. At 9 p.m. the conversation faded as the radio was switched on. The voice of the announcer was calm, but the events he described could not have been more dramatic. Throughout the day huge formations of German bombers, protected by large fighter escorts, had been flying from their bases in northern France to pound targets in the south of England.

The pilots listened in silence, until the newsreader revealed the day's score. At least 182 enemy aircraft had been destroyed, he claimed. Only 34 British fighters had been lost. The quiet was swept away by a wave of cheering and a wall of blue serge backs sprang up at the bar, yelling for celebratory pints. In his report the journalist wrote that he "found it incredible that these noisy youngsters were in fact front-line troops, even then in the thick of battle". The figures given for the day's fighting by the BBC were a vast exaggeration, the result of a process of official inflation and the confusion of battle, and the true "scores" of both sides would not emerge until much later. But the rest of the picture is accurate enough.

The depredations of the Battle of France and the air fighting at Dunkirk had taken a heavy toll of Fighter Command, but after the fall of France in June 1940 there was a breathing space of a few weeks. Hitler wanted to give Britain time to contemplate its isolation, and the consequent apparent hopelessness of its situation. It would surely then come to its senses and sue for peace. Besides, the army and the Luftwaffe deserved a rest after their heroic exertions. The lull gave Dowding an opportunity to reshuffle his squadrons, sending the most depleted off to rest, and to absorb new pilots and rehearse the command-and-control system that was vital to success when the Germans came.

Looking back, Dowding admitted that "it is difficult to fix the exact date when the Battle of Britain can be said to have begun. Operations of various kinds merged into one another almost insensibly." There were grounds for choosing 10 August 1940 when the Luftwaffe began full-scale attacks on objectives on land. Instead, he chose, "somewhat arbitrarily", 10 July, when German formations began hitting convoys in the Channel. His reasoning was that "the weight and scale of the attack indicates that the primary object was rather to bring our Fighters to battle than to destroy the hulls and cargoes of the small ships engaged in the coastal trade."

The intention then was to drag Fighter Command into a battle of attrition. Thus, Hitler could continue to exert military pressure on Britain in a measured fashion in keeping with his aim of cowing the country into submission without the necessity for invasion and conquest.

"Stuffy" Dowding's personality sat oddly with the dashing image of the outfit he commanded. Trenchard, with whom he clashed in the early days, branded him a "dismal Jimmy". His fellow aviators on the Western Front also found the non-drinking, non-smoking loner hard-going. In 1918 he married Clarice, the widow of a soldier killed in the war, and the following year they had a son, Derek, who went to Cranwell and flew with 74 Squadron during the Battle. In 1920 Clarice died after a short illness. Dowding moved in with his father, then with his sister. He devoted himself to work, becoming the RAF's Director of Training in 1926 and working his way up to take over Fighter Command when it was formed in 1936. Behind the buttoned-up facade lurked an inquiring mind. "Since I was a child, I have never accepted ideas purely because they were orthodox," he once said. He proved it by countering the prevailing, Trenchardian, pro-bomber view that reigned at the Air Ministry, and he fought fiercely to ensure there were enough Spitfires, Hurricanes and men to fly them when the great test came. For all his stiffness, he felt emotions intensely. It was Dowding who gave currency to the name by which his pilots became known and loved, in a letter he wrote to "My Dear Fighter Boys" in June 1940, telling them "how proud I am of you and the way you have fought since the 'Blitzkrieg' started." Later his affection for them manifested itself in a fashion many regarded as cranky. He was a keen spiritualist and announced that he had been visited by the ghosts of departed pilots.

In the summer of 1940 he was fifty-eight years old and had been due to retire in 1939. In view of the looming crisis the Air Ministry had asked him to stay on until March 1940, then to July, then to October. Then Churchill retired him. This was seen by himself and his supporters as a slight. But his time was more than up and anyway he was worn out.

That summer of 1940 he exercised superb control over his squadrons, making countless vital decisions, almost all of them correct. He was later criticized for not throwing more of his reserves against the Luftwaffe at an early stage. The debate is sterile. The point is that he won the battle. He was helped very effectively by Air Vice Marshal Keith Park, commanding 11 Group, which covered London and the South East and bore the brunt of the German assault. The forty-four-year-old New Zealander gave personal encouragement to his men, flying round the bases in his own Hurricane, listening as much as talking.

At the start of July Dowding had fifty-nine squadrons available. Thirty were equipped with Hurricanes, nineteen with Spitfires, eight with Blenheims and two with the Boulton-Paul Defiant, a hybrid which, although it had its uses, was hopeless as a day fighter. Most of the squadrons had between fifteen and twenty pilots "on state". Many of them, though, were exhausted and some units had been savagely reduced — 73 Squadron, for example, had only seven pilots. There were also serious shortages of aircraft. The ravages of the early summer were still being repaired. Twenty-two units had fewer than twelve fighters. The ability to fight a war of attrition depended on the aircraft factories maintaining a steady flow of replacements. This was possible thanks to the existence of the shadow factory system — another example of British foresight, and also of the energy of the Minister for Aircraft Production, the Canadian newspaper magnate and Churchill crony Max Beaverbrook. By the end of the battle, production was more than keeping pace with losses.

The efficiency of the command-and-control structure was a crucial factor if Fighter Command was to be nursed through its recovery period. It operated like a nervous system which conveyed information from the extremities to the centre, where data was analysed and action initiated. The nerve endings were the radar stations and Observer Corps posts, which picked up raiders and noted their type, numbers, height and direction. The brain was Fighter Command headquarters at Bentley Priory, an elegant mansion perched on the heights above north London at Stanmore in Middlesex. The arms and hands were the group and sector stations.

The Bentley Priory filter room would ascertain whether the aircraft were friend or foe and deal with the inevitable inconsistencies in the reports. The processed details were then passed to the Operations Room next door, where the raid was plotted on a large map table which provided a striking visual representation of the threat.

At the same time the information was flashed to the relevant groups — 10 Group (South West), 11 Group (South East), 12 Group (Central England and Wales), 13 Group (the North and Scotland) — which had their own ops rooms and maps. The maps were constantly updated by plotters wearing headphones. Using what looked like a long-handled croupier's rake they pushed arrows across the squares, each marked with an "F" for friendly, "H" for hostile and "X" for unknown, and colour-coded to show the time of the report. When the system was working smoothly it was reckoned to be possible to get fighters airborne within six minutes of a raid being detected.

Once an attack was confirmed, the controller of the sector or sectors affected would scramble his fighters and guide them to meet the attackers. The ideal interception was from above, when the German fighters which escorted the bomber fleets were at the limit of their endurance and with little fuel to spare for dog-fighting, and before the bombardment began. If the defenders took off too early they might themselves be running low on petrol by the time the raiders appeared, or back on the ground. Too late and they would fail to disrupt the attack. Once the enemy was sighted and the controller heard the cry of "Tally Ho!" the pilots were left alone.

Controllers also had to consider the limits of pilots and machines. Time was needed for men to recuperate and for aircraft to be patched up. To manage this, commanders maintained their squadrons at various stages of availability. "Released" meant that usually they were free to leave the station for short periods. "Available" required them to be ready to take off at ten, fifteen, thirty or sixty minutes notice. At "Readiness" they had to be able to run to their aircraft and take off within five minutes.

"Readiness meant that you were sitting in the dispersal hut togged up in your 'Mae West' life vest, your aeroplane all ready for instant departure," remembered Flying Officer John Young of 249 Squadron. "Standby meant that you were sitting in the cockpit with your helmet on, your hood slid back, listening on the radio for start-up." For some the hanging around was the most nerve-wracking part of the experience. "The most stressful thing in the Battle of Britain was sitting at readiness, waiting for the scramble telephone to ring," said Sergeant Cyril "Bam" Bamberger of 610 and 41 Squadrons. "I couldn't relax. You tried to read a book or you tried to play draughts or you pretended to doze. The phone would ring and immediately you jumped up, but it was probably that the NAAFI van was coming with tea. Then you flopped back and tried to relax again."

When dawn broke on 10 July 1940 the Channel was smothered with cloud and rain drenched the sandbagged Observer Corps posts on clifftops and headlands. Behind them the radar stations probed the skies for intruders. The station at West Beckham on the Norfolk coast was the first to register a blip on one of the cathode-ray tube displays. At 7.30 a.m. pilots of 66 Squadron, based at Coltishall in Essex, got the order to scramble and three of its Spitfires took off into the wet skies. Led by Pilot Officer Charles Cooke, the section climbed fast through the rain and cloud and at 10,000 feet broke through into brilliant sunshine. Cooke was given a vector bearing, which led him to where the enemy aircraft had been last spotted. At 8.15 a.m. the intruder came into sight. It was a lone Dornier 17 bomber, probably on a reconnaissance mission to

199

report back on the weather over the coast. One by one the Spitfires peeled off to attack. As they swooped down, the pilot of the Dornier threw his aircraft around the sky in a desperate attempt to avoid the stream of fire floating towards him and to give his gunners a chance to shoot back. One bullet from the Dornier's 7.9 mm machine guns smashed through Cooke's windscreen, flooding the cockpit with freezing air.

Then one fighter, attacking from underneath, found the belly of the bomber with its eight Browning machine guns. Smoke began to spout from the Dornier. It went into a banking turn and glided smoothly down, until it struck the grey seas off Yarmouth to be swallowed, swiftly, by the waves. All four crew were killed. The Spitfires returned to base, the victors of the first small clash of the battle.

It turned into a busy day. There were eight convoys at sea. The biggest, code-named "Bread", was rounding the North Foreland at about 10 a.m. when it was spotted by another Dornier reconnaissance aircraft — this one accompanied by thirty Messerschmitt 109 fighters. These were the Luftwaffe's quickest, nimblest aeroplanes, the equal of the Spitfire and faster than the Hurricane. Their objective, apart from protecting the lone recce plane, was to pick a fight with the British defenders. Fighter Command obliged. Six Spitfires of 74 Squadron took off from Manston, perched high on the North Foreland, and raced to intercept. They concentrated first on the bomber — a mistake. The Me 109s pounced and a series of wheeling dogfights developed that brought the aircraft over Margate, where the citizens got the first of many ringside seats at an air battle. Two Spitfires were damaged, but their pilots were unhurt and managed to make it back to Manston. None of the Messerschmitts was shot down and the Dornier limped back across the Channel to make a crash-landing.

Historians have tended to divide the Battle of Britain into three phases, with the first period characterized by attacks on shipping, the second on Fighter Command infrastructure targets, and the third on cities and London in particular. This suggests a method and concentration in the German approach that was, in reality, quite lacking. On that day, 10 July 1940, a large German formation also bombed Swansea, damaging ships, railways, a power station and a munitions factory, and killing thirty people. Among the pilots that launched a fruitless attempt to catch them was Wing Commander Ira Jones, Mick Mannock's old comrade and now in charge of the training airfield at Worthy Down. He took off in a Hawker Henley, used for towing targets, armed with only a Very signal pistol, which he discharged eloquently but uselessly at the raiders.

The biggest clash, however, was over the "Bread" convoy. At 1.30p.m. radar noticed what seemed to be a large cluster of aircraft building up over the Pas de Calais. Twenty minutes later the sky above the convoy was crowded with hostile aircraft — nearly thirty Dornier bombers protected by sixty Me 110 twin-engined fighter bombers and Me109s. The convoy was being shadowed by a protective patrol of only six

201

Hurricanes from 32 Squadron. They called for help. The first to ride to the rescue were Hurricanes from 111 Squadron, who attacked the bomber formation head-on. It was a very risky tactic, but the effect was devastating. "You could see the front of the aircraft crumple," said Flying Officer Ben Bowring of 111 Squadron. The shock tended to cause the pilots to break formation, losing the limited mutual protection it gave, leaving individual aircraft easier prey for the fighters. "A head-on attack did far more to destroy the morale of German bombers than anything else," said Flying Officer Brian Kingcome of 92 Squadron. "It upset the poor old pilot so much that he turned tail. When he was sitting and couldn't see the attack, and he was protected by a nice sheet of metal behind him and he could hear his gunners firing away, he was in a much more relaxed state of mind than when we were coming straight at him and there was nothing between himself and the guns."

Soon squadrons from five airfields had answered the call and a huge dogfight involving 100 aircraft developed, by far the biggest seen in the war or indeed ever. Every pilot was on his own and co-ordination was impossible. Flying Officer Henry Ferriss arrived with 111 Squadron just as the first bombs began to plunge around the merchantmen. "It was a thrilling sight I must confess," he told a BBC Radio interviewer. "I looked down on the tiny ships below and saw two long lines of broken water where the first bombs had fallen." Ferris led his flight in an attack on the second wave of

Dorniers. "We went screaming down and pumped lead into our targets. We shook them up quite a bit."

As the formation split up he latched onto an Me 109 that was heading for home, chasing it far out to sea. It was a dangerous thing to do, inviting the possibility of being "bounced" from above by an unseen enemy and with very little chance of rescue if he survived the attack and managed to bail out. This day, his luck was in. The German "was going very fast and I had to do 400 miles an hour to catch him up. Then, before I could fire, he flattened out to no more than fifty feet above the sea level and went streaking for home." Ferriss managed to get in five short bursts, "all aimed very deliberately. Suddenly the Messerschmitt's port wing dropped down. The starboard wing went up, and then in a flash his nose went down and he was gone. He simply vanished into the sea."

It was only then that Ferriss noticed a stinging sensation in his leg. He had been hit and now there were two Me109s on his tail. They followed him back to the coast, launching several attacks and smashing his port aileron. Just before landfall they turned away and he managed to touch down safely. He was given a fresh aeroplane and took off on another sortie. Ferriss, who had been a medical student before joining the RAF in 1937, did not survive the Battle. Five weeks later he was killed in a collision with a bomber while executing a head-on attack.

At the end of the month, Britain was winning the battle of attrition. Seventy-seven RAF aircraft had been lost of all types, and sixty-seven pilots killed. The

Luftwaffe had lost 216 aircraft and 495 aircrew. The figures were not as comforting as they seemed. The Germans, initially at least, had numbers on their side. They had their huge bomber fleet and a fighter strength that was slightly larger than the RAF's. Each force had its job to do. The bombers bombed. The fighters protected them. The Fighter Boys had a double duty. As well as trying to shoot down the bombers, they had to protect themselves — and sometimes each other — from the fighters who were striving to destroy them.

In August the strain increased. The Germans switched tactics. Instead of trying to draw the enemy into battle by attacking convoys, they now concentrated on trying to blitz the bases from which Fighter Command operated. Hitler had given up hope of a negotiated settlement after his public "appeal to reason" was rejected. Under his orders, Goering prepared a maximum effort, a knockout assault to gain air superiority over Britain that would either force surrender or clear the way for invasion. The attack would come — after a postponement due to bad weather — on 13 August, codenamed Adlertag, Eagle Day. The day dawned cloudy and rainy, but improvement was predicted and operations were scheduled for early afternoon. Some units never received the order and took off anyway, bombers flying without fighters and fighters without bombers, confusing both defenders and attackers.

By mid-afternoon the confusion and the weather had cleared. At 3.30p.m. radar spotted a huge force advancing across the Channel from the direction of

Cherbourg along a forty-mile front. There were nearly 300 aircraft, the largest formation yet seen, many of them Junkers 87 Stuka dive-bombers. Eighty Hurricanes and Spitfires from 10 Group bases rose up to meet them. The Spitfires of 609 Squadron — an Auxiliary unit drawn from the gentry of the West Riding of Yorkshire, based at Warmwell in Dorset — had plenty of time to gain the height needed for them to swoop down out of the sun on a formation of Stukas. The dive-bombers were slow and cumbersome and weighed down with bombs, and they made easy meat for the delighted pilots. "Thirteen Spitfires left Warmwell for a memorable Tea-time party over Lyme Bay and an unlucky day for the species Ju87," wrote Flying Officer John Dundas in his diary. "No less than fourteen suffered destruction or damage." The true number was five destroyed, but the punishment inflicted on the Luftwaffe that day was heavy. They had lost forty-five aircraft, the RAF thirteen.

Most of the British casualties were suffered by squadrons attacking the escorts. No. 238 Squadron, based at Middle Wallop, had four pilots killed in fighting two days previously. Now they lost another two, with a third shot down and badly burned. All had been the victims of Me 109s. The following day the unit was withdrawn from the battle to lick its wounds in the relative quiet of St Eval in Cornwall. One of the surviving pilots, Sergeant Eric Bann, wrote to his parents: "I am afraid that our duty on the front line has told its tale on our systems. Our engagements have been really hectic . . . we are all up and down with nerve trouble and have been sent to the rest camp . . . just Gordon Batt and I remain among the sergeants and many of our officers have gone." Bann lived until the end of September. His Hurricane was damaged in combat over Fareham. He baled out, but his parachute failed. His friend Gordon Batt survived the war.

Morale would decide the contest. The defenders were blessed with many advantages. They had radar and, by and large, sufficient aircraft and pilots to put the boon of early warning to maximum use. There were, for sure, periodic crises when there were shortages of men and machine. But there was an underlying strength in the system and the production lines of both fighters and pilots were picking up speed. However, the dismal example of France had shown that equipment and numbers did not decide a battle. The crucial question was: did the pilots have the skill and the nerve to keep going? By now they had the skill. In air-fighting you learned fast or died. Collectively, pilots did not achieve anything like the same degree of proficiency. In any squadron it was soon clear that there were some who had a sharper edge, whose reactions were a nanosecond quicker, whose eyesight was keener and whose determination a little stronger, which put them above the others. A minority of pilots shot down a majority of the enemy aircraft. Most pilots shot down nothing at all. It was resolve and *esprit* that counted. The Battle of Britain proved that the British pilots had more of it than their opponents.

They enjoyed one enormous practical and psychological benefit: they were fighting over their own territory.

That meant that pilots who baled out could, if they escaped serious injury, be back in action in days or in some cases hours. Crashed aircraft were patched up and recycled by special recovery teams. Surviving Luftwaffe aircrew, on the other hand, or downed but repairable aircraft, were lost to the German war effort for ever.

The fact that the battle was fought was over the land they were defending also gave the pilots a huge motivational boost. The writings and recollections of those who took part are full of quiet patriotism. In the case of the many pilots from the Dominions who took part in the battle and who had never seen the Old Country before they came to fight for it, the loyalty was to an ideal more than a reality. This patriotic mood seemed to affect everybody. An extrovert character like Pilot Officer Crelin "Bogle" Bodie of 66 Squadron grew poetical when describing his return to Coltishall at the end of a day in which he had shot down four Dornier 17s. "I flew to the coast and set course for home. Passing low over the fields and villages, rivers and towns, I looked down at labourers working, children at play beside a big red-brick schoolhouse, a bomb crater two streets away; little black heads in the streets, turning to white blobs as they heard my engine and looked up. I thought of workers in shops and factories, of stretcher-parties and ARP wardens. I hoped the 'All Clear' had gone. I was tired. I'd done my best for them."

Bodie, who was later killed in a flying accident, was writing about the events of 15 September 1940. This was subsequently taken as the point when the battle turned in Britain's favour — though it did not feel like that to the pilots. The Luftwaffe had spent August following the sensible course of battering Fighter Command on the ground. Six of the seven sector stations in 11 Group had been bombed almost to the point of collapse and five of the advanced airfields were severely damaged. In the air, just over 300 RAF pilots had been lost and only 260 had arrived to replace them, and the factories were struggling to keep replacement aircraft flowing to the squadrons. This did not mean that Fighter Command was on the point of collapse. The system was strong and even if the 11 Group stations had been knocked out there were other lines of defence to fall back on in the West and Midlands.

As it was, miraculously, the pressure lifted. On 7 September the Luftwaffe changed direction. The 11 Group bases were left alone. The target now was London. The decision was based on Goering's natural impatience and the belief (stubbornly maintained, despite the evidence that the RAF was still well-stocked with aircraft) that Fighter Command was on its last legs. That hot, sunny Saturday the Blitz began. Just before 4.45 that afternoon the sirens sounded and soon great fleets of bombers were laying waste the East End. Twenty-three squadrons raced to catch them and an epic dogfight involving more than 1,000 aircraft developed over the city.

The raids went on all night and Londoners were at last plunged into the long-anticipated reality of aerial bombardment. For the RAF, however, the German tactical switch allowed its bases and infrastructure to be repaired rapidly. The squadrons had been unable to inflict much damage on the raiders. Only thirty-eight enemy aircraft were shot down, while RAF losses totalled twenty-eight, with nineteen pilots killed. As the raids continued, the defenders refined their responses. On 15 September, when the Luftwaffe attempted a repeat of the great attack of eight days before, Fighter Command was ready and waiting. For Pilot Officer Tom "Ginger" Neil, a tall, elegant twenty-one-year-old who had joined through the volunteer reserve, it was "a very special day". After a frustrating morning when he failed to shoot anything down, he and 249 Squadron were directed at a group of Dorniers flying over Maidstone on their way to London. "I found myself behind a Dornier and as I was firing at it, the crew suddenly bailed out," he recalled. "I was so close behind it that as one of the bodies came out, I ducked in the aeroplane, thinking, 'My God, he's going to hit me!' " His interest was deflected by the swarm of German fighters who "set about me furiously and I defended myself." Then, as he and so many other pilots were to remark, the violence suddenly evaporated. "You're surrounded by aeroplanes like bees round a honey pot, and suddenly everything is quiet and there are no aeroplanes. It happens instantaneously."

Then ahead, only a mile away, another target appeared: a lone Dornier was heading down the Estuary. "It took some time for me to catch up, because it was going in a slight dive. Eventually I caught it up and I suddenly found that a Spitfire was to my left. And thereafter it was fairly straightforward. A single aeroplane on its own, two of us. We took it in turns to fire. It went down and down and down, out to sea, across a convoy of ships." Both fighters were out of ammunition. Neil thought, "Oh God, we're going to lose this one, he's going to get home." They flew alongside their victim, close enough to "read all the letters on the cockpit and I could see the damage that had been done. And then it got slower and slower and slower and the nose came up and up and up, and suddenly the tail hit the sea and it splashed down and I felt satisfaction, total satisfaction." As they flew back, "over the convoy, the ships all blew their whistles".

By the end of the day the same satisfaction was being felt all across Fighter Command. Wreckage of German aircraft and burned bodies lay in fields, lanes and streets all over south-east England. The figure of destroyed aircraft was given: 183 — a considerable exaggeration, as the true figure was nearer 60. RAF losses were light: 25 aircraft lost and 13 pilots killed.

This mauling did not cause the Luftwaffe to abandon its attacks. It had learned the lesson, however, that air superiority was not achievable, and the Spitfires and Hurricanes that came out to attack them were not — as German intelligence reports persisted in claiming — the last scrapings of the RAF barrel. By the end of October the daytime bomber attacks ceased and the Germans concentrated on the marginal policy of bringing about a collapse of morale by nocturnal blitz.

Thus ended one of the great battles of history. The pilots had not simply blunted Hitler's invasion plans, which were half-hearted at the best of times. Their achievement was more strategically significant — and glorious — than that.

The victory lit a beacon of hope. This was the first time since German territorial expansion began in 1938 that Hitler's forces had suffered a major defeat. Out of this came practical consequences that would profoundly affect the course of the war. The most crucial effect was that — as Churchill always intended — our performance persuaded the Americans that we were worthy partners in the event of them joining the conflict. It was the Japanese attack on Pearl Harbor in 1941, of course, that pushed America into the war. But it was the survival of Britain as a base that allowed the United States to fight in Europe.

There was also a moral aspect to the Battle of Britain that reached beyond mere realpolitik. It was a great triumph of the spirit that exalted the value of doing the right thing, no matter how painful and costly that might have seemed at the time. That summer, the British people were truly as they liked to imagine themselves — unperturbed, generous-spirited, heroic in a modest sort of way. And it was the RAF, the pilots in the air and the crews supporting them on the ground, who had led the nation in this finest hour.

CHAPTER
ELEVEN

Flying Blind

In Churchill's famous speech of 20 August 1940 there is a passage that no one now remembers. While praising the fighter pilots, he also emphasized that "we must never forget that all the time, night after night, month after month, our bomber squadrons travel far into Germany, find their targets in the darkness by the highest navigational skill, aim their attacks, often under the heaviest fire, often with serious loss, with deliberate careful discrimination, and inflict shattering blows upon the whole of the technical and war-making structure of the Nazi power."

Almost every assertion in this statement was untrue. The RAF's navigational ability was embryonic and targets were located as much by luck as judgement. The aiming of bombs was rudimentary and the damage they inflicted trifling. Only the parts of the Prime Minister's speech referring to the regularity of operations and the losses suffered were correct.

For most of its short life, bombing had been the RAF's *raison d'être*. When the campaign was finally launched at the start of the Battle of France it was a severe disappointment and continued to be so for another two years. Culpability lay not with the crews but with the aircraft they flew and the navigational devices, bomb sights and bombs available to them. The senior officers who had talked up bombing as a war-winning device must also take some of the blame.

The start of the Blitz generated a hatred of Germany that had previously been latent or absent. On 14 November 1940 the city of Coventry was devastated with more than 40,000 homes destroyed or damaged, 554 people killed and nearly a thousand seriously injured. The attack created an upsurge in popular pressure for retaliation and revenge. Before Coventry there were some — perhaps many — who felt it was unwise to provoke the Germans. Afterwards most shared the view of the young man who told a Mass Observation reporter: "We're fighting gangsters, so we've got to be gangsters ourselves. We've been gentlemen too long." From now on the bombing of Germany had the backing of the nation, even when everybody knew what that meant for the townsfolk of Cologne, Hamburg and the Ruhr, names that soon became very familiar from the radio and press bulletins.

Bombing also satisfied another need. It showed that Britain could still do something, even when it had no soldiers in the field to face the enemy. Allied armies would later pursue German armies through North Africa, Italy, France and the Lowlands. But for much of the war the Strategic Air Campaign, as it became known, was the only way of striking directly at the enemy's territory.

It was generally accepted that Germany would have to be defeated at home if the Nazi plague was to be eradicated. Bombing was a good — and for the time being the only — way to start. Churchill summed it up in a phrase: "The fighters are our salvation, but the bombers alone provide the means of victory."

Some of the flood of young men clamouring to join the RAF were glad to be channelled off to Bomber Command. "I thought that the defence of Great Britain was over and the next step was to smash the Germans up," said Noble Frankland, a young Oxford undergraduate and member of the University Air Squadron. "I was quite keen to take part in smashing up the Germans, which I think was a fairly common sort of instinct, but I actually had the opportunity to do it."

Others, however, brought up like so many would-be aviators on the Biggles novels of Captain W. E. Johns, and inspired by the deeds of the Fighter Boys, longed to be flying Spitfires and Hurricanes. After the Battle of Britain the call for fighter pilots dwindled. The demands of the Strategic Air Campaign meant the majority of men who flew with the RAF in the war did so with Bomber Command.

Some who had volunteered for flying duties were dismayed when they learned what it was they would be flying. Dennis Field had done his initial instruction on single-engined Harvards and was looking forward to going to a fighter squadron. But as he moved to the next stage of his training "a special parade was called and the CO announced that the whole course would be trained for multi-engined aircraft and, we inferred, four-engined bombers. I felt totally deflated at the news. The very little I knew about them gave the impression that I should become a glorified bus driver."

It would be some time before the volunteers arrived on operational squadrons. The training could afford to be lengthy and rigorous. There was nothing for them to fly until the big four-engined bombers that had been ordered as part of the pre-war rearmament programme arrived in service. The first of the series — the Short Stirling — started to be fed into squadrons in August 1940, the Halifax in 1941 and the mighty Lancaster not until the beginning of 1942.

In this interim period Bomber Command struggled on with its inadequate Blenheims, Hampdens, Wellingtons and Whitleys, trying to make the Air Staff's assertions that bombing was capable of inflicting precise and painful damage on the German war machine a reality. In the course of 1941 it lost 1,338 aeroplanes on operations — more than the number of German aircraft the RAF had shot down during the Battle of Britain. Another 154 were destroyed in training and other accidents, a scandalous rate that persisted throughout the war.

The official progress of the campaign was reported in bulletins that conveyed an impression of continuous success. Typical was a broadcast made by Flight Lieutenant J. C. Mackintosh, a Hampden bomb-aimer. His script — almost certainly prepared for him by a Ministry of Information hack — made night-bombing seem like a cool, precise science. It started with the claim that "when the war began we were well trained in finding targets in the dark and were therefore never compelled to bomb indiscriminately through the clouds". He went on to describe a recent attack on an oil refinery. The crew had imagined it would be a tricky target. But the fact that it was sited on a bend in a river which would provide a useful navigational point led them to decide that "perhaps, after all, it would not be such a difficult job to find".

As they entered the target area they located the river, but after three runs through anti-aircraft fire they had still not spotted the objective. Mackintosh called on the skipper to go round again. Then, "there it was. The dim outline of an oil refinery wonderfully camouflaged. It was getting more and more into the centre of the sights. I pressed the button and my stick of bombs went hurtling towards Germany's precious oil. The rear-gunner watched the bombs burst and in a very few seconds those thousands of tons of valuable oil had become hundreds of feet of black and acrid smoke."

This was bombing as optimistically imagined in the Air Ministry's pre-war plans. The reality was much closer to the experience of Eric Woods, a navigator who joined 144 Squadron in the autumn of 1940 and carried out his first operation on the night of 9–10 October. The target was the Krupp factory in Essen, an objective that the RAF would return to again and again.

At the briefing the crews were told to expect only scattered cloud over the town. As they neared their destination "it was obvious that the Met people had got it wrong, as a solid mass of cloud was clearly visible below, and as we progressed eastwards we saw that the cloud was becoming denser ahead. We pressed on, but two ominous developments took place. A film of ice appeared on the windscreen and an opaque mass of rime ice began to spread out along the leading edge of each wing." The Hampden's two engines began to splutter as ice worked its way into the fuel lines. "There was a hurried conference, since it was pretty obvious that the target was unlikely to be identifiable, so the decision was taken to fly on and see what happened when we reached our ETA [estimated time of arrival]. In the event, at that time we were still in dense cloud, the whole mass being lit up by searchlights sweeping below, with frequent bright flashes which could have been anti-aircraft fire or bomb bursts, I certainly knew not what."

With the ground invisible a decision was made not to bomb but to head for home, looking for a target of opportunity on the way. Shortly after they turned "the cloud began to break up to the west — quite the opposite of what the weatherman had said . . . We did, in fact, fly along the Scheldt Estuary and as we passed over the port of Flushing the navigator let go with our total load and I clearly saw bomb bursts, though I wasn't sure precisely where they landed." Only three of the twenty Hampdens that set out reached Essen.

The basic problem was navigation. Pre-war planning had assumed that most bombing would take place in daylight. In night-time bombing the navigator became the most important man on board, and he had only basic instruments to get his comrades to the target and back. Before the advent of radio and electronic aids — the Gee, Oboe and H2S systems — the navigator operated like a yachtsman at sea, by dead reckoning, drawing a line between two points on a map and factoring in speed and wind to calculate progress. He gave his pilot a course on take-off and then, if the skies were clear and a moon was shining, looked below for landmarks to check they were on track.

On a trip to Germany they left England over the chalk cliffs of Flamborough Head in Yorkshire, turning right at the Friesian Islands. If the night was clear he might try and get a fix from the stars using a sextant, but only if the pilot was prepared to fly straight and level for long enough, increasing his vulnerability to night-fighter attack. Winds that were forecast failed to blow. Unpredicted ones arrived to whisk them off their course. It was no wonder that German targets were sometimes unaware that they had been the subject of an attempted attack.

Initially, the only real means of measuring success were the reports brought back by the crews. In 1941 some aircraft were fitted with cameras triggered by the release of the bombs. That summer Frederick Lindemann, Churchill's friend and chief scientific adviser to the Cabinet, initiated an investigation to compare crew reports with the information that could be gleaned from the admittedly blurred and monochrome images available. Lindemann was the son of a German emigré and brilliant, but argumentative and obstinate. He demonstrated his faith in his own judgement by learning to fly to test his theory about how pilots could recover from a spin. He took off, deliberately stalled the aeroplane, spiralled earthwards, then pulled out. The theory was proved and by an act of great bravery the technique became the standard procedure, saving the lives of countless aviators.

The job of analysing the bombing data was given to a clever young assistant, David Bensusan-Butt, a civil servant in the War Cabinet secretariat. He studied more than 600 operational photographs, compared them with the debriefing reports of the crews and arrived at some shocking conclusions. He found that only a third of the aircraft claiming to reach the target did, in fact, do so. Of those recorded as attacking the target, "only one in three got within five miles".

The Butt Report was a devastating challenge to the Air Staff's prevailing wisdom and came at a very bad time for the advocates of strategic bombing. All summer the Battle of the Atlantic had been raging, a struggle that was just as vital to Britain's survival as had been the Battle of Britain. Army and navy critics and some politicians were pressing hard for RAF resources to be switched from what they regarded as the wasteful and ineffective business of bombing Germans to come to the aid of the convoys being sunk willy-nilly by the U-boats of the Kriegsmarine and the Condor bombers of the Luftwaffe.

The reaction of the Air Staff, now headed by Air Chief Marshal Charles Portal, a strategic bombing enthusiast and previously the head of Bomber Command, was to deny the findings and commission another survey. The Directorate of Bombing Operations investigation took as its model the bomb damage caused to British cities by the Blitz. Its conclusion was much more favourable to the bombing lobby. By their calculations, a force of 4,000 bombers would be able to destroy forty-three of the biggest towns in Germany. The message was that far from diverting bombers away from Germany, more should be thrown into the fight.

It had been shown that estimates of what bombing could achieve were exaggerated. It was now clear — from the example of the Blitz and the failures of the RAF's bombing of Germany — that there was no such thing as a knockout blow. Instead of abandoning the theory, though, its advocates were in the process of refining it. In place of one devastating punch, the enemy could be defeated by a continuous volley of body shots. The argument was given scientific legs by the indefatigable Lindemann, who, in the spring of 1942, produced a report advocating the abandonment of the futile pursuit of "precision bombing". The air force simply did not have the means of systematically hitting oil refineries, war factories and so on, he argued. The large numbers of four-engined heavy bombers, now starting to arrive on squadrons, and Gee electronic navigation were not going to significantly improve accuracy. What the bolstered force should be concentrating on now was hitting towns.

Lindemann's report used statistics to make it all sound very simple. The language was bloodless, with no mention of killing. According to the "Prof", as Churchill called him, Britain should have a force of about 10,000 bombers by mid-1943. Each bomber had an average life expectancy of fourteen bombing trips, meaning it could deliver a total load of forty tons. Judging from the data collected in Birmingham, Hull and other blitzed towns, this meant that one bomber could make between 4,000 and 8,000 people homeless. If only half the projected bomber force reached its target, a third of the German population could be "dehoused". Investigation of the British experience "seemed to show that having one's home demolished is most damaging to morale. People seem to mind it more than losing their relatives." The report concluded that "there seems little doubt that this would break the spirit of the people".

The debate flowed back and forth with Lindemann's great rival, the chairman of the Aeronautical Research Committee, Henry Tizard, maintaining the projections were inflated. It was a technical argument. The morality of "dehousing" did not enter the discussion. In the intensity of total war, in the face of the enemy's utter absence of scruples, pre-war squeamishness about harming civilians had vanished like snow in spring. The debate was settled after the Cabinet asked a High Court judge to weigh the competing views. Mr Justice Singleton concluded that Germany would not be able to stand twelve or eighteen months "continuous, intensified and increased bombing, affecting as it must, her war production, her power of resistance, her industries and her will to resist (by which I mean morale)". This view became enshrined as official policy in the Directive issued to Bomber Command on 14 February 1942, which stated that "the primary object

221

of your operations should now be focused on the morale of the enemy civilian population and in particular of the industrial workers".

Eight days after it was issued, Bomber Command got a new leader. Arthur Harris — "Bert" to his peers, "Bomber" to the public and "Butch" to the crews he led — took over on 20 February 1942. He was undoubtedly the man for the job. He had spent his early years seeking his fortune in Rhodesia, a part of the world he loved, and the crack of an invisible *sjambok* could often be heard in his dealings with subordinates. After early war service in Africa he joined the Royal Flying Corps in 1915, stayed on in peacetime and, after his service bombing natives on the North-West Frontier and in Iraq, had moved through a succession of staff jobs. He knew Whitehall and its ways from a stint as Director of Plans at the Air Ministry. He also understood and got on with Americans, following a tour as head of the RAF delegation in Washington in 1941.

Harris would later complain that "there is a widespread impression that I not only invented the policy of area bombing, but also insisted on carrying it out in the face of a natural reluctance to kill women and children that was felt by everybody else . . . the decision to attack large industrial areas was taken long before I became Commander-in-Chief." He certainly supported the policy with all his heart, pursuing it with dogged determination, even when the progress of the war eroded its value and justification. But it was true that he had not been one of the plan's progenitors. Its most vehement advocate inside the RAF was his boss, Sir Charles Portal, the short, beaky-nosed, highly intelligent and obsessively hard-working Chief of the Air Staff. If anyone in the RAF was responsible for area bombing it was him. Yet he escaped all the post-war opprobrium and it was Harris who would forever be associated with the flattening of German cities.

Harris was just fifty in the spring of 1942, but looked rather older, due perhaps to a bristly moustache, which added to the initial impression he gave of impatience and irascibility. It was more than an impression. Harris was rude, arrogant, pig-headed. He disliked being challenged and in the words of Bomber Command's official historians had "a tendency to confuse advice with interference, criticism with sabotage and evidence with propaganda". The belligerence he radiated translated into an intense passion for the business of "smashing up the Germans". He was an eloquent talker and writer and he came up with a succinct description of the situation he inherited. "The Nazis entered this war under the rather childish delusion that they were going to bomb everyone else and nobody was going to bomb them," he declared in a broadcast. "At Rotterdam, London, Warsaw and half a dozen other places, they put their rather naive theory into operation. They sowed the wind, and now they are going to reap the whirlwind."

He arrived at Bomber Command at a moment when the materials were being assembled that would make it possible for the prophesy to be fulfilled. Many squadrons were already equipped with Handley Page

Halifaxes and in March 1942 the AVRO Lancaster began to arrive. Both planes were powered by four Merlin engines and they were bigger and stronger than any other bombers in the world. The Halifax got mixed notices from those who flew in it. Wing Commander James "Willie" Tait, one of the great aviators of the Second World War, who commanded three bomber squadrons, hated it. The Mark II, he thought, was "far from satisfactory. It had accumulated a weight of extra gear, including a mid-upper turret, and the last straw was the exhaust cowls." These emitted flames which provided "night-fighters with a good target" and created drag, which affected handling so that the "performance of the loaded aeroplane at operational height on a warm summer's night can be better described as 'waffling' than flying".

To a Canadian flier, Ralph Wood, who switched from Whitleys in May 1942, the "Hallybag" was a "beautiful four-engined bird". He occupied the "dinky little navigator's compartment [which] was below and in front of the pilot's cockpit. You went down a few steps and entered a small section with a navigator's table down one side, ahead and below the pilot's feet." Wood doubled as front-gunner when needed. His weapon was a twin-barrelled Vickers, mounted on a swivel and stuck through the perspex canopy, which pumped out .303 calibre rifle bullets. They were regarded as "pop-guns" by the crews and were little protection against being shot down by a night-fighter.

The Lancaster inspired universal trust. It was a masterpiece of military aviation design. It was capable of carrying loads of up to about seven tons, yet despite its great strength was fast and manoeuvrable. It could reach nearly 290 mph and was nimble enough to "corkscrew" out of trouble when under attack from a night-fighter. It also had the lowest accident rate of the bombers. Tony Iveson, an ex-fighter pilot who had already notched up about 1,800 hours flying time in many different types before he encountered the "Lanc", remembered it as "a lovely aircraft, splendid night and day". Pilot Ken Newman "liked the Lanc from the first moment that I climbed aboard". The cockpit layout was "much more sensible than that of the Halifax" with everything within easy reach. It was only in an emergency that the main design fault became apparent. The thick spar that lay across the fuselage supporting the wings had to be clambered over when moving forward and aft, and was an impediment when trying to bale out.

These greatly improved aircraft now had a means of finding their way in the dark. It was called Gee (for the "grid" mapping system on which it worked) and it sent out radio pulses which were picked up on a cathode-ray tube in the navigator's cabin. Because of the Earth's curvature, the range was limited to 350 miles and navigators had to contend with German jamming. Nonetheless, Gee was a great improvement. It set the bombers on a correct course on the outward journey and helped to guide them back home.

The new heavy bombers conveyed a feeling of might and strength that inspired those who flew in them. Noble Frankland thought them "incredibly sinister and powerful". Nobody looking at them could doubt that they meant business.

By now there was a large pool of trained men to fly the "heavies". The aircrews of Bomber Command were an extraordinarily mixed bunch. If the fighter squadrons were a microcosm of British society, bomber squadrons were a microcosm of the English-speaking world. In any crew there might be Canadians, Australians, New Zealanders, Irishmen, as well as British from all regions and every layer of society. There were also Poles, French and Czechs, eager to do to the Germans what had been done to their own people. Every one of them was a volunteer. Those who put themselves forward for Pathfinder Force, which identified targets for the following bombers, were volunteers twice over. By 1942 the increasing complexity and size of bombers had created distinct roles for each crew member. There were six categories: pilot, navigator, engineer, bomb-aimer, wireless operator and air-gunner. After the initial vetting process, candidates were sent to an Aircrew Selection Centre. On the first day they faced a fairly demanding set of academic tests. These were marked on the spot and those who failed were sent home. The following morning there was a strict medical and anyone less than A1 was weeded out. The aspirant was then quizzed by a panel, a process that was "more of a chat than an interview". If deemed acceptable, the candidate was sworn in, issued with an RAF number, placed on "deferred service" and told to go home and wait.

The applicants all shared an enthusiasm which in retrospect struck some as excessive. "Why did it seem to us such a good idea at the time?" mused Jim Auton, who joined up in 1940. "Our side didn't appear to stand any chance of winning the war. The United States had not yet shown any signs of joining in as combatants . . . Stalin with his millions of troops was allied with Hitler. Our gallant allies the French had swiftly capitulated to the Germans, and the British Army had been humiliatingly kicked out of the continent at Dunkirk." Auton decided that in his case it was "the chance to leave home and fly an aeroplane" that was the ultimate lure. "Joining the Air Force made us feel that we were real men. Little did we realize what was in store for us — some of it good, much of it bad."

The waiting could last months. Eventually the volunteer was summoned to an Aircrew Reception Centre for basic training, where they marched, saluted, went on endless runs and listened to terrifying lectures from the medical officer. These, according to James Hampton, the youngest of three brothers who volunteered for aircrew and the only one to survive, warned the new arrivals, virgins almost to a man, about "some of the shocking and terrifying diseases that abounded and of which they had previously been unaware. These diseases had certain things in common. They could not be caught from lavatory seats and they invariably ended with general paralysis of the insane, followed shortly by death."

One of the main reception centres was at Lord's Cricket Ground. Jim Auton recalled the members of his

227

intake lining up in the Long Room while a civilian medic inspected their private parts. "'Get your balls up," he bellowed at the top of his voice as he paused in front of each of us. We were rather surprised by his vulgarity and we could not understand why he seemed to be so angry. I suppose he thought the whole process was a waste of his time. We certainly thought it was a waste of ours. 'Get fell in for an FFI!' the corporal had shouted. 'What on earth does that mean?' we had asked each other." A worldly volunteer explained that "They want to see if you've got a dose of the clap." They "tried not to stare at each other's works as we stood there exposed and red-faced".

Then the corporal ordered someone to fall out. "We craned our neck to see what was happening. Was it the clap? If so, what did it look like? As one of our number was hauled out of the ranks, we saw that one of his testicles was rather larger than an orange. The other was the usual size. How the hell did that happen? Surely not the clap — but we didn't know the symptoms." The volunteers were barely out of school and "most of us were virgins, but keen to learn the ropes as soon as the opportunity presented itself".

The cadets were eventually sifted into the "trades" in which they would fight the war. Their paths now diverged as they went off to specialized flying, engineering, navigation, bombing and wireless schools. The lucky ones found themselves on a ship to one of the 333 training schools in Canada, Australia, South Africa, Rhodesia, India and the United States, where they enjoyed a sybaritic break from the austerity of wartime Britain.

Training was fun and for many a great social adventure. Young men who would normally never have rubbed shoulders as equals found themselves flung together. Assumptions and prejudices tended to evaporate. Denholm Elliot was at RADA when the war began and volunteered for the RAF on his eighteenth birthday. He found service life "rather exciting. I was mixing for the first time with many different types of men from different strata of society and I found that I was [getting] on really quite well with them." Elliot was shot down and spent most of the war in a prison camp, before going on to become one of Britain's best-known actors.

At the end of specialist training everyone was promoted. About two thirds became sergeants. The rest were commissioned as pilot officers. It was here that the submerged issue of class resurfaced. Despite the supposedly meritocratic nature of the RAF (in the early years, at least), there seemed to have been an institutional conviction that those whose parents were wealthy enough to send them to fee-paying schools were automatically considered officer material.

They then moved on to Operational Training Units (OTUs), the final stage before being launched into the air battle. It was here that individuals were welded into teams — the crews that would fly and die together in the cold and dark over occupied Europe. The crew henceforth became the centre of the airman's existence. Life beyond the base — the world of family and friends

— took on a distant and secondary importance. The process was called "crewing up" and it showed the RAF at its most inventive and imaginative. Instead of trying to apply scientific methods to decide likely compatibility, the anonymous devisers of the system took an enormous leap of faith and allowed human chemistry to work its magic. Essentially the crews selected themselves.

The procedure was very straightforward. The requisite numbers of each aircrew category were put in a room together and told to team up. As they were all arriving from different specialist schools, no one knew anyone in the other categories. Jack Currie, a sergeant pilot who reached his OTU at the end of 1942, had "imagined that the process would be just as impersonal as most others that we went through in the RAF. I thought I would just see an order on the noticeboard detailing who was crewed with whom. But what happened was quite different. When we had all paraded in the hangar and the roll had been called, the chief ground instructor got up on a dais. He wished us good morning . . . and said: 'Right chaps, sort yourselves out.' "

Currie looked around, trying not to stare. "There were bomb-aimers, navigators, wireless operators and gunners, and I needed one of each to form my crew . . . This was a crowd of strangers. I had a sudden recollection of standing in a suburban dance hall wondering which girl I should approach. I remembered that it wasn't always the prettiest or the smartest girl who made the best companion for the evening. Anyway, this wasn't the same as choosing a dancing partner, it was more like picking out a sweetheart or a wife, for better or for worse."

He started off trying to find a navigator and approached a knot of them who were standing chatting together, hoping instinct would guide him to the right one. "I couldn't assess what his aptitude with a map and dividers might be from his face, or his skill with a sextant from the size of his feet." Then he "noticed that a wiry little Australian was looking at me anxiously. He took a few steps forward, eyes puckered in a diffident smile and spoke: 'Looking for a good navigator?' " Currie formed an immediate impression of "honesty, intelligence and nervousness". They teamed up and soon had acquired the rest of the crew. As they walked off together for a cup of tea, Currie realized that he "hadn't made a single conscious choice".

Once formed, a crew stood by to await posting to a squadron. The process had been long and expensive. It took about £10,000 to train each crew member, the equivalent of about £800,000 in today's money. However, the expense of getting them into battle did not mean that once they got there, their lives would be worth very much.

The revelation of how little Bomber Command was achieving meant operations had been scaled down during the winter of 1941–2 to husband resources and await the arrival of the heavies.

In the spring of 1942 the force was better equipped and had a new, aggressive and ambitious officer at its head. Harris came armed with some new ideas on how

231

bombers should be used. He believed strongly in the principle of concentration. Instead of smallish numbers of aircraft being despatched to two or three different targets in a night, large numbers would saturate one objective. Harris favoured fire as the principle tool of destruction. It was easier, he calculated, to burn down a city than to blow it up. Very small, light incendiary bombs were horribly effective when showered on old buildings. The method would be to first drop high explosive bombs that would rip off roofs and blow down walls, choking the streets with rubble that would hamper the work of firemen and rescue teams. Then the four-pound magnesium incendiaries would float down into the wreckage, starting fires that would be whipped up by the winds generated by the blasts. The aim was, he stated bluntly, to "start so many fires at the same time that no fire-fighting services, however efficiently and quickly they were reinforced by the fire brigades of other towns, could get them under control."

Harris selected an easy target on which to try out the method. Lübeck, an old Hanseatic port on the Baltic, had only minor strategic importance, but it was easy to find and given that many of the houses were partly built of wood was easier than most cities to set on fire. On the night of 28–29 March — Palm Sunday — 234 aircraft took off into clear skies and headed north and east, guided on their way for much of the journey by Gee, with which the first wave of bombers was equipped. Wellingtons made up most of the force with twenty-six Stirlings and twenty-one Manchesters, the unsatisfactory precursor of the Lancaster. The target was only lightly defended and pilots felt safe enough to bomb from a mere 2,000 feet. More than 400 tons of bombs were dropped. Of these, two thirds were incendiaries. The aiming point was the centre of the Altstadt, the old town, a quaint jumble of narrow streets and half-timbered houses. They went up like tinder. Harris had organized the attack into three waves, with the idea that the fires set by the first wave would make it easier for the succeeding one to find and bomb. So it turned out.

In the days following the raid the images brought back by aircraft from the RAF's Photo Reconnaissance Unit were studied eagerly. The story they told was very different from the catalogue of failure analysed by David Bensusan-Butt. For once an air raid had achieved what it set out to do. The purpose had been, unashamedly, to lay waste the town and that is what had happened, by and large. It was calculated that 190 acres of Lübeck — 30 per cent of the built-up area — had been burned down. It was an overestimate, but not a wild one. By the Germans' reckoning, 3,401 buildings had been destroyed or seriously damaged. Among them was a factory that made oxygen equipment for U-boats. But the beautiful Marienkirche had also gone up in the conflagration. Up to 320 people were killed, the largest number in a raid on Germany so far, but still considerably fewer than the more than 1,400 who died when the Luftwaffe blitzed London on the night of 10–11 May 1941. Only twelve aircraft were lost, most on the outward journey.

Harris was delighted. Even with the limited force of obsolescent aircraft available, the formula of concentration plus incendiaries, when applied to a target the size of a town, produced devastating results. He repeated the feat a month later with four raids in quick succession on Rostock, another old Hanseatic town.

By the end of May Harris was ready for a real spectacular. He understood the power of publicity and was keen to mount an operation that would win him and his men attention and prestige, as well as boosting British morale. He hit on the idea of launching a "thousand-bomber raid". The phrase would resonate in the press in Britain and across the Atlantic. He took the idea to Churchill. The Prime Minister was a sucker for a grand gesture. The project was irresistible. The problem was that Harris had nothing like a thousand serviceable bombers standing by. To reach the magic number he had to drag in aircraft and crews from Operational Training Units.

On the night of 30–31 May, a bright, clear, moonlit night, the great raid was launched. There were 1,047 aircraft, most of them old types, but including seventy-three Lancasters. The volume of aircraft meant they had to move in a "bomber stream", flying through different air corridors to reduce the risk of collisions. The target was Cologne, Germany's third largest city and an important industrial centre. In his departing address to the crews, Harris left them in no doubt about the significance of the mission. The force, he told them, was "at least twice the size and has at least four times the carrying capacity of the largest air force ever before concentrated on one objective." They were making history. "You have an opportunity," he declared, "to strike a blow at the enemy which will resound, not only throughout Germany but throughout the world."

They were carrying 1,455 tons of bombs, two thirds of which were incendiaries, and the results were awe-inspiring. One airman, Ralph Wood, looking down from his Halifax, saw what looked like "the embers of a huge bonfire". The conflagration destroyed more than 13,000 homes, mostly apartments, and seriously damaged 6,360 more. Nine hospitals, seventeen churches, sixteen schools and four university buildings were either burnt or blown down. The death toll set a new record: at least 469 people were killed, almost all of them civilians.

News of the raid was received with enthusiasm by a British public eager for revenge for Coventry. It was, for the time being, exceptional. Bomber Command did not have the men or machines to keep up the tempo, and a rhythm of regular mass raids would not be established until the following year. The importance of the Cologne raid was that it established the feasibility of the concept, and by extension the value of the strategic bombing campaign. Henceforth, strategic bombing was at the heart of Allied war planning. It meant a crucial prioritization in the allocation of resources. Aircraft that were dedicated to blasting Germany could not be used in other theatres, even one so vital to Britain's survival as the war being fought in the sea lanes of the Atlantic.

CHAPTER
TWELVE

Seabirds

The Battle of the Atlantic could be said to have begun in the first days of the war. It would be just as vital for Britain's survival as a free nation as the Battle of Britain. Aircraft had a crucial part to play if the struggle was to be won. Unlike their counterparts in Fighter Command, Coastal Command and the Fleet Air Arm went into the contest woefully equipped, and although a procurement programme promised better days to come, it would be some time before they arrived.

Coastal Command's duties, as laid out in 1937, were "trade protection, reconnaissance and co-operation with the Royal Navy". Of these, "trade protection" would be the most important. The innocuous phrase disguised the enormity of what was at stake. "Dominating all our power to carry on the war, or even keep ourselves alive, lay our mastery of the ocean routes and the free approach and entry to our ports," observed Winston Churchill. What that meant was that unless Britain could keep the sea lanes to the Americas open, the war machine would sputter to a halt for lack of fuel and the population would start to starve.

236

Remarkably little attention was paid in the interwar years to the business of securing the trade routes. The experience of the spring of 1917, when U-boats sank almost a million tons of shipping in a single month, had been soon forgotten. Then, it had seemed possible to the First Sea Lord, Admiral Jellicoe, that the war might be lost if no antidote were found to the German submarines. One was: the adoption of a convoy system where merchantmen sailed protected by warships and, latterly, air escorts. By the time the new war started, new technology had arrived and convoys were out of fashion. The development of Asdic — underwater sonic detection — had advanced to the point where the naval staff felt able to state that "the submarine should never again be able to present us with the problem we were faced with in 1917". The Admiralty was therefore confident that only a small air element would be needed to handle the underwater threat. As to attack by enemy aircraft, the development of the multiple pom-pom gun was thought to be an adequate defence and deterrent.

This hubris was soon punished. Asdic was valuable, but not infallible. After the great conquests of the spring and early summer of 1940, Germany controlled a coastline that stretched from the North Cape in northern Norway to Bordeaux. U-boats, long-range bombers and surface raiders had a multitude of bases on the French Atlantic seaboard from which to sally out. The toll rose steadily. In June 1940 they sank ships totalling nearly 400,000 tons. These disasters forced a change of heart. The navy reverted to the convoy system and the task of providing aerial protection from the ravages of U-boats and long-range bombers fell largely on Coastal Command's willing but pitifully equipped squadrons.

At the start of the war it had thirteen squadrons of aircraft and six of flying boats, organized in three groups. Their commander was Air Marshal Sir Frederick Bowhill, then fifty-nine. He had started life as a merchant seaman. After taking flying lessons, he joined the RNAS and commanded HMS *Empress* during the Cuxhaven raid on Christmas Day 1914. According to the Air Ministry mandarin Maurice Dean, "he had seawater in his veins (and) an appreciation of naval needs based on a lifetime's experience".

Bases were scattered around the fringes of Scotland, England, Wales and Northern Ireland. It had been estimated that 261 shore-based aircraft would be needed to secure Britain's maritime defence; 165 for convoy escort duty and 96 for reconnaissance. When war broke out, there were 259, which seemed to bode well. However, the paper strength disguised a fundamental weakness. At this stage Coastal Command was the "Cinderella Service", jostled aside in the rush for resources by the demands of Fighter and Bomber Commands. Only one of the aeroplane squadrons had an aeroplane that was up to the job: the American-manufactured Lockheed Hudson. Eight of the rest had Ansons, and two had torpedo-carrying and obsolescent Vildebeests. The crews called the Anson "Faithful Annie" and it was as dependable and unexciting as the nickname suggests. It had been built as a six-seater passenger plane with a maximum speed of about 190 mph. Despite this, its reach was inadequate for its function. An Anson was incapable of getting all the way to the Norwegian coast — a vital area of naval activity — and back. It also posed very little threat to any enemy vessel it might encounter. "The Anson was quite useless in any active wartime role, except a limited anti-submarine patrol to protect shipping, and was really obsolete before 1939," judged Wing Commander Guy Bolland, who commanded Coastal Command's 217 Squadron, based at St Eval. "The performance bomb load and armament were totally inadequate."

All of the bombs available were feeble. The experience of the previous war suggested that the best weapon for an air attack on a submarine was a bomb carrying at least 300 lbs of high explosive. With the weight of the casing, that amounted to a bomb of 520 lbs. But in 1934, when a new stock of bombs was ordered, the sizes were 500 lb, 250 lb and 100 lb. Why they were chosen when so obviously inadequate was never explained. The puny effect of the hundred-pounders was demonstrated when an Anson dropped one by mistake on a submarine, HMS *Snapper*. The only damage suffered, it was said, was four broken light bulbs in the control room. Was the story true? Perhaps not, but the fact that it did the rounds gave some idea of the low regard those who would have to drop the bombs had for their destructive powers.

Coastal Command's effectiveness was further hampered by the lack of on-board radar, so crews had only their eyes to depend on as, hour after hour, on North Sea patrol or convoy escort, they scoured the monotonous grey ridges below for signs of a small, dark shape. It was recognized that the activity could induce trances — similar to the "empty-field myopia" experienced by pilots in the Falklands — which could have fatal consequences. On convoy duty the method was to fly back and forth across a fifteen-mile "box" ahead of and on either side of the merchantmen. It was decided that it was good for morale if they remained in sight of the ship's crews, so deeper searching was ruled out. At night there was no flying at all.

It was hardly surprising that of the eighty-five attacks carried out by Coastal Command against U-boats in the first eight months of the war, only one resulted in a sinking, and that was with the help of surface ships. During this period, as the official narrative admitted, "all we could do was harass and frighten," hoping to cause prowling U-boats to at least hang back. Depth charges, which were far more effective than bombs, eventually took their place. But it was not until 1941 that Coastal Command could claim a "kill" of its own.

The change in fortunes began with the arrival of better aircraft and on-board radar. The aircraft flying to the rescue were American not British. The PBY Catalina flying boats and Liberators were both made by Consolidated Aircraft in California. The Catalina acted as a replacement to the Sunderland flying boat, which went out of production when the manufacturer, Short's, were told to switch to churning out Stirlings. It was a marvellous aircraft, initially intended for reconnaissance and bombing over the vast spaces of the Pacific. It was slow but had formidable endurance and its twin Pratt and Whitney engines were famously reliable. It was also highly versatile. Flying boats did not need airstrips. They had two thirds of the earth's surface to land on. A Catalina could spend two hours on station at a distance of 800 miles, 200 miles further than the Sunderland could manage for that amount of time. By June 1941 fifteen squadrons were due to be supplied with them.

The four-engined Liberator, which carried 2,500 gallons of fuel, could manage three hours patrolling at a distance of 1,100 miles. The Liberators' great range was needed if the "Atlantic Gap" was to be closed. This was the area of greatest peril for the convoys when they were beyond the reach of the air umbrellas that could be pushed out from Britain, Northern Ireland and Iceland on one side of the ocean and Canada on the other. These were slower to come and by the end of 1942 had reached only four squadrons. It was not until well into 1943 that some degree of cover could be provided by a combination of reconnaissance aircraft, bombers and long-range fighters.

Work on airborne radar had begun in 1936 and by 1940 twelve Coastal Command Hudsons carried an early version. The ASV (Air to Surface Vessel) Mark I was large and heavy. Its range was short and found it hard to distinguish between a ship and the myriad signals sent back by the sea's surface. Work persisted and an improved version emerged. The ASV II had a more powerful transmitter and a more sensitive receiver and was more robust than its predecessor. It could scan twelve miles ahead and twenty miles to the side. Four thousand sets were ordered and by August 1942 most of the squadrons had them.

Although the land-based aircraft of Coastal Command belonged to the Royal Air Force, the Air Ministry had been sensible enough to cede effective control of it to the Admiralty. Relations between the two were good on the whole and the arrangements were recognized as a model of the not always easy practice of inter-service co-operation.

The decision to return control of ship-borne aircraft to the navy had been made in July 1937. This brought to an end the highly complicated and unsatisfactory sharing arrangement that had existed with the RAF since 1942. But it left the Admiralty with only two years in which to recruit and train air and ground crews and build or adapt shore bases and aerodromes to support their extended duties. At this stage it was not clear what exactly they would be. The navy had few trained pilots at senior levels and — unlike the navies of the United States or Germany — had devoted very little time to thinking about where naval aviation was heading. Initially it was thought that its passive tasks would be confined to reconnaissance and shadowing and spotting for the fleet's guns. Its active roles would include attacking a faster enemy in order to slow it down until the pursuing force could catch up, and fighting off hostile aircraft and submarines. These would turn out to be only a few of the functions they would be called on to perform. In time they would be involved in convoy protection, covering amphibious landings, attacking enemy ships in harbour and cutting enemy supply lines. It became in the words of Hugh Popham, a FAA fighter pilot and historian, "one of the hardest worked of any of the services". For most of them, however, it was "severely — and for some of them, ludicrously — ill-equipped".

One thing the navy did have was suitable ships. A new, modern aircraft carrier, *Ark Royal*, went into service in 1938 to add to the existing six older ones, and between 1936 and 1939 three more were laid down. Plans were made to train up the men and form the squadrons to fly off them. They envisaged a front-line strength of 540 aircraft and 1,570 aircrew by 1942. A recruitment drive for short-service commission officers was launched and air-minded ratings started pilot- and observer-training. By the time the war started and the FAA was fighting its first actions, these men were squadron and flight commanders. Beneath them were the men of the Royal Naval Volunteer Reserve, who, like their RAF counterparts, had signed up when war loomed. The result was that the squadrons were full of "lawyers and teachers, draughtsmen and geologists, actors and civil servants", who all took the rank of Temporary Sub-Lieutenant (A).

Among the short-service officers was Charles Friend, an ex-grammar schoolboy who was working as a laboratory assistant in the Paint Research Station in Teddington, near London, and "apparently set to earn my bread in useful industrial scientific work" when the

Munich crisis broke. Friend spent those anxious days with the rest of the staff, "digging an enormous hole outside with the intention of getting in it when the bombs began to fall". The experience gave him a "full realization that the war was coming. I decided that I would not wait to be conscripted, but that I would volunteer." The decision set him off on a career that was packed with adventure and peril.

In March 1939 he joined the carrier HMS *Hermes* at Plymouth to start training. Friend had been impelled into the FAA primarily by a desire to fly, but it was made very clear that it was the navy he was joining. He and the rest of the intake spent their initial time "exhaustedly pulling boats around the harbour before breakfast to sailing them for both duty and pleasure; from proper behaviour in the Gunroom or Wardroom mess to the necessity to snatch a tiddy-oggy [pasty] at action stations", before moving on to specialized training as an air observer at Portsmouth.

They started on simulators. In "mock-up cockpits which bumped, yawed and generally gave a realistic impression of flying, we looked at a green floor through binoculars. Model ships manoeuvred on it and spots of light were projected down around them as shell splashes." They reported in Morse code to instructors who marked their ability and progress. It was three months before they actually took to the air.

The new boys were a mixture of grammar and public school boys entering an enclosed world peopled by officers who had been in the navy since they were thirteen. Like many of the outsiders thrust into the

244

services by the advent of war, Friend found much to like and admire in the environment. The "loss of complete independence inherent in service life at all levels was compensated for by an abiding sense of belonging to an organization with a purpose".

Friend first saw action in what was to be the FAA's first big engagement of the war. In April 1940 he was attached to 801 Squadron aboard *Ark Royal* and in the thick of Britain's calamitous military debut on the still winter-bound shores of Norway.

He was flying as observer in a Blackburn Skua, the navy's first monoplane aircraft, which was intended as a dual-role bomber and fighter, with a fellow midshipman A. S. Griffiths as pilot. Their first mission was with a flight of six Skuas that set off to bomb a frozen lake that the Germans were using as an airfield. They were carrying under their wings eight 100 lb anti-submarine bombs. "The flight bombed the lake in line astern," he wrote. "The ice split satisfactorily into large slabs. The aircraft parked on it slid into the water. As we — 'tail-end, Charlie' — pulled up from our dive, some tracer bullets came up past us. Griffiths said, 'Someone's firing at us — let's go back and fire at him,' and then turned to dive back, firing the front guns at a machine-gun position on the edge of the lake." As well as its four front-firing Brownings, the Skua had a Vickers mounted in the rear cockpit from which Friend did his observing. Griffiths invited Friend to have a go and "flew back low past it whilst I fired half a pan of bullets at it too". He had no idea whether or not he hit anything, but "it was pleasing to see the Germans running for shelter when we made our dive on them".

As with many experiencing their first taste of combat, Friend "had no sense of dangerous conflict as we were doing all this. Either of us could have and possibly did hit the men below, but I did not understand the enormity of my actions until long after, when I had seen the results of similar deeds by others — wounded pilots, observers and air-gunners, aeroplanes so damaged that they crashed, and ships damaged or sunk."

For all its shortcomings, the Fleet Air Arm was to achieve early glory in a spectacular action which showed what could be achieved with enough planning, preparation and skill, even with the limited aircraft and weapons available. In the Mediterranean, the loss of the French fleet (and the sinking of a significant part of it by Britain at Mers-el-Kébir) had sharpened the necessity to deal with the Italian navy. Various plans had been drawn up to attack the Italian navy, the Regia Marina, at its home base of Taranto, a bowl-shaped inlet tucked inside the heel of Italy. In the autumn of 1940 it was activated. The operation was preceded by extensive reconnaissance and the men detailed to take part were among the most experienced aviators in the service. On the evening of 11 November from the brand-new carrier *Illustrious*, which had just arrived in the Mediterranean, twenty-one Fairey Swordfish from 813, 815, 810 and 824 Naval Air Squadrons took off in two waves from a position off Cephalonia about 200 miles to the south, armed with torpedoes and bombs.

The first wave was led by Lieutenant Commander M. N. Williamson, to be followed an hour later by the follow-up force under Lieutenant Commander "Ginger" Hale, a former England rugby player. Charles Lamb of 815 Squadron was charged with dropping flares to illuminate the targets. As he and his observer Sub-Lieutenant Kiggell approached at 5,000 feet, Lamb "realized that I was watching something that had never happened before and was unlikely to be repeated ever again. It was a one-off job. 815 Squadron had been flying operationally for nearly twelve of the fifteen months of the war and for the last six months, almost without a break, we had attracted the enemy's fire for an average of at least an hour a week; but I had never imagined anything like this to be possible."

The intense reconnaissance of the preceding days had alerted the Italians to what was coming. "Before the Swordfish had dived to the attack, the full-throated roar from the guns of six battleships and the blast from the cruisers and destroyers made the harbour defences seem like a sideshow . . . into that inferno, one hour apart, two waves of six, then five Swordfish, painted a dull bluey-grey for camouflage, danced a weaving arabesque of death and destruction with their torpedoes, flying into the harbour only a few feet above sea level — so low that one or two of them actually touched the water with their wheels as they sped through the harbour entrance."

The Italian gunners had had three levels of attacking aircraft to fire at: the low-level torpedo planes, the dive-bombers and the flare-droppers. But if they aimed at the sea-skimming attackers, they would hit their own ships and positions. They kept their guns angled upwards, allowing the Swordfish to weave underneath the umbrella of fire and drop their "fish". As Lamb turned away, he saw burning craft "surrounded by floating oil, which belched from the ship's interiors as the bottoms and sides and decks were torn apart".

One torpedo ripped an enormous hole below the waterline of the battleship *Conte di Cavour*. Two other battleships were also sunk at their moorings. They were eventually repaired, but the *Cavour* was out of action for the rest of the Italians' war. The Swordfish made their own way home. "All the way back to our rendezvous with the ship off Cephalonia the moon was on my starboard bow, which helped me to relax," Lamb recalled. "The clouds had all dispersed and the shimmering path of watery gold, lighting up the sea's surface from the horizon to the water below us made night flying easy." A terrible thought kept troubling him. He spoke to his rear-gunner, Grieve, over the voice pipe. "'I'm a bit worried,' I said. 'We may be the only survivors.'" His fears were unfounded. Incredibly, only two aircraft were lost. Williamson's Swordfish was shot down, but he survived with his observer to be taken prisoner. Another, from the second wave, was destroyed by flak and the crew killed.

Taranto signalled the beginning of the end for the Regia Marina. "Thus was British maritime power reasserted in the central basin of the Mediterranean in no uncertain fashion," recorded the official historian of the war at sea, Captain Stephen Roskill. The following year the rest of the Italian fleet was neutralized at the Battle of Cape Matapan and the Allied navies had mastery of the Mediterranean.

The victory of Taranto was remarkable. It was an extraordinarily destructive action given the featherweight lightness of the attacking force. "Taranto Night" is celebrated by the Fleet Air Arm each year with the same fervour that the navy marks Trafalgar Day. It was, however, a singular event. Success on this scale was never repeated, although, as we shall see, six months later the FAA played a key part in another famous victory.

Much of the work the naval fliers did in the Mediterranean was routine, protecting convoys on "club runs" that supplied aircraft to Malta and war supplies from Gibraltar to Alexandria. For much of the time it was quite congenial. John Moffat joined Ark Royal as a Swordfish pilot shortly after Taranto. This was the last stop in a journey that began when, suffering the "soul-destroying boredom" of a job with a bus company in Kelso, he answered a newspaper advertisement for volunteers for the navy's air service.

He found that even in the middle of war there were still moments of ennui and that "much of my time flying was not the heart-stopping drama of a dive-bombing attack or the stomach-turning tension of a torpedo run, but long uneventful patrols over mile after mile of flat, featureless ocean". There were compensations, such as when "the sun was just striking the tops of the mountains of Spain and beginning to burn off the haze lying over the surface of the

Mediterranean. [Then] I would feel that upsurge of exhilaration that I have always associated with flying . . . the open cockpit of the Swordfish was marvellous for the full experience, which really did sometimes seem like a miracle." Then there were the times when "the clouds were low and dark, and the sea was a cold, white-flecked steel grey, and the rain beat against my face [and] the patrols became an endurance test".

In May 1941 Moffat was propelled into a drama that provided more than enough excitement. Both he and Charles Friend were aboard *Ark Royal* when it was sent north to join the hunt for the battleship *Bismarck*, which had fought its way through to the Atlantic via the Denmark Strait and now, damaged but very much afloat, was running for the safety of Saint Nazaire. By mid-morning on Monday, 26 May, she was only a day from port and the pursuing British fleet had lost the scent.

The sequence which led to her destruction began with a coup by Coastal Command. At 10.30a.m. a Catalina operated by 209 Squadron from Lough Erne saw *Bismarck* through a hole in the ragged clouds, about 790 miles north-west of Brest. The men at the controls were not British but Americans. US Navy Flying Officer Dennis Briggs and Ensign Leonard B. Smith had volunteered to go with an assignment of Catalinas supplied to the RAF under the Lend-Lease agreement and help train crews. In their anxiety to get close they came under fire from the battleship. Bullets and shells punched through wings and fuselage and one round smashed through the floor of the pilot's cabin, but then they were swallowed up in cloud and radioing back the sensational news. From then on *Bismarck* was under constant air surveillance.

Ark Royal was about a hundred miles away when news of the sighting came through. Swordfish were flown off and soon located the target. Admiral James "Slim" Somerville, the commander of the force, reckoned his own ships were too slow and old to be able to offer battle with any chance of success. The best hope was to slow *Bismarck* down until the pursuing fleet could catch up and deal with her. At 2.50p.m. fifteen Swordfish from 818 and 820 Squadrons took off to attempt an attack. The weather had been foul all day. Even *Ark Royal*, which stood sixty feet above the water, had waves coursing over her bow and down the flight deck. The business of getting to their aircraft was a trial. "The after-end of the flight deck was pitching something like fifty feet up and down," said Charles Friend. "The take-offs were awesome in the extreme. The aircraft, as their throttles were opened, instead of charging forward on a level deck were at one moment breasting a slippery slope and the next plunging downhill towards the huge seas ahead and below."

The force was led by Lieutenant Commander James Stewart-Moore, who flew as an observer. He was a pre-war professional and it seemed to him that the mission was "fairly straightforward". One of the Swordfish carried radar that would help the hunt, which appeared to have been simplified by the assurance, given in the pre-operational briefing, that there were no friendly ships in the area.

251

Despite the Force 8 gale, all aircraft got off safely with the radar-equipped machine leading. It was operated by the observer, Sub-Lieutenant N. C. Cooper. There was no wireless link between the aircraft and they had to use hand signals. Stewart-Moore recalled that "after a while I saw Cooper waving to me". He managed to convey the message that something was showing up twenty miles to starboard. This was unexpected. *Bismarck* had not been heading in that direction. As no other ships were meant to be in the area Stewart-Moore ordered the force to begin their attack.

Descending through the cloud they sighted the ship and prepared to drop their torpedoes. "Everything looked promising," remembered Stewart-Moore. It was then that his pilot, Lieutenant Hugh de Graff Hunter, realized their mistake. It was not *Bismarck*, but the cruiser *Sheffield*, which Somerville had detached to shadow the battleships at a distance. Hunter waggled his wings to try and warn the others, but it was too late. Their torpedoes were plunging into the sea and racing off towards the cruiser, while Stewart-Moore "watched from above, horrified and praying for a miracle". God was listening. "Without any apparent reason, all the torpedoes except one or two, blew up within half a minute of striking the water."

Back on board they were met with "profuse apologies" and another attack was prepared. The dud torpedoes had been fitted with "Duplex" firing pistols, which were supposed to be activated by the magnetic field of a ship's hull. Stewart-Moore persuaded

Somerville to let them use torpedoes with conventional pistols for the next attempt.

Six sub-flights of Swordfish, fifteen aircraft in all, were ranged for the attack. It would be led by Lieutenant Commander Tim Coode of 818 Squadron. John Moffat was his wing man. "It was all on us now," he remembered. "It was a question of salvaging our reputations . . . We were under no illusions about how important this was to the navy and to Churchill and we felt under enormous pressure to pull it off."

The weather had not improved. On the flight deck "the wind hit you like a hammer threatening to knock you down . . . the deck crews were really struggling with the aircraft, spray was coming over the side and the waves were breaking over the front of the flight deck." He felt he was "thrown into the air rather than lifting off". They were helped on their way by the Deck Control Officer, Lieutenant Commander Pat Stringer, who stood well over six feet and had to be harnessed to a stanchion to avoid being blown overboard. He seemed to be able to gauge the ship's surges and plunges to perfection. "He would signal to start the take-off when he sensed that the ship was at the bottom of a big wave, so that even if I thought that I was taking-off downhill, the bows would swing up at the last moment and I would be flying above the big Atlantic swell rather than into it."

Eventually all the aircraft were airborne and they formed up and headed off. On their way to the target they passed *Sheffield*, which this time they correctly identified. From the deck a lamp winked the signal that

253

Bismarck was only twelve miles ahead. They approached at 6,000 feet above a thick blanket of murk. Coode ordered them into line astern and they dived down. When he emerged from the cloud at 300 feet Moffat was alone. *Bismarck* was about two miles away and "even at this distance the brute seemed enormous to me". He turned to starboard and towards her. Immediately there was "a red glow in the clouds ahead of me about a hundred yards away as anti-aircraft shells exploded". The gunners were aiming just ahead of him and their fire threw up "walls of water". Two shells exploded below him, knocking him off course, but he pressed on, only fifty feet above the waves, sure that "every gun on the ship was aiming at me".

He retained enough composure to calculate the amount he would have to lay off when aiming to be sure of hitting the target and, with *Bismarck* looming, he felt he could not miss. He was about to press the release button when he heard his observer Sub-Lieutenant John "Dusty" Miller shouting, "Not yet, John, not yet!" It dawned on Moffat that Miller was waiting for a trough in the waves, so the torpedo would not get knocked off-track. "Then he shouted, 'Let her go!' and the next [moment he] was saying, 'John, we've got a runner.'"

As the torpedo fell away the Swordfish leapt upwards. Moffat was desperate to keep it below the trajectory of the *Bismarck*'s guns and managed to execute a ski turn. The slow speed of the machine allowed him to skid round and set off, skimming the wavetops until he felt it safe enough to climb into the cover of the clouds.

At the debriefing it emerged that two and possibly three torpedoes had found the target. This did not mean success, as *Bismarck*'s flanks were thickly armoured and a torpedo strike earlier in the pursuit had failed to do fatal damage. But then news began to filter in of astonishing developments. *Bismarck* had turned round and was heading straight into the path of the battleship *King George V*.

One of the torpedoes had hit the stern, jamming her rudders at 12 degrees and making steering impossible. All she could do was await the end, which came after a night of torpedo attacks and three-quarters of an hour of battering by the fleet's big guns before she went down, with the loss of all but 118 of the 2,224 men on board.

The essential part that the FAA had played in the removal of the *Bismarck* menace was acknowledged. But the poor quality of its equipment meant that the courage and skill of its crews were often employed in vain. Its performance was exemplified by the heroic failure of Lieutenant Commander Eugene Esmonde and 825 Squadron to stop the cruisers *Scharnhorst* and *Gneisenau* as they made their "Channel Dash" from the Atlantic to home waters in February 1942. Esmonde was killed and received a posthumous VC, but the German ships got through.

When modern dive-bombers such as the Fairey Barracuda came into service on the carriers, they failed to deliver ostentatious results. Churchill's natural impatience led to an unfortunate outburst in which he appeared to accuse the FAA of not trying hard enough. In July 1943 he sent a memo to the First Lord of the Admiralty, Albert Alexander, noting the "rather pregnant fact" that out of the 45,000 officers and ratings in the service "only thirty should have been killed, missing or prisoners during the three months ending April 30". This was despite the "immense demands . . . made on us by the Fleet Air Arm in respect of men and machines".

This outburst understandably sparked anger in the Admiralty. Churchill seemed to imply that the performance of a military organization could be measured by the number of its members who got themselves killed. The FAA defended its record, claiming that it was "a matter beyond dispute that, in proportion to its size, the Fleet Air Arm has given bigger results than any branch of any other service". It was, however, a matter of fact that when Churchill made his stinging observation it had been more than a year since the FAA had sunk a ship. The criticism provoked action. When it seemed that the German battleship *Tirpitz*, which had been badly damaged in a daring attack by midget submarines in the autumn of 1943, might be ready to go to sea again, the navy pushed the FAA forward to deal with her. Throughout the middle months of 1944 large carrier forces were engaged in laborious operations to launch Barracuda attacks on *Tirpitz* as she lay in Kaafjord in Northern Norway. The FAA aviators flew with their customary bravery, skill and determination, but the results were disappointing. At the end of the summer the Admiralty had to admit defeat and hand the job to Bomber Command.

Much of the work of both the FAA and Coastal Command was carried out unseen and unsung. Coastal Command's motto was "Constant Endeavour" and that summed up its fate, carrying out endless, unglamorous duties, the crucial importance of which would only be noticed if they ceased to be performed.

They flew from the first to the last day of the war, conducting over 240,000 operations of all varieties. They attacked German seaborne supply lines, in the Mediterranean, the Bay of Biscay and Scandinavian waters. They flew endless photo-reconnaissance and meteorological missions. And they roamed the seas hunting U-boats, destroying 212 of them. It was all lonely and dangerous work, and costly in machines and men. Coastal Command lost more than 2,000 aircraft and nearly 6,000 aircrew in the course of the war.

John Slessor, who was in charge for the crucial months from February 1943 to January 1944 when the Battle of the Atlantic was at its height, gave a memorable description of what was involved. It meant "junior commanders and crews — hundreds of miles out in the Bay [of Biscay] or on the convoy routes, fighting the elements almost as much as the enemy, but when the tense moment came, going in undaunted at point-blank range against heavy fire, knowing full well that if they were shot down into the cruel sea their chances of survival were slender indeed." Their reward was the heartfelt thanks of the merchant seamen, who

257

looked up from heaving decks and felt a comforting presence amid the harshness and perils of their existence.

Many stricken bomber crews, limping home after a night over Germany, and many a shipwrecked mariner, also had reason to be profoundly grateful to the Command's air sea rescue squadrons, which saved the lives of 10,663. Landing flying boats on anything but flat seas was perilous, so aircraft instead dropped rubber dinghies and supplies. Then powered lifeboats were developed that were designed to be dropped from converted bombers by parachute. In May 1943 279 Squadron, based at Bircham Newton, King's Lynn, had just received the new boats, which had two engines and could carry up to a dozen men and weighed three-quarters of a ton. On 5 May, Flight Sergeant A. Mogridge and his crew were told that a Halifax had ditched 50 miles east of Spurn Head in Yorkshire. They took off in their Vickers Warwick and "after about an hour's flying we sighted another [aircraft] circling. We made for it and were able to see a large dinghy with a number of chaps waving like the dickens." After a careful approach they dropped the lifeboat, whereupon the Warwick "rose like a balloon for about a hundred feet". Mogridge "turned sharply and we watched the boat going down. The three 'chutes had opened OK and it was floating down nicely, a bit faster than a man would. It hit the water about fifteen to twenty yards from the dinghy with a large splash . . . we were all tremendously pleased and felt on top of the world . . .

the boys in the drink who had by this time climbed aboard the boat, they seemed cheerful too."

The ASR squadrons shared the same hazards as the men they were rescuing. A few weeks later Mogridge was summoned by his CO and told that a dinghy had been spotted by Coastal Command Beaufighters a few miles north-west of the North Sea island of Borkum. As the Beaufighters were on their way to carry out a shipping strike, they could not divert. Mogridge was given the option of waiting until dusk before attempting a rescue, but after consulting with his crew decided to risk a daylight mission when there would be a greater chance of locating the dinghy. They flew out low, but as they approached the place where the dinghy had last been seen they saw a Dornier circling the area. They pressed on nonetheless. "All of us were ready for action with fingers near the gun tits," he wrote. "We couldn't see if they were over a dinghy and were reluctant to leave until this was established. However, the rear gunner must have spotted us because he started to spray us wildly. There didn't seem to be much direction to his fire." Some of his shots, though, found a target. A single round pierced the rear turret, hitting the gunner, Flight Sergeant Ted Rusby instantly.

"This made me feel very bitter," wrote Mogridge. "Pushing the throttle open we went after the Hun. I gave him a couple of long bursts with the front guns and saw strikes on the fuselage and engines." The Dornier was still firing back, though, and now "Mac" the navigator had been hit in the thigh. Mogridge broke off the attack and headed for home. There were ambulances standing by when they landed. "Mac" had a nasty wound but would survive. Ted was dead from a bullet to the heart. Death was never far away, but its sting was still painful. The intimacy of operations made brothers out of strangers. "We all grieved the loss of a gallant airman and a great personal friend," wrote Mogridge. "We had been together for over a year."

CHAPTER
THIRTEEN

Wind, Sand and Stars

Wherever Britain sent soldiers, the air force went with them. In the first years of the Second World War RAF Squadrons would serve in Greece, Iraq, Kenya, Palestine, Sudan, Singapore and points east, and, above all, in the deserts and skies of North Africa. The assets Britain and its dominions could deploy against the Axis powers were severely limited. It was essential that they combined in the most efficient and frictionless manner. By and large, co-operation between the air force and its naval and military comrades was good. Middle East Command's frequent requests for more aircraft and men were often supported by the other services in the field — an unusual circumstance that caused the brass fighting the war from desks in Whitehall to wonder what was going on.

Egypt duty could seem at times like a holiday. The main RAF depot was at Aboukir, close to sandy Mediterranean beaches and the bars and nightclubs of cosmopolitan Alexandria. It could also feel like hell. The desert was a testing environment in which to operate aircraft. Arthur Tedder, who would go on to lead the force, left a description of arriving at a place where "everything was covered with a fine, very soft yellow powder — though it did not feel soft with a thirty or forty mile an hour wind behind it. Eyes blinked and teeth gritted with the sand. Outside one had to wear goggles and some people occasionally even used their gas masks. On one occasion I had the front mud flaps of my car literally sand-blasted down to the bare metal in the course of an hour's drive against the dust."

Nothing could stop the march of dust and grit. Air-cleaners for Blenheims had to be cleaned after five hours flying — a job that took three hours. Sand got into instruments and worked its way into the propeller bearings so that the blades could not be moved to coarse-pitch when cruising. The desert sun cracked and buckled canopy perspex. The problems were multiplied by the chronic shortage of spares.

The RAF was trying to run a long-distance campaign through tortuous supply lines. With the entry of the Italians into the war the passing of convoys through the Mediterranean became hazardous and most reinforcements and supplies came round the Cape of Good Hope, a journey that took eight weeks. The problem of supplying aircraft was alleviated by the opening of a staging post at Takoradi on the Gold Coast, modern-day Ghana. Airfields were laid down, hangars and workshops and accommodation blocks built, so that by the end of 1940 a first-class service was in place to speed machines into theatre. They would arrive by ship in crates, to be reassembled, then were flown on by delivery pilots and crews. The 3,600-mile, six-day journey took them via Lagos, Kano, Maiduguri, Fort Lamy, Geneina and Khartoum, before ending at Aboukir. By the close of 1943 more than 5,000 aeroplanes had been sent to Egypt by the Takoradi air bridge.

The RAF's initial enemies in North Africa were the Italians. The Regia Aeronautica looked good on paper with more than 2,000 aircraft in the region. Their Savoia-Marchetti bomber was more effective than the Blenheim and could outpace the biplane Gladiator fighters, which were all that were available until Hurricanes began to come in from Takoradi. Some of the crews had been blooded fighting for the Francoists during the Spanish Civil War (1936–9). Like their earthbound brothers-in-arms, however, the hearts of the Italian aviators were not in it. On 9 December 1940 General Richard O'Connor launched Operation Compass to counter a tentative Italian offensive. Before the battle started, RAF bombers from Malta and Egypt pounded enemy airfields, destroying many aircraft on the ground. Ports, ammunition and supply dumps, and troop formations were all targeted relentlessly as the Italian retreat collapsed into rout and mass surrenders. When the fighting finished, the victory in the air was as complete as the success on the ground. The Italians lost fifty-eight aircraft in combat. Another ninety-one were captured intact and a staggering 1,100 damaged machines overrun during the helter-skelter advance. Henceforth the Italian air force was crippled and offered no serious threat to British operations until Italy surrendered in 1943. The price of victory was minimal. For the period from 9 December 1940 to February 6 1941 the total losses amounted to six Hurricanes, eleven Blenheims, five Gladiators, three Wellingtons and one Vickers Valentia cargo biplane.

With the arrival of the Germans in North Africa in early 1941 the RAF were confronted with a far more dangerous opponent. As Rommel's forces swept away the gains of O'Connor's offensive, the air force — already weakened by the decision to detach squadrons to assist in the doomed attempt to keep Hitler out of Greece — fell back to Egypt.

A long pause followed, during which both sides prepared for what was expected to be the decisive encounter. In that time aeroplanes poured in through Takoradi, including American Tomahawk, then Kittyhawk fighters. The expanding force needed a vast number of ground staff to keep it in the air. The technical nature of flying meant the RAF trailed a longer logistics "tail" than the other services, a necessity that was nonetheless a source of continual irritation to Churchill, who calculated that it took more than a thousand men to operate one squadron of sixteen aircraft.

The ground crew airmen were mainly British. They included my father Ernest, a fitter at Aboukir, who also flew on operations ranging from spraying the local marshes with DDT to clandestine missions landing agents on Mediterranean islands. The fliers came from everywhere that Britain had planted a flag, and beyond. There were South Africans, Rhodesians, Australians, New Zealanders and Free French. The South Africans were to play a particularly prominent part in the Desert

Air Force (as it became known), providing crews for half the light bomber force and a large part of the fighter strength. South Africans starred in some of the great stories of the campaign. In March 1941, as British forces were pushing the Italians out of Somaliland, No. 3 (Fighter) Squadron raided an enemy air base at Dire Dawa in Ethiopia. During the attack a Hurricane piloted by Captain[1] John Frost was hit and forced-landed on the airfield. Frost jumped out and set fire to his machine. His wingman, Lieutenant Bob Kershaw, saw his predicament and brought his Hurricane down through a hail of enemy fire to land alongside him. Frost clambered into the narrow cockpit and sat down on Kershaw's lap. The two then took off, as rounds flashed about them, with Frost operating the joystick and rudder, while Kershaw worked the flaps and the undercarriage lever.

After a summer of preparations the storm broke. On 18 November the Eighth Army launched Operation Crusader to relieve Tobruk. For the six weeks of the campaign the RAF had mastery of the skies. The Desert Air Force was now commanded by a brisk, forty-six-year-old New Zealander, Air Vice Marshal Arthur Coningham, whose nickname "Maori" had somehow been mangled to "Mary". Coningham was determined on an effective combination of air power and ground forces. He set up his headquarters next door to that of the army commander, his near-namesake Lieutenant-General Sir Alan Cunningham,

---

[1] The South African Air Force stuck to army ranks.

and their staffs messed together. Co-operation in the air matched the closeness on the ground. Of the twenty-seven squadrons at Coningham's disposal, sixteen of them were fighter units — fourteen equipped with Hurricanes and Tomahawks and two with the longer-range Beaufighters. Hitherto air support for a major ground action had been thought of as the domain of bombers. But the new generation of fighters showed they could function in much the same way as the Luftwaffe had in the Blitzkrieg, bombing and strafing enemy troops and communications with powerful effect. By the end of the year, after some setbacks, the Eighth Army had pushed Rommel back to Agedabia (modern-day Ajdabiya) on the Gulf of Sirte, well to the West of Tobruk. Operation Crusader was a victory — albeit not a decisive one.

The stalemate on the ground that followed did not take hold in the air. Fighters and bombers kept up a continuing campaign of harassment. For the fighters it meant regular sweeps looking for targets of opportunity, during which the prospect of an encounter with their Luftwaffe opponents was always present. In the first six months of 1942 Neville Duke of 112 Squadron was constantly embroiled in the action. Duke was the epitome of coolness. He was tall, handsome, a brilliant flyer, whose undoubted enthusiasm for the kill was tempered by a sardonic and easy-going manner. He was brought up in Tonbridge, Kent, not far from the Kenley and Biggin Hill fighter stations. He went on his first "flip" aged ten and was bitten. Thereafter his main ambition was to become a pilot. In June 1940, having been turned down by the Fleet Air Arm, he was accepted by the RAF. In the New Year he bought a three-shilling diary and the entries he kept fairly faithfully thereafter provide us with a privileged glimpse into the thoughts of a lively, civilized young man who went on to become the most successful RAF fighter pilot in the Middle East. He began it in the detached, philosophical tone that suffuses all the entries thereafter: "Decided to keep a diary this year ... I started flying last August. Some of my friends are dead, but many of my other brother pupils will last this war out; perhaps, if I should one day fall, this diary will be of some slight interest to those who will in the future become pilots."

At the end of January 1942, aged barely twenty, Duke was in North Africa, living the life of a front-line pilot flying Kitthawks, operating from desert air strips and based in a tent. By now a counter-attack by Rommel was pushing the British back to the Gazala line. Duke's entry of Sunday 25 January gives us a flavour of the uncertainty and discomfort of the time: "Flew escort for nine Blenheims in the afternoon. They were to bomb any target they could find and it was not until they had wandered all over the desert that they bombed near Agedabia. The road from there to Antelat was packed with Huns and after the bombing the Blenheims went down to 2,000 feet along this road, getting all the AA [anti-aircraft fire] available! I saw three EA [enemy aircraft] take off from Agedabia and as I took a potshot at them, Sgt Leu hit one head-on and shot the wing-tip off. It was seen to go in near Msus."

To "go in" was Fighter Boy-speak for screaming down at several hundred miles an hour to collide with the earth in a shattering explosion and eruption of smoke and flame. Duke recorded everything in the same laconic tone. "Ground strafing this morning," reads the next day's entry. "Hunk led the squadron off before lunch and we started strafing along the Antelat road and up to Msus. I was to stay above the section and attract the AA . . . I went down around Msus and shot up a truck which was seen to catch fire. Got quite a bit of AA fire all to myself."

Duke does not disguise the fact that, whatever the dangers, he was thoroughly enjoying what he was doing and despite the subsequent portrayal of the fighting in the Western Desert as a "war without hate" had little time for his enemies, though as this entry shows, human sympathy did sometimes intrude. "The squadron has done quite a bit of strafing lately," he wrote at the end of the month. "It is good sport if gone about the right way . . . It is a terrific thrill to come belting down out of the sun to let rip at the Huns with the .5s [the six heavy-calibre machine guns which the Kittyhawk carried]. To see your bullets making little spurts in the sand in front of a truck and then pull the nose up a bit until the spurts no longer rise and your bullets are hitting home. Pulling out just before you hit the target as the tendency is to be so engrossed . . . that you forget the ground. Then making your escape, taking advantage of every little rise in the ground and dodging the hate thrown up by the swines." He finished on a softer note: "You can't help feeling sorry for the Jerry soldier when you ground strafe them. They run, poor pitiful little figures, trying to dodge the spurts of dust racing towards them."

He found encounters with enemy fighters equally exhilarating. On 14 February 1942 the squadron ran into some Italian Macchis and Bredas. "A general dogfight started and I enjoyed myself more than I have ever done before. The cloud was just right and we dived down, had a squirt and climbed up into the cloud again." Duke ended up joining an Australian Air Force pilot to chase a Macchi, which, "after two or three attacks . . . crashed and burst into flames in an army camp where they had been strafing". For soldiers on the ground, the sight of their tormentors being despatched by friendly aircraft was heartening and the pilots were much appreciated.

Life in between sorties was trying. Like everyone Duke hated the dust, as well as the rain and wind in winter and the awful heat in summer. The memories of British bases with their flower beds, squash courts and elegant anterooms where white-coated orderlies served pre-luncheon and dinner drinks seemed like distant dreams. Instead they kipped under canvas and ate bully-beef stew and drank tea, heated over petrol fires.

They relaxed doing what airmen had always done. Duke's diaries are studded with references to "pissys" on leave in Cairo bars or when a beer wagon made a welcome stop. "Golly, what a session it was last night," he wrote on 12 March. "I faded away at 1.30, but it was still going strong then. I just couldn't get my glass empty. No sooner had I taken a sip than it was topped up again by some passing, staggering body." There was no question of official disapproval, as Duke made clear. He recorded that earlier that day "the CO rather put up a 'black'. We had been drinking good and hard since lunchtime and at sunset he announced he was going to drop a bomb. He took off and it appears he dropped it on Martuba. He landed and when taxiing in put the machine on its nose! Then at dinner time he was sitting at the head of the table chattering away, and he suddenly disappeared from my sight. I thought I had had one too many, but no. He had gone over backwards and a sepulchral voice from the depths enquired as to the whereabouts of his bloody beer. Oh, yes, it was a good session." It is easy to forget that behind the extremes of experience to which these desert warriors were exposed, in years they were not much more than schoolboys.

Rommel was down but not out. Mounting a serious offensive, however, depended on his ability to re-equip and reinforce. His supply lines back to his Italian allies were blocked by the island of Malta, which was perfectly strategically placed in the middle of the Mediterranean, halfway between the toe of Italy and the shores of Tripoli. Malta was of paramount importance to both sides. Britain needed to hold it to hang on in the Middle East. The Germans needed to capture or neutralize it if they were to sustain their campaign. An initial attempt had been made to starve and bomb Malta into submission in the first half of

1941. When Hitler attacked the Soviet Union in June, the Luftwaffe had been diverted to the new campaign. Britain took this chance to stockpile supplies and ferry aircraft into Malta, including cannon-armed Hurricanes, Blenheims and Beaufighters. Together with the navy's submarines and destroyers, Malta-based aircraft slashed at the Afrika Korps's sea communications, so that in the month before Operation Crusader was launched Rommel lost 63 per cent of his expected supplies. Something had to be done. Late in 1941 Luftwaffe units were shifted to Sicily, some from the Eastern Front, to begin a long assault on the island. On New Year's Day 1942, 200 aircraft under the command of Feldmarschall Albert Kesselring began pounding the Grand Harbour and docks at Valletta, where the British fleet lay. The battle raged through the spring of 1942, by which time the docks had been pounded to rubble and the Luftwaffe had moved on to the RAF bases. The arrival of a small batch of Spitfires in March blunted the German assault for a while, but the respite was temporary and the Germans, supported by the Regia Aeronautica, enjoyed control of the air and, increasingly, the seas around the island.

Relief came in May when the carriers *Wasp* and *Eagle* managed to deliver 140 more Spitfires. In heavy midsummer fighting the RAF whittled away Kesselring's force so that by the end of June he was down to thirty-six fighters and thirty-four bombers. Among the defenders was one of the most publicized pilots of the war. George Buerling, sallow, tousle-haired and equipped with amazingly sharp blue eyes, had first

271

taken the controls of an aeroplane in his native Canada at the age of thirteen, and at seventeen he was flying solo. When the war began he was desperate to join it, but lacked the academic qualifications to enter the Royal Canadian Air Force. In the summer of 1940 he risked an Atlantic crossing in a convoy and was eventually accepted by the RAF. In the spring of 1941 he was with Fighter Command, taking part in its costly and pointless campaign of cross-Channel sweeps to stir up enemy airfields. After volunteering for overseas service he was posted to 249 Squadron and Malta.

He arrived there on 9 June, having flown his Spitfire off the deck of the *Eagle*, and promptly set about creating his own legend. Beurling was one of those men for whom war is a liberation, allowing them a freedom to demonstrate a prowess for which there is no great demand in peacetime. In the summer of 1942 he shot down seventeen Axis aircraft, four of them in a single day.

Beurling brought brilliance to the business of flying an aeroplane. In the judgement of Percy "Laddie" Lucas, another superb 249 Squadron pilot, "he had an instinctive 'feel' for an aircraft. He quickly got to know its characteristics and extremes . . . He wasn't a wild pilot who went in for all sorts of hair-raising manoeuvres, throwing his aircraft all over the sky . . . a pair of sensitive hands gave his flying a smoothness unusual in a wartime fighter pilot."

Beurling's exceptional eyesight was matched with phenomenal marksmanship and the ability to instinctively calculate the precise amount of lay-off needed for a perfect deflection shot. "I never saw Beurling shoot haphazardly at an aircraft which was too far away," wrote Lucas. "He only fired when he thought he could destroy. Two hundred and fifty yards was the distance from which he liked best to fire. A couple of short, hard bursts from there and that was usually it."

Beurling was also "highly strung, brash and outspoken", characteristics which had made him unpopular in Britain. Lucas sensed that his "rebelliousness came from some mistaken feeling of inferiority" and that "what Beurling most needed was not to be smacked down but encouraged" and made to feel part of the team.

One morning they were sitting at readiness in a dispersal hut on the palm-shaded airfield at Takali in the centre of the island. In the corner lay a half-eaten slice of bully beef, which was being devoured by a swarm of flies. Lucas watched as "Beurling pulled up a chair. He sat there, bent over this moving mass of activity, his eyes riveted on it, preparing for the kill. Every few minutes he would slowly lift his foot, taking particular care not to frighten the multitude, pause and thump! Down would go his flying boot to crush another hundred or so flies to death. Those bright eyes sparkled with delight . . . each time he stamped his foot to swell the total destroyed, a satisfied transatlantic voice would be heard to mutter 'the goddam screwballs!' "

Thus was born the nickname by which he was known thereafter, to his comrades and then, thanks to the publicity that attached to his exploits, the wider world. It fitted him well. "Screwball" Buerling was a strange man, restless, unsocialized and unfitted for normal life. On returning to Britain he was hijacked by the Government's propaganda machine and sent back to Canada to help with a war bond-selling drive, a job he hated. He found a wife in Vancouver, but the marriage was brief. Back in Britain on operations he failed to add much to his score. When the war finished he was left high and dry. In an attempt to find refuge in the only world in which he felt comfortable, he signed up to fly Mustangs for the Israeli air force. He was killed on his way there, in a crash at the Aeroporto dell'Urbe in the northern suburbs of Rome.

The long siege of Malta came to an end with Rommel's defeat at Alamein in November 1942. The battle witnessed the most perfect melding to date of land and air power in the desert war. Lieutenant-General Sir Bernard Montgomery, who took command of the Eighth Army in August, was a fervent believer in integration of effort and expressed himself on the subject with his usual, ringing self-assurance: "Fighting against a good enemy — and the German is extremely good . . . you cannot operate successfully unless you have the full support of the air. If you do not win the air battle first, you will probably lose the land battle. I would go further. There used to be an accepted term of 'army co-operation'. We never talk about that now. The Desert Air Force and the Eighth Army are one . . . If you knit together the power of the Army on the land and the power of the Air in the sky, then nothing will stand against you and you will never lose a battle."

"Monty" and "Mary" set up their headquarters side by side. Rommel's preparations to break out of the defensive box he had been pushed into at First Alamein were crippled by nine days of bombing. At the battle of Alam el Halfa that followed, waves of Hurricanes, Spitfires and Tomahawks strafed and blasted the Afrika Corps on the ground, turning away only for the bombers to continue the work. They met little opposition from an exhausted, depleted and fuel-starved Luftwaffe as they took lives, smashed up armour and vehicles, made rest impossible and wore down nerves. On 2 September 1942 light bombers delivered what was effectively the battle-winning blow, dropping 112 tons of bombs on the Germans. Rommel folded and the German withdrawal began. The overwhelming strength of the RAF had played a key part in the outcome. Rommel reflected later that "anyone who has to fight, even with the most modern weapons, against an enemy in complete control of the air fights like a savage against modern European troops, with the same handicaps and the same chances of success."

The relationship between aeroplanes and soldiers had come a long way in the space of less than thirty years. The air force had moved from being a useful adjunct to military operations to a crucial necessity, and air superiority had become accepted as a prerequisite of victory. When the Eighth Army met the Afrika Korps again at Second Alamein, Monty had overwhelming mastery of the skies to complement the overmatch he enjoyed on the ground, and he had no excuse for not delivering the first great British success of the land war.

Throughout October 1942 new aircraft flooded in, supplemented by the men and machines of the United States Ninth Air Force. By the time the battle opened on 23 October, the Allied air forces mustered ninety-six squadrons. By its end, the RAF had flown 10,405 sorties, and the Americans 1,181. The Axis air forces managed just over 3,000. Though outnumbered, they could still bite. The Allies lost nearly a hundred aeroplanes against the Germans' and Italians' eighty-four.

Such intensity of air operations was dependent on the matching energy and efficiency of ground crews. Not a single sortie could take place without fitters and riggers preparing the aircraft before it set off, and maintaining and repairing it when it returned. Inevitably, public attention had always focused on the men in the air. The achievements of the men on the ground were as remarkable in their way, and if they did not endure the same hazards, they were often exposed to danger and frequently to hardship. Between the wars maintaining aircraft was largely carried out by the squadrons themselves. The demands of wartime meant a new system was needed and the Air Ministry set up a series of maintenance units at home and abroad.

Often the arrangements were improvised and unusual. In Egypt the workshops were situated in various suburbs of Cairo. No. 1 Engine Repair Section (ERS) was situated in "a rather distasteful slum quarter", according to Philip Joubert. "The pungency of the surrounding atmosphere was almost visible, so intense were the odours, but this had to be endured as the men entered into the spirit of the job and appreciated all it entailed." A small nucleus of RAF tradesmen worked alongside Egyptians, Greeks, Cypriots, Palestinians, Jews and Armenians, recruited locally.

The British presence was not welcomed by the locals and a phalanx of Indian soldiers was needed to protect the mechanics. Personnel came and went in a truck, which had to carry out "a number of intricate manoeuvres to dodge the hordes of men, women, children, donkeys, camels, taxis, gharrys . . . in time it was possible to judge reasonably accurately where to expect a shower of filth, garbage, chewed sugar cane and spit as the truck wended its way to the shop. Craftily thrown stones and plenty of abuse announced the point of arrival."

The section received all the aero engines from the Desert Air Force, stripped them down to their last nut and bolt and, after an overhaul and bench-test, sent them back to the squadrons for another lease of life. The engines came from Malta and Syria, as well as all over the desert, and by the time they arrived were often "completely covered with a coating of sand at least a quarter of an inch thick. Some had been dragged by tanks on to rocky ground before they could be loaded and suffered considerably in doing so, yet those engines left No. 1 ERS as jet-black, gleaming power units with the guarantee of the RAF behind them." The same feats were repeated all over the globe where the RAF's footprint fell.

By now women were an intrinsic part of the enormous logistical support force. The Women's Royal Air Force had been disbanded after the First World War. Following the Munich crisis in 1938, the Auxiliary Territorial Service (ATS) was set up to engage women for work in the event of a war. Two offshoots emerged, the Women's Royal Naval Service (WRNS) and the Women's Auxiliary Air Force (WAAF). It was officially founded on 28 June 1939 and its first Director was Jane Trefusis-Forbes, an independent-minded thirty-nine-year-old who had left school early to volunteer for war work in the previous conflict, and had built up a dog-breeding and kennel business before becoming an instructor in the ATS. She had vitality and organizational gifts and a streak of unorthodoxy, roaring into work each day on a motorbike. At the outbreak of war there were 1,734 Waafs. Three years later there were 181,835 — 16 per cent of the entire RAF. They served in a dozen trades — from drudgery as mess orderlies, cooks and clerks to skilled work as ops-room plotters and radar operators, a category which by 1944 was predominantly female. Some served as intelligence officers, a tough calling in a masculine world in which pre-operation briefings were always regarded with scepticism when delivered by a woman. More than 160 women served as pilots with the Air Transport Auxiliary (ATA), ferrying new or repaired aircraft from factories to maintenance units and squadrons.

The influx of personnel from the Waafs released many men for flying and other operational duties. It was calculated that without their support, the RAF would have needed another 150,000 extra men. Volunteers had to be between seventeen-and-a-half and forty-three years old. Most were eighteen or nineteen. The first influx seemed to contain a disproportionate number of the wealthy and the well-educated. "At the start there were a whole lot of titled people," remembered a former Waaf, Marian Orley. "But a lot of them couldn't take it. Out of sixty of us, thirty didn't come back after a week's leave at Christmas."

Among the more socially prominent were the Prime Minister's daughter, Sarah Churchill, the British Ladies Golf Champion Pam Barton, and an airwoman cook who rode to hounds and asked permission to keep her two hunters on the station. However, there were also a number from the other end of the class spectrum. On a tour of inspection of RAF bases in 1943 Joubert was horrified to find "Borstal girls, trollops and thieves amongst a mass of decent women".

Many of the volunteers came from the dominions and colonies, which in the early days lacked organizations of their own. Others were refugees from occupied Belgium, Poland, Czechoslovakia and France. "There were many reasons that brought all these girls to enrol," wrote Squadron Leader Beryl Escott, the WAAF historian. "Patriotism, money, freedom, escape from unpleasant jobs, the promise of companionship, revenge on fathers or boyfriends, or for a husband's death. Many chose the air force out of a fascination for flying and a spirit of adventure."

Conservative fathers disliked the idea of their daughters joining up. "My father was very service-oriented and his memory of the women's services from the First World War was that they had bad reputations," said Vera King, a WAAF NCO. "His theme was, if you go into the services, no decent man will want to marry you." So did some mothers. "I shall always remember my mother, tears streaming down her face, at the door," said Hazel Williams. "Then she called me back and said, 'Don't sit on strange lavatory seats' and, pointing to my bosom, 'Don't let any man touch you there.' "

Some of the older pre-war professionals bristled at this influx of females. "A very high percentage of the regular RAF officers regarded them as an unmitigated nuisance and gave them no help," wrote Philip Joubert. "Their accommodation was abominable, their food most unsuitable and their uniform unattractive. But the volunteers that came forward to enrol had amongst them some outstanding characters, and all had a burning desire to be of use to their country in whatever capacity they were called upon to work."

Most of the war-service airmen were delighted to see them. Serving on bases where there were plenty of women around was a significant factor in attracting recruits to the RAF. Morfydd Brooks, a young, married woman, had joined the WAAF after her husband was called up to the RAF and posted overseas. In the spring of 1943 she was working in the sergeants' mess at Scampton, where 617 Squadron was preparing for the Dams Raid. "We would hear the planes, then after they discussed and analysed the day's training, they entered the mess," she wrote. "The doors would burst open and the aircrews would swarm in shouting boisterously as we served their food. We young Waafs had to endure a barrage of good-natured banter. 'How about a date, darling?' 'How is your sex life?' 'I dreamed about you all night.' 'Would you like to sleep with me?' 'Please serve us in the nude.' " The stations and depots served as gigantic dating agencies and tens of thousands of marriages and children had their genesis in an encounter in a canteen or at a Saturday night hop. For many couples, though, the war deprived them of a happy ending. Pip Beck was a young radio telephony operator at Waddington, a Lincolnshire bomber base, when she went to a dance in the sergeants' mess. Nervous and alone, she hovered in the anteroom until a tall sergeant with an air-gunner's brevet and wireless operator's badge approached.

"'You're new around here, aren't you?' he enquired. 'I don't think I've seen you around before. Look, I'm a bit tight just now, but I promise I won't drink any more if you'll come and dance with me.' " Pip finished her sherry and followed him to the dance floor where they joined the crush of couples, the smoky air making her eyes tingle. "The smell of alcohol near the bar was now overpowering and the floor wet with spilt beer," she recalled. "We kept away from that area as much as possible and my partner stuck to his promise and drank no more. He told me that his name was Ron Atkinson, and his home was in Hull. We danced and danced — I was having a wonderful time. Sometimes we slipped back into the anteroom again, just to talk. He teased me and we both laughed a lot. I studied his angular, intelligent face and large grey eyes; the dark hair and the rather youthful moustache . . . We fell in love — what else could we do?"

When Ron proposed marriage, however, Pip shied away. "Marriage was something I hadn't thought about. I was just in love." When she tried to explain this to him he "turned away, hurt and angry". They didn't see each other for three days. Then, as she was leaving the cookhouse after tea she ran into him. "He was wearing battledress, flying boots, thick white roll-necked pullover — and a little black cat charm dangling from the button of his breast pocket. So he was 'on' tonight. My anxieties rose in full force — and yet I felt a surge of fierce pride." Ron had been looking for her. He asked her to phone him the following day in the mess, after he got back from the raid on Le Havre. Pip felt a shiver of fear. She could not sleep and went to the control-tower roof, praying to see his bomber H-Harry looming out of the dawn. But Ron never returned. "Loss was an unknown experience until now — and it was painful." She talked to no one about it "and tried to behave normally. I was silently grateful to those who *did* know and were unobtrusively kind. And at eighteen, one recovers quickly."

Initially, all but a handful of Waafs did their service in Britain, but in the middle of 1944 they started to be posted abroad. By the end they were present in twenty-nine countries, from the Arctic to the tropics. For many of the quarter of a million young women who passed through the WAAF their service was a high point in their life, a liberation, an adventure, an awakening. When Phyllis Smart was demobilized it felt as if a deep emotional bond was being severed. After queuing up in a large hall in Birmingham to collect her back pay, clothing coupons and ration book she was called into a small office where a young WAAF officer solemnly shook her hand and bade her farewell. "I was out! I have never felt so forsaken in my life. After being part of a huge family for so long, I was on my own. I lay in bed that night and cried."

CHAPTER
FOURTEEN

No Moon Tonight

In North Africa, where air power was used in conjunction with land forces, the record was one of almost continuous success from late 1942 onwards. The pattern was repeated after the landings in Italy and then in north-west Europe and a dozen other places. Over the sea, Coastal Command grew in numbers and confidence. It was in the realm of strategic bombing — the activity by which the RAF hoped to make its greatest contribution — that the story grew darker and more complicated.

The destruction visited on Cologne by the first "Thousand" raid in May 1942 had generated high hopes. The effects, however, were short-lived. Contrary to the belief (held by even highly intelligent men like Sir Charles Portal) that enemy civilians were less able to "take it" than their British counterparts, German public morale did not crack. Within a fortnight of the raid, Cologne was functioning more or less as normal and the loss of industrial production was temporary — perhaps no more than a month's worth.

This was not known at the time, however. The raid seemed a sort of victory, providing an illusion of power and bringing the satisfaction of revenge at a time when there was nothing else to celebrate. Harris was given the green light to press on with the "Thousands". On the night of 1–2 June Essen was attacked by 957 aircraft. There was cloud over the city. Many of the crews could not be sure they had identified the target. Little damage was done to Essen and the Krupp works was untouched. Three weeks later there was another raid on Bremen. Harris plundered Coastal Command to scrape together the aircraft to reach the magic number. Once again, the weather intervened and results were disappointing. Casualties, though, were high. Fifty-three aircraft failed to return.

These failures were glossed over in official reports and public enthusiasm remained high. But until he had more Lancasters and Halifaxes, Harris simply did not have the resources to maintain operations on this scale, at this tempo. He was forced into the unwelcome step of having to lower expectations about what his command could achieve.

Inside the Air Ministry there were those who believed that while not immediately possible, precision bombing of vital German war industry targets was attainable. They were led by Group Captain Syd Bufton, the Director of Bomber Operations. Bufton pressed Harris to concentrate on objectives where area bombing would have a definite effect. A favourite was Schweinfurt in Bavaria, where most of Germany's ball bearings were thought to be made. His argument was backed up by data from the experts at the Ministry of Economic Warfare. Harris did not welcome the intervention. He countered that the town was very difficult to locate. At any rate, he held "experts" in low esteem and was highly suspicious of claims that destroying this or that factory would significantly shorten the war, deriding them as "panacea targets".

As far as he was concerned, area bombing was an end itself, and, if vigorously enough pursued, could lead to victory. The argument between Harris and the advocates of precision bombing would rage until the end of the war, and, as the methodology of bombing became more and more accurate, his continued opposition became increasingly difficult to justify.

Bufton had another proposal which put him squarely in the path of Harris. Earlier in the war he had led Bomber Command's 10 Squadron and pioneered a technique of using his best crews to locate the target with flares, then to direct the others on to it by firing signal lights. He argued strongly for a small, elite spearhead that would guide the main force to the target area and then drop markers to identify the aiming points. The idea of a Pathfinder Force was strenuously opposed by Harris, who complained that it would mean creaming off the best crews from his squadrons and undermining their performance and morale. His doubts were shared by the bombing group commanders. Eventually, Portal stepped in to overrule Harris and in August 1942 one squadron was detached from each of the command's four heavy groups to operate from bases in Huntingdonshire and Cambridgeshire.

The operations they would lead were overwhelmingly area attacks. By the end of 1942 obliterating cities had become official policy, thanks to the advocacy of Portal and the acquiescence of both politicians and the other service chiefs. With the Americans bringing their assets to the air war, he reckoned that a fleet of up to 6,000 heavy bombers could be amassed which could blast 25 million Germans from their homes and kill 900,000 of them, fatally weakening Germany's home defences before the land invasion was launched. That Portal could coolly present such a proposal is proof of the brutalizing consequences of going to war with the Germans. Appalling choices were necessary to crush the evil of Nazism, and the critical judgements on Bomber Command that followed in peacetime, delivered by those who had never had to endure the appalling ethical pressures of war, were arrogant and unjust. Few knew the reality better than Noble Frankland, the Bomber Command navigator and historian of the campaign. In his words, "the great immorality open to us in 1940 and 1941 was to lose the war against Hitler's Germany. To have abandoned the only means of direct attack which we had at our disposal would have been a long step in that direction."

The crews were now caught up in a horrible process that inevitably resulted in the large-scale deaths of civilians. They, too, would experience their share of suffering. By the spring of 1943 all the elements for a full-scale assault against German cities were in place. Harris had a regular front-line strength of more than 600 new heavy bombers at his disposal and the numbers would keep on growing.

He had his orders, delivered from the highest level. In January 1943 Winston Churchill and President Franklin D. Roosevelt met at Casablanca to plan the next stage of a war that was now irrevocably going their way. The role of Bomber Command was spelled out in what became known as the Casablanca Directive, which informed Harris: "Your primary objective will be the progressive destruction of the German military and economic system and the undermining of the morale of the German people to a point where their armed resistance is fatally weakened." Throughout spring and summer the crews would be hurled against the industrial conglomerations clustered between the Rhine and the Lippe, an area which became familiar to the British public through countless progress reports, in the press and on the BBC, as the Ruhr.

Rapidly constructed bases sprang up on the flat fields of the eastern counties of England, and placid market towns filled with men and women in grey-blue serge. Bomberland started where East Anglia juts out into the North Sea, reaching out towards the Low Countries and Germany, and stretched north to Lincolnshire and Yorkshire. The American journalist Martha Gellhorn, who visited a bomber base to report for *Collier*'s magazine, found it "cold and dun-coloured. The land seems unused and almost not lived in."

There was not much to divert your mind from contemplation of the operations that lay ahead or to celebrate your safe return. At the end of a mission, crews came back to a monochrome world of muddy potato fields, Nissen huts with smoky stoves, weak beer and dull food. The experience of the fighter pilots of 1940 was sometimes portrayed by them as something of an idyll, and that the trauma of a day of dogfighting might be soothed way by evenings in old pubs nestling picturesquely in downland and weald. No Bomber Boy ever made this claim. Life on base was as dank and unappetizing as a raw Lincolnshire spud, and letters home are full of yearning for decent food and drink. George Hull, arriving at the Heavy Conversion Unit at Wigsley near Newark in Nottinghamshire in the autumn of 1943, wrote to his friend Joan Hull: "I seem to have fallen decidedly into the soup or what have you in being posted to this station. Even the name is obnoxious. Wigsley, ugh! Pigsley would be more appropriate, yet I doubt that any pig would care to be associated with it. The camp is dispersed beyond reason. If I [didn't have] a bike I doubt if I could cope with the endless route marches that would otherwise be necessary. Messing is terrible, both for food and room to eat it. Normally we queue for half an hour before we can even sit, waiting for it. Washing facilities are confined to a few dozen filthy bowls and two sets of showers an inch deep in mud and water."

There was nowhere to escape to. The local towns were dreary, even by provincial standards. For the many airmen in Lincolnshire the choice was between the tearooms of the cathedral city or Scunthorpe's handful of dance halls, where hundreds of men competed for the favours of a handful of local girls. Drink provided a little solace and piss-ups in pubs or mess were frequent. Sex was sometimes available, from a variety of

289

amateurs, professionals and lonely wives whose men were away at the war. No one wanted to die a virgin and descriptions of first encounters make them sound more than usually like a job to be done rather than a sensual experience.

The bleakness of life was to some extent compensated for by the warmth of companionship. "Thank God for the crew," wrote George Hull from his dreary base. "A fierce bond has sprung up between us . . . we sleep together, we shower together, and yes we even arrange to occupy adjacent bogs and sing each other into a state of satisfaction."

They were fighting a very peculiar sort of war. They attacked an enemy they couldn't see, night after night. Their targets were not soldiers or fellow aviators but buildings and those who lived in or near them. There was no way of measuring success, no territory or strongpoint they could say they had captured, no enemy put to flight. The fights were brief. There was nothing connecting them to the battlefield. They visited, then left.

"Life on the squadron was seldom far from fantasy," wrote Don Charlwood, a thoughtful Australian navigator. "We might at eight, be in a chair beside a fire, but at ten in an empty world above a floor of cloud. Or at eight walking . . . with a girl whose nearness denied all possibility of death."

Even inside the bomber the airmen could feel disassociated from the lethal events they were engaged in. Reg Fayers, a navigator with 78 Squadron, described the feeling to his wife Phyllis in the summer

of 1943. "Lately in letters I've mentioned that I've
flown by night and that I've been tired by day, but I
haven't said that I can now claim battle honours —
Krefeld, Mülheim, Gelsenkirchen, Wuppertal and
Cologne. I suppose I've been fighting in the Battle of
the Ruhr. But it hasn't felt like that."

"Battles" were how Harris chose to describe certain
phases of the campaign. It was a misleadingly neat term
for something that was repetitive, widespread and
lacking a focused objective. There was no measure of
success. There was, however, a yardstick for failure —
the ability of his force to soak up punishment, which, in
the winter of 1943, the German defences were
efficiently meting out.

As had always been the case in the short history of
aerial warfare, when one side developed a new
technology or technique, the other was not long in
countering it. So it was when Harris unleashed his
assault on German cities. German reactions sharpened.
Around the big towns, searchlights and radar-directed
batteries evolved systems that created a cauldron of fire
that unnerved all but the most self-contained or the
least imaginative. It was a civilian, the BBC reporter
Richard Dimbleby, who put into words the bowel-
melting, yet awe-inspiring nature of the sight, when he
bravely flew to Berlin with Guy Gibson and 106
Squadron on the night of 16–17 January 1943. They
took off from Syerston at tea time. "It was a big show as
heavy bomber ops go," he broadcast later. "It was also
quite a long raid, as the Wing Commander who took
me [Gibson] stayed over Berlin for half an hour. The

flak was hot, but it has been hotter. For me it was a pretty hair-raising experience and I was glad when it was all over, though I wouldn't have missed it for the world. But we must all remember that these men do it as a regular routine job."

The journey out had been trouble-free, but they "knew well enough" how bad things could get when they were approaching Berlin. "There was a complete ring of powerful searchlights, waving and crossing," he reported. "There was also intense flak. First of all they didn't seem to be aiming at us. It was bursting away to starboard and away to port in thick yellow clusters and dark, smoky puffs. As we turned in for our first run across the city it closed in right around us. For a moment it seemed impossible that we could miss it. And one burst lifted us into the air, as if a giant hand had pushed up the belly of the machine. But we flew on, and just then another Lancaster dropped a load of incendiaries. And where a moment before there had been a dark patch of the city, a dazzling silver pattern spread itself, a rectangle of brilliant lights, hundreds, thousands of them, winking and gleaming and lighting the outlines of the city around them. As though this unloading had been a signal, score after score of fire bombs went down and all over the dark face of the German capital these great, incandescent flower beds spread themselves . . . as I watched and tried to photograph the flares with a cine camera, I saw the pinpoints merge and the white glare turning to a dull, ugly red as the fires of bricks and mortar and wood spread from the chemical flares."

Dimbleby was very impressed by Gibson's skill and coolness, which would be demonstrated brilliantly a few months later when he led 617 Squadron on their dambusting mission. The Dams Raid, however, was a spectacular side show, which did more for Allied morale than for the war effort. The real business of Bomber Command during 1943 and 1944 was city-bashing.

The industrial nature of the campaign meant that by 1944 operations had settled down into a regular routine that was no less harrowing for its familiarity. After breakfast, aircrew would report to their flight officers to learn whether or not ops were on that night. The decision lay in the hands of the group headquarters. During the winter of 1943–44 the campaign went on relentlessly, night after night, interrupted only by the most extreme weather conditions. Details of the destination and the size of the force were telephoned through to the bases. Further information on routes, bomb loads and the time of departure — H-hour — would follow later.

As yet, none of this was relayed to the crews, who simply busied themselves with preparations. Their first task was to drive out to the dispersal areas to check with the ground crews on the serviceability of their aircraft, going over engines, instruments, radar and wireless. Later, the aircraft would be fuelled, armed and bombed-up. They returned to the base for lunch, officers and NCOs heading off to their respective messes.

In the afternoon the briefings would begin. The crews gathered in a large briefing room filled with

293

chairs. At one end was a platform and behind it a large map shielded from view by a blackout curtain. A roll call was held, and when it was confirmed that all crews were present the assembly got to its feet and the station, squadron and senior flight commanders walked in to join the meteorological, intelligence, engineering and flying control officers already on the stage. The doors were shut behind them by an RAF policeman who stood guard outside.

The CO then rose and approached the large cloth-covered rectangle. He whisked the cloth away and declared. "Gentlemen, your target for tonight is . . ." Hundreds of eyes took in the red tape leading to their destination. An "easy" target where the flak was light was greeted with relieved laughter. A tough one like Berlin, with groans and muttering. The briefing then commenced, invariably stressing the importance of the target and the significance of the contribution the operation would make to the war effort. Peter Johnson, attending his first briefing before his first op, was struck by the crews' indifference to these exhortations. The intelligence officer was a WAAF, a "formidable lady who minced no words. The target, for the umpteenth time, was the Krupp factory at Essen. 'Yes, they've been damaged!' she shouted over the chorus of groans and expletives. 'But make no mistake, they're still turning out guns and shells aimed at you!' " She went on to warn that the defences would be stronger than ever, and gave details of the known searchlight and flak battery positions. "'They're going to give you hell!' she spat. 'See that you give it them back!' "

Johnson found this theatricality distasteful coming from a non-combatant, but he was impressed by the dangers she had described. Looking around, though, he noted that the others "seemed almost totally untouched by what they had heard". Many were sitting back with their eyes closed. All they wanted to know was "the details of route and navigation, which colour of target indicator they were to bomb and what they could do to make sure they arrived on time and got home safely".

With the detailed briefings on start-up times, designated runways, weather on route and bombing routines completed, each squadron commander gave a briefing to his unit, then the station commander rounded off by wishing them good luck and a safe return.

They then filed out, navigators to pick up maps, wireless operators the "flimsies" telling the radio frequencies for the night, before heading off to the mess for the traditional "operational meal" of bacon and eggs. Sometimes there were a few, fretful hours to kill before H-Hour. They spent these trying to sleep, writing letters to family, wives and girlfriends, mooching around the mess, listening to the bittersweet tunes of the time. In the mess at Elsham Wolds an arrangement of "Tristesse" was forever turning on the gramophone. "I wondered why it was that this recording happened to be played so often as we waited to leave," wrote Don Charlwood. "To me it was a song without hope, full of urgent pleadings we could never heed." He recalled finishing off a letter back to his folk in Australia, while around him men dozed in armchairs waiting to go. As they were roused by their comrades he "noticed how child-like they appeared in the moment they woke". Outside "the rain had increased and as they passed through the door they put on their coats and turned up their collars". Charlwood followed. "Outside the night was empty and very dark, the rain heavier. I shuddered and pulled on my coat. As I left the building the last words of the song followed me, as on other nights they had followed men now no longer there. 'No moon tonight, no moon tonight.' "

The next stop was the crew room where they climbed into their flying gear — layers and layers of it to combat the cold: electrically heated vests, long johns, trousers, roll-neck pullovers, tunics, sheepskin jackets and helmets, fur-lined boots. They collected parachutes, Mae Wests and escape kits containing maps, currency and false ID cards, as well as a few comforts for the trip — Thermos flasks of coffee, sandwiches, barley-sugar sweets and Fry's chocolate bars. They were ferried to dispersal by lorries or buses. There was time for a last once-over of the aircraft, a final cigarette and perhaps a communal piss against the tail wheel for good luck.

Even the most rational succumbed to superstition. Panic could ensue if someone arrived at the aircraft to find they had left behind their lucky charm. "Luck and a Lancaster were our daily bread," wrote Harry Yates. "We loved the one and couldn't expect to live without a large slice of the other. We all carried a keepsake, a sign of our trust worn around the neck or pocketed next to the heart. It could be the ubiquitous rabbit's foot or a rosary, letter, St Christopher, coin, photograph, playing card . . ."

Then they mounted the ladder at the rear of the fuselage and clambered past the many sharp edges of the interior to reach their stations. For many it brought a temporary relief to be in their place, going through familiar routines waiting for the churning of the ignition, the splutter of engines, the cough and bark of the exhaust and the judder of turning propellers. You were shackled to your fate and nothing you could do now could change its course.

The bombers followed each other around the perimeter track, then onto the designated runway, lumbering down the tarmac until the four engines hauled airborne bomber, bombs and the seven small men inside the fuselage. Always, whatever the weather, a knot of WAAFs and ground crew would be standing at the end, waving them off. After they had formed up and set off over the sea a sort of calm descended. Willie Lewis, a flight engineer, wrote of how the "powerful mechanism of the aircraft had overborne [our] individuality and welded it into the machine".

The pitch of the engine notes produced a curious effect, so that some thought they were hearing celestial music. The calm was first broken by the thud of the gunners test-firing their weapons. In his cramped station amidships the wireless operator tuned his set to receive the latest meteorological data on wind direction and speed, while the navigator adjusted his Gee cathode-ray tube to get the best picture.

Then, from the nose, the bomb aimer was calling "Enemy coast ahead!" and they tensed for the flak rising to meet them from the anti-aircraft ships and batteries below. They were above 5,000 feet now and breathing oxygen, which made a sinister rasping noise as they inhaled and exhaled, an unwelcome reminder of the tenuous mechanics of life.

By now the Germans were watching, following them on radar from a string of stations stretched the length of the approaches to the Reich. To confuse the Germans, bundles of alumunium foil — "Window' — were shoved through the chute used for dropping flares to swamp the operators" screens with a cloud of false signals. Once the raid was detected, enemy night-fighters took off to circle a radio beacon and await orders from a central control room. By mid-1943, the Luftwaffe had about 400 of them fitted with short-range radar sets, which, once they were set on the right track, would guide them on their target. They were armed with 20 mm or 30 mm cannon, and some with upward firing guns which allowed them to creep up under the belly of the victim's plane and fire into the bomb bay, which was packed with incendiaries and high explosive.

Night-fighters accounted for the majority of Bomber Command's losses in 1943 and the first six months of 1944, the most dangerous period in the Bomber Boys' war. In those eighteen months the Luftwaffe destroyed 1,625 Allied aircraft, against 878 shot down by flak, a ratio of two to one.

Attacks almost always came without warning. Donald Falgate, a bomb-aimer with 49 Squadron, was peering through his perspex nose-cone on the approach to a raid on Magdeburg when he saw tracer from a night-fighter's guns floating past.

"He was on to us before we saw him," he remembered. "He made the first attack from the rear and from above, which was unusual. He'd obviously come upon us quite by mistake. If it was a radar interception, they usually picked up from below."

The attacker, a Ju 88, fired a brief burst then broke away, swinging around immediately for a second attempt. He got in too close and the shots went wide. Undeterred, he latched on to the bomber's tail. The rear-gunner yelled for the captain to "corkscrew". For all its weight and size, the Lancaster was a remarkably nimble aeroplane. A good pilot could send it into a screaming, twisting 300 mph dive then jerk it upwards, a manoeuvre which, with luck, could shake off an attacker. Falgate's skipper "managed to evade him and get into cloud, but it was a very scary time. It wasn't until we got back to base that we found bullet holes in the fuselage and two huge holes in the mid-upper turret where the shells had gone through. The poor gunner nearly froze to death."

By early 1944 Pathfinders equipped with H2S downward-looking radar were usually at the spearhead of major attacks. They played a variety of roles, dropping Window and using colour-coded pyrotechnics to mark the route, then, once they had reached the target, to light it up and identify the aiming points for the main force squadrons to bomb on as designated.

The system achieved a grim efficiency. In a typical raid on the Ruhr in late 1944, a stream of 550 bombers could pass through the target area in just fourteen minutes. By this time the erosion of the Luftwaffe's strength meant that some of the dangers of flying by night to Germany had subsided. In 1943 and early 1944 it was probably the most harrowing and hazardous activity open to any Allied fighting man. In the year from September 1943 a total of 16,483 British and Dominion airmen were killed flying with Bomber Command. Another 2,413 lives were squandered in non-operational accidents.

This was the price that was paid for Harris's stubborn belief that the Germans could be blasted into submission. The policy reached its height — or nadir — with the Battle of Berlin, waged between the end of the summer of 1943 until the end of March 1944. It opened with three attacks in late August and early September. The results were disappointing and the losses sobering. On the first raid, in which 727 aircraft took part, nearly 8 per cent of the force was lost. Most of them were Halifaxes and Stirlings. By the time of the third, only the better-performing Lancasters were sent. Even so, twenty-two of the 316 bomber force were destroyed, a loss rate of 7 per cent.

Harris waited for the nights to close in before he sent another large force. His pugnacious mind was set on proving the righteousness of his vision, which was now under attack from the Americans, whose strategic preference was for a much more precise choice of targets and in particular the German aircraft industry. In November 1943 Harris promised Churchill that with American help "We can wreck Berlin from end to end . . . it will cost between us 400–500 aircraft. It will cost Germany the war."

In all there were sixteen major attacks on Berlin, as well as an equal number of heavy diversionary raids designed to confuse and divide the defences. It was a dreadful task to set anyone, as Harris himself acknowledged. He wrote afterwards that "the whole battle was fought in appalling weather and in conditions resembling those of no other campaign in the history of warfare. Scarcely a single crew caught a single glimpse of the objective they were attacking . . . unbroken cloud . . . concealed everything below it except the confused glare of fires."

Berlin suffered. In the second raid of the winter, 2,000 were killed; 1,500 in the third raid; 4,330 in the fourth. By the end of the sixth raid, a quarter of the city's housing was unusable. But Berlin is a large place — "The Big City" in crew parlance. Its eighty square miles of brick and stone apartment blocks were spread out between woods and parks, lakes and waterways. There was no tinderbox old town to spark a catastrophic inferno. It was also a long way — an eight-hour round trip, and it was frequently covered by cloud. There was despair, panic, terror in the streets, but nothing like the paralysis that Harris hoped to induce. Many bombs fell in open countryside. The authorities began an evacuation programme and casualties fell. Industry was damaged, but not knocked out.

The strength of the capital's defences and the long journey in and out meant Bomber Command's casualties were high. On the night of 28–29 January, 677 aircraft, most of them Lancasters, raided Berlin. Forty-six of them were shot down by night-fighters over the city. Two nights later another thirty-three were brought down. Harris was now exhibiting the "one more push" mentality that he had derided in the trench generals of the previous war. On 15 — 16 February he amassed the biggest force so far: 826 aircraft. They dropped 2,642 tons of bombs, another record. Forty-three aircraft were destroyed, but the results seemed hardly to merit the loss. The battle was effectively over, although Harris would not admit defeat until April, when he conceded that the clear conditions needed for good bombing handed an equal advantage to the defenders. In other words, the costs incurred did not match the results.

As the battle drew to a close another terrible trauma awaited the crews. On the night of 30–31 March 1944 the distant city of Nuremburg was chosen for a full-scale raid. The weather forecast predicting concealing cloud for most of the journey, but clear skies over the town. Then a Meteorological Flight Mosquito returned from a reconnaissance reporting just the opposite: the likelihood was that there would be clear skies en route and poor visibility over the target. These were the worst conditions possible, but the operation nonetheless went ahead. There is a famous photograph of the pre-operational briefing, taken at 51 Squadron's base at Snaith. Squadron Leader Peter Hill is standing in the aisle, looking confidently ahead as he instructs the crews. In front and behind him, men stare, expressionless, at the board on the platform and the red ribbons stretching far into the heart of Germany. Hill did not return from the trip. Nor did another thirty-four men in the picture.

Gordon Webb was flying a Halifax that night, but felt confident in the quality of the men around him. "We were by all standards a capable and efficient crew," he wrote. "Each man knew his job thoroughly and we had been together and flown on operations long enough so that we were now considered a seasoned crew." They had no illusions about what they were facing. "We knew all about the percentages for and against finishing a tour. We had all long since come to terms with the possibility of one night not coming back." That night's operation "would be, we were quite certain, a one-way trip for many".

At the end of the briefing the horror of what lay ahead was apparent. "What this . . . really told us was that we were going to challenge the full might of the Luftwaffe's night-fighter squadrons, plus the deadly, highly sophisticated German radar and flak defensive system. And we were going to do this under weather conditions which gave the defenders, who already held a big edge, an overwhelming advantage. It must be admitted that to a man we felt that Bomber Command HQ was being uncommonly generous with our lives."

On the way in they were lit up by "the brightest moon any enemy night-fighter could have asked for". Cloud cover "simply did not exist". The forecast winds were wrong. At the height the airmen were flying at, the engines left vapour trails that it seemed to Webb the defenders could not miss. And so it turned out. "The night sky seemed to be full of Jerry fighters," he wrote. "You could almost find your way to the target by navigating along the line of shattered and burning aircraft scattered across Germany . . . Death, sudden and violent, was everywhere. I lost count of the aircraft I saw shot down or blown up."

They reached the target and dropped their bombs. Their Halifax, "Pistol Packing Mama", leapt 200 feet as the load dropped away. Then Webb had to "fly precisely straight and level for thirty seconds, the longest thirty seconds anyone will ever know", in order to take the photographs demanded by operational orders to show to the intelligence officers back at base. They touched down eight and a half hours after taking off, but "bone tired, mentally beat though we were, sleep was out of the question".

It did not take long to confirm what they had suspected. Bomber Command had suffered its worst defeat of the war. Of the 795 aircraft despatched, ninety-five were lost, nearly 12 per cent of the force. Almost everything that could go wrong did go wrong, starting with the route chosen, which placed the bomber stream in exceptional peril, channelling it between two radio beacons around which the night-fighters circled to await details of targets.

The Nuremberg Raid was the darkest hour in Bomber Command's war. What now seems extraordinary is that it did not cause a collapse in confidence in Harris, either by his masters or by the men he led.

The vast majority of the Bomber Boys believed in the necessity and the justice of what they were doing. It was, though, little discussed. Their ability to resist fear, their fortitude, was reserved for getting through their tour of thirty trips, and the life that beckoned beyond. For some the burden was just too great. Jack Currie described, at the start of the Battle of Berlin, coming across a newly arrived sergeant pilot who was "a casualty neither of flak nor fighters, but of an enemy within himself. He came back early from the mission and gave as a reason the fact that he was feeling ill. Next night he took off again, but was back over Wickenby twenty minutes later. Again he said that he had felt ill in the air. I had seen the crew together in the locker room, clustered protectively around their white-faced pilot. They may have thought that some of us would vilify him, but no one except officialdom did that."

That there were failures of nerve was inevitable. The problem had been recognized in the First World War when rest homes were set up in the smart Channel resort of Le Touquet, where pilots were sent to recuperate from attacks of "nerves". It was accepted that such a reaction was a natural response to abnormal circumstances. By the time the next war came this commonsensical and humane view had been replaced by a more scientific approach, set out in a pamphlet circulated to base Medical Officers. While it recognized that stress was cumulative and "everyone has a breaking point", it tended to blame character flaws for psychological breakdown. "Morale," it stated, "depends largely upon the individual's possession of those controlling forces which inhibit the free expression of the primitive instinctive tendencies." In translation this meant that faced with great danger, those with the right stuff would be able to stifle their urge to run away. Procedures were set up whereby MOs examined those who were unable to carry out their duties to establish if there was a physical or nervous explanation, which could be dealt with by treatment or rest. But in an Air Ministry document, issued in April 1940, a third category was introduced. "It must be recognized that there will be a residuum of cases where there is no physical disability, no justification for the granting of a rest from operational employment and, in fact, nothing wrong except a lack of moral fibre."

LMF, as the condition became known, was a stigma and intended as such. Sympathetic MOs tried hard to avoid such a diagnosis. But when they did the punishment was harsh and humiliating. The final judgement lay in the hands of Harold Balfour, the Under Secretary of State for Air, who had experience of combat flying from his time in the RFC in the previous war. "In reviewing a case my sympathies always started off with the poor fellow, as I knew only too well myself what it was like to be scared stiff in air warfare," he wrote. However, he also believed LMF to be "dangerously contagious. One crew member could start a rot, which might spread not only through his own crew, but through the whole squadron." If an officer was judged LMF, the punishment "was to take his wings away, order him to resign his commission and arrange for the army to pick him up for enlistment, probably in a labour battalion. In the case of an aircrew sergeant his flying badge was forfeited, he was reduced to the lowest rank or AC2 and put on the worst fatigues." Such was the treatment of men — all volunteers — who had gone through the rigours and dangers of training and the trauma of ops, but whose courage had run dry. What is surprising to contemporary eyes is that there were so few cases of LMF. Between February 1942 and the end of the war, only 1,029 RAF airmen were thus diagnosed, most of them from Bomber Command.

As spring turned to summer in 1944, the almost unimaginable stresses of flying bombers began to ease a little. Normandy was approaching and the final phase of a war in which the skies would belong in the main to the Allies.

CHAPTER
FIFTEEN

Air Supremacy

By the summer of 1944 the Allied air forces had achieved virtual mastery of the skies of Europe. The process had begun in the long campaign to clear the Axis powers from North Africa and continued with the invasions of Sicily and Italy in 1943. As the British and American air forces grew in size and quality, as their tactics and systems increased in efficiency and sophistication, the fortunes of the Luftwaffe declined.

In northern Europe Bomber Command and the US Army Air Forces continued their epic campaign independently, there being no troops on the ground for them to support. In the Mediterranean theatre, however, the lessons of co-operation had been well-learned by now and ground attack fighters and fighter-bombers, light and heavy bombers, were meshed structurally into the overall effort. Two vital lessons had been learned from the breakout from Egypt and the advance through Libya and Tunis. One was that air superiority had to be established before any major operation could be launched with any hope of success. The second was that once the assault had begun it was essential to capture enemy airfields to maintain the air advantage and keep the momentum going.

Gaining control of the skies was an easier proposition now as the Axis air forces went into a long downward spiral. The Luftwaffe had been bled white during the monster battles on the Eastern Front, throwing up to 1,800 aircraft into the Battle of Kursk in July 1943 to no avail. The assault by the USAAF on the German aircraft industry — Operation Pointblank — which reached its climax during 20–25 February 1944, also had a devastating effect. During those days a thousand bombers pounded fifteen aviation hubs. They were escorted by an almost equal number of P-51B Mustang fighters, which had a range of 1,650 miles and were able to provide cover all the way to the objectives and back. The Luftwaffe came up to defend the infrastructure, just as Fighter Command had over Britain in 1940. Instead of simply surrounding their charges, the Mustangs ranged ahead of the bomber fleets, intercepting the German fighters before they arrived. In the ensuing air battles the Americans won a clear victory. By some calculations the Luftwaffe lost about 600 aircraft and 17 per cent of their pilots.

These depredations tipped the German air force in all theatres into terminal decline. In the twelve months from July 1943 German first-line air strength in the Mediterranean theatre fell from 1,280 to 475. At the end of 1943 the Allies had 7,000 aircraft at their disposal, served by 315,000 air and ground crew.

The enormous disparity in resources meant that when Operation Husky was launched to capture Sicily,

600 aircraft operating from Malta (under the direction of the Battle of Britain tactical wizard Sir Keith Park) kept the Germans away. Some claimed to be disappointed. "The Sicilian campaign has been the reverse of our anticipations," wrote the anonymous keeper of the 244 Fighter Wing Operations Record Book. "We expected the Hun to come out of his lair in droves, but though when we were in Malta there were enticing stories of formations of forty-plus lurking at judicious distances from the operations we covered and the sweeps we did, in the main he just refused to play." This was written after the wing, equipped with Spitfires, had flown more than 3,000 sorties, but had engaged only 131 enemy aircraft, claiming eleven destroyed and fifteen damaged.

By the spring of 1944 there were so many Allied aircraft in the skies that fighters were often directed onto targets only to discover they were "friendlies". "Lunch-time patrol of Anzio," wrote Neville Duke, who now had a confirmed "victory" for each of his twenty-two years, on 19 March. "On way out was sent to chase two bogeys coming in towards Naples. Intercepted and found a P38 [Lockheed Lightning fighter]. Then was sent to chase two bogeys at 26,000 feet over Cassino area. Chased around and found another P38. In fact, I think we chased ourselves quite a lot."

The following morning they ran into some real opposition, more than thirty Messerschmitt 109s and Focke-Wulf 190s, but the German pilots did not stay to fight. Even so, Duke's patrol shot down three and a further two in the afternoon, pushing the squadron's score past the 200 mark. Inevitably, this was the excuse for a "big party in the Mess, including all the ground crews, Squadron Cos, etc".

Air superiority had been gained. The Italian experience, however, revealed an unpalatable truth. The possession of a great armada of aircraft and the delivery of vast amounts of high explosive did not guarantee victory, or even smooth progress for the forces on the ground. In December 1943 alone Allied aircraft (a category increasingly dominated by the Americans) flew 27,500 sorties and dropped 10,500 tons of bombs. Progress up the narrow, bony spine of Italy was depressingly and painfully slow, as the Germans resisted with their habitual deadly resolution.

The lack of correlation between destructive effort and practical effect was shockingly demonstrated at Monte Cassino, the ancient Benedictine Abbey which dominated the Liri Valley and the main highway to Rome. On 15 February 1944 the Sixth Century foundation where St Benedict's bones were laid was pounded to rubble by American bombers in the belief that it was occupied by German troops. It turned out there were none there. As John Slessor, by then commanding the RAF in the Mediterranean and Middle East, pointed out, even if this were known at the time it was unlikely to have made much difference, for "no man among the troops detailed to attack the Cassino position would have believed it for a moment . . . Private Doe from Detroit, Smith from Wigan, Jones from Dunedin or Yusuf Ali from Campbellpore eyed it

311

and felt that behind those windows there must be at least an enemy observer waiting to turn the guns on him personally when the time came to attack. So the Abbey had to go." It was the Catholic convictions of the German commander, General Fridolin von Senger und Etterlin that underlay the decision not to place troops there. Now, though, he wrote later, "we could occupy the Abbey without scruple, especially as ruins are better for defence than intact buildings . . . Now the Germans had a mighty commanding strongpoint, which paid for itself in all the subsequent fighting."

It took until 18 May for a Polish force to occupy the ruins. Monte Cassino would have proved an enormous obstacle to the Allied advance, whether or not the Abbey had been left standing. The narrow river valleys that led northwards were dominated by high, rocky ridges that provided perfect defensive positions for an enemy as obstinate and resourceful as the Germans.

The difficulties of the march to Rome, which did not fall until June 1944, led Slessor to set down his thoughts on the things that "air power can-*not* be expected to do in a land campaign". The first was that "it cannot by itself defeat a highly organized and disciplined army, even when that army is virtually without air support of its own. The German will fight defensively, without air support or cover, and does not become demoralized by constant air attack against his communications and back areas. The heaviest and most concentrated air bombardment or organized defensive positions cannot be relied upon to obliterate resistance and enable our land forces to advance without loss."

What air power could do, however, to a degree which would have seemed inconceivable even two years before was "so to dominate the air in the battle area and in the enemy's rear that our army can make its dispositions, supply and administrative arrangements in the most convenient manner virtually regardless of the enemy threat". This meant that the vast organization of the invasion, involving huge supply convoys, nose-to-tail on narrow mountain roads, unprotected ammunition dumps and the great fleets of merchant vessels clogging Naples Harbour were at little risk from the arrival of a Luftwaffe bomber formation.

For the Germans, the opposite was true. It was one of Trenchard's maxims that "all land battles are confusion and muddle and the job of the air is to accentuate that confusion and muddle in the enemy's army to a point when it gets beyond the capacity of anyone to control". This, as Slessor was proud to point out, was what the RAF and the USAAF achieved on the road to Rome in those critical last days. "Roads were cratered and blocked by destroyed vehicles, telecommunications were cut, villages became a mass of rubble barring through movement, local reserves could not be moved because there was no petrol available, forward troops were out of ammunition and out of touch with their controlling headquarters, nobody knew for certain where anyone else was . . ."

The Allies were able to achieve this degree of disruption through a system of air control known as the "cab rank". Fighter-bombers already airborne on missions against preselected targets were told to leave twenty minutes before they attacked to await instructions from a ground-based air controller. He would pass on by VHF radio telephone details of any enemy targets of opportunity — convoys, concentrations of troops, etc. — which showed up fleetingly, close to the front lines, for obliteration. It was a system that would work well in Normandy and the march to Berlin. It is still in use now by British forces fighting the Taliban in southern Afghanistan.

By the time Rome was captured the greatest military operation in history was only two days away. Air superiority had been an essential prerequisite of Operation Overlord, and D-Day had been preceded by months of aerial operations aimed not just at gaining control of the skies, but the systematic erosion of the German's ability to recover when the invasion began. Fighters, fighter-bombers and heavy bombers were all employed in the assault. In June 1943 the RAF had established the Second Tactical Air Force (2 TAF), whose role was to support the army in the field when the troops went ashore. In January it came under the command of Air Marshal Sir Arthur "Mary" Coningham, who had turned the Desert Air Force into a model of effective co-operation with ground forces in North Africa and Italy.

Much of this would involve using fighters and fighter-bombers in a ground attack role. Ever since the Battle of Britain the RAF had been engaged in sweeps across the Channel to maintain an offensive against tactical targets, using Spitfires and Hawker Typhoons, which had replaced the trusty but now dangerously outmoded Hurricanes. In 1943 the trains that supplied the occupation forces in France and Belgium were a favourite target. One of the masters of the art of "train-busting" was Roland Beamont, a brilliant aviator who had fought with Fighter Command in the summer of 1940 and now commanded 609 Squadron, based at Manston, perched on the North Foreland in Kent. It specialized in night attacks, when most movements were made to avoid the attentions of the daytime Spitfire sweeps. According to his official biographer, under the squadrons' cannons and rockets "locomotives blew up in vivid yellow-white flashes or died in clouds of gasping steam. Goods trains were raked from stem to stern." The armoured flak wagons hitched to the back of trains failed to provide much protection. In reaching its first century of "busted" trains, the squadron lost only two pilots.

The work of softening up the Germans was shared with Bomber Command. The squadrons were shifted away from the deadly drudgery of area attacks on German cities to the far more precise business of raids on targets in the hinterland of the invasion coast. The operations began in April 1944 and the date marked a new and happier phase in the lives of the crews after the nightmare of the Battle of Berlin and the Nuremburg Raid. They were now engaged in attacks on railway targets in France and Belgium aimed at stopping the flow of reinforcements once the battle began. There were also raids on military camps, ammunition dumps and armaments factories in France, and (as the date for Overlord approached)

315

against radio and radar stations and coastal artillery batteries. In the two months before D-Day, 2 TAF and Bomber Command would carry out 71,800 sorties and drop 195,400 tons of bombs. The USAAF was almost twice as active, but due to the smaller carrying capacity of their bombers dropped nearly the same tonnage. They were to bear the brunt of the Allied total losses of 1,953 aircraft for the period, with the deaths of more than 12,000 aircrew. These sacrifices had brought enormous advantages to the Allies. With the approach of D-Day, the railway network of the north of France was approaching paralysis. Those trains still running moved very slowly, under cover of darkness, and were forced to make long detours, crippling the enemy's freedom of movement.

This exercise demonstrated that when sent against small targets (with strict instructions to avoid casualties among the civilians they were about to liberate) Bomber Command could now achieve a considerable degree of accuracy. The use of a Master Bomber to go in low and mark the objective became standard. One of the greatest practitioners was Leonard Cheshire, commander of 617 Squadron — the Dambusters — and "very learned in the art of bombing the enemy".

In March 1944 Cheshire and Group Captain Monty Philpott, the station commander at Woodhall Spa in Lincolnshire where 617 was based, had prepared a paper on how the squadron's bombing performance might be improved. It could already count on getting 60 per cent of the bombs it dropped within 100 yards of the target. Cheshire hoped to better that. At that stage, aircraft tasked with dropping markers arrived at the objective at the same time as the main force, which had to hang around in the flak-filled skies while Target Indicators (TIs) were dropped from heights of 5,000 to 8,000 feet. The memorandum argued that the target should already be marked before the bombers arrived. Also, to ensure precision, the marking should take palce at the lowest possible level. To do so in a Lancaster was suicidal. Cheshire and Philpott proposed that smaller aircraft should be used, preferably a Mosquito, perhaps the finest of the great flock of aeroplanes that had taken flight from the inspired drawing board of Geoffrey de Havilland. The proposal was accepted by Ralph Cochrane, the commander of 5 Group to which 617 belonged, and two Mosquitoes were duly delivered.

The new technique was called "Mossie marking" and it was pioneered in a raid on Brunswick on 22 April 1944, with good results. The first time it was used in France, however, it resulted in a qualified disaster. The target was a panzer base near the village of Mailly in the Champagne-Ardennes region and the attack was due to go in just before midnight. The operation required expert marking and 617 Squadron, which by now had four trained Mosquito crews, was brought in. Cheshire led the team and the marking was good, so he called the main force to tell the bombers to begin their runs. By an appalling mischance, however, the controller's VHF set was swamped with an American forces radio broadcast and he could not communicate the order. In the ensuing delay, the target had to be marked again. In the meantime German fighters appeared and shot down forty-two Lancasters, more than 11 per cent of the force. The raid was nonetheless a success. But there were misplaced accusations that Cheshire's perfectionism had contributed to the debacle.

Cheshire possessed an extraordinary serenity that enabled him to tarry with danger for protracted periods with apparent unconcern. He combined this quality with a charisma that touched everyone he came into contact with. "He was not shy. He was not reserved," remembered one of his men. "On the other hand he was not gushing, alarmist or boastful. He had no side. He was cool, calm, sympathetic. He was impressive. He was patient with us and he was kind . . . above all else to me, he was magnetic."

617 Squadron would play a major part in the immediate post-operational air strikes to disrupt the German counter-attack, and on the V-weapons sites that menaced London and the South East. Their role on D-Day itself was psychological. They were tasked with executing Operation Taxable, which was part of the great deception strategy utilized in the run-up to the invasion to convince the Germans that the landings would be in the Pas de Calais. Research suggested that Window — the alumunium strips dropped on bombing raids to blind radar defences — could also mimic the presence of a mass of shipping. After dusk on 5 June 1944 the squadron took off from Woodhall and headed to a point off the Sussex coast to line up with a small dummy fleet. They then began flying back and forth towards the cliffs of Cap d'Antifer near Etretat along a

fourteen-mile front, dropping Window all the while. When dawn came up at 4 a.m., their task was over. As they flew back for the last time they could see the skies to the south, full of aircraft and gliders heading for the Normandy beaches and below them, the real invasion fleet.

The invasion of Normandy was the greatest amphibious operation in history, a one-off event that will never conceivably be repeated, and the role played by aeroplanes was of a matching magnitude. During the night 1,056 Lancasters, Halifaxes and Mosquitoes launched bombing raids on the coastal batteries with bombs, and when dawn came up the fighters, fighter-bombers and medium bombers of 2 TAF, and the heavies and mediums of the Eighth and Ninth US Army Air Forces joined the battle. The soldiers arrived by air as well as by sea. About 24,000 flew into action. The Americans of the 82nd and 101st Airborne divisions were carried there by fifty-six squadrons of transport aircraft. Most of the British arrived by Horsa glider, which could carry twenty-nine soldiers.

The memory of the carpet of aircraft overhead that morning, their wings decorated with thick black-and-white stripes, stayed with those who saw it for the rest of their lives. John Keegan, the great military historian, was a small boy in the West Country when one evening "the sky over our house began to fill with the sound of aircraft, which swelled until it overflowed the darkness from edge to edge. Its first tremors had taken my parents into the garden, and as the roar grew I followed and stood between them to gaze awestruck at the

319

constellation of red, green and yellow lights which rode across the heavens and streamed southward towards the sea. It seemed as if every aircraft in the world was in flight, as wave after wave followed without intermission, dimly discernible as dark corpuscles on the black plasma of the clouds, which the moon had not yet risen to illuminate. The element of noise in which they swam became solid, blocking our ears, entering our lungs and beating the ground beneath our feet with the relentless surge of an ocean swell. Long after the last had passed from view and the thunder of their passage had died into the silence of the night, restoring to our consciousness the familiar and timeless elements of our surroundings, elms, hedges, rooftops, clouds and stars, we remained transfixed and wordless on the spot where we stood, gripped by a wild surmise at what the power, majesty and menace of the great migratory flight could portend."

Among the carpet of aircraft rolling overhead were gliders, packed with troops, being towed to the landing areas. Around them buzzed a bodyguard of fighters, protection against any Luftwaffe marauders. The pilots and aircrews included men for whom the coming liberation was the answer to their most fervent prayers. Jean Accart who had escaped from France in 1943, was flying with a Spitfire squadron to cover the landing. "0.4.30 hours . . . over the Channel," he recorded. "The twelve aircraft fly in three columns in close formation so as not to lose contact . . . against a gradually lightening sky, the fleeting shadows of the fighters become sharper as they sweep over their sector in stacked groups, crowding in between the water and the clouds. We make out the powerful silhouettes of the Thunderbolts which pass above us, dipping a little to check our identity, and of the suspicious Lightnings, which come in and sniff at our tails. It is a miracle that all these squadrons can manoeuvre in so small an area without colliding."

Turning back at the end of his patrol Accart saw "in the early morning mist and precisely at the appointed time and place columns of towing planes and gliders appear and move onwards in a procession more than forty-five miles long. As far as the eye can see the lines of heavy aircraft and huge gliders fly low over the Channel, covered by swarms of fighters weaving over them like watchful sheepdogs. The French coast appears and becomes clearer as the gliders pass over precisely on time amid the puffs of a few bursts of flak. One after the other the gliders cast off, spiral down and land lightly on their designated field, assembling with masterly skill on a pocket handkerchief. Above them the fighters provide an impenetrable defence — and impenetrable it is for the problem is to avoid collisions. Never before had we possessed such absolute domination of the skies."

The picture painted by Accart was somewhat idealized. Many gliders were whisked off course by high winds or lost their way after jinking to avoid flak; troops were scattered far and wide and stores lost. The weather was against them, with a thick cloak of cloud overlaying the landing zones at 2,000 feet. But despite the conditions and the huge volume of missions, losses were mercifully low. Only 113 aircraft were shot down, most of them by flak, a rate of only 0.77 per cent.

On that vital day the Luftwaffe defenders could only muster 319 sorties. Their presence over the beach head remained sparse. It was not until D plus 2 that Roland Beamont, now leading 150 Wing and flying the new Hawker Tempest, met the enemy. It is a measure of the state of the German air defences that it was the first time in two years of regular cross-Channel operational flying that he had done battle with a German fighter.

They crossed the coast at Dieppe and the controller passed the welcome news that there were "bogeys in the vicinity of Lisieux". A few minutes later he saw a smattering of black specks outlined against the cloud, two miles away and 6,000 feet below. With the skies so full of Allied aircraft it was vital to make a positive identification before going in to attack and Beamont dived down to investigate. As they grew closer to what he now saw were five fighters, weaving in line astern, he noted the thin fuselages and narrow, tapered wings. They were Messerschmitt 109s. The aeroplane's superb basic design had, like the Spitfire, enabled it to undergo numerous mutations to keep it in service even at this late stage of the war. Beamont called on one of his two squadrons to cover him, while he took the other in on the attack.

"Already he was rolling over into a steep dive to cut off the Messerschmitts, which were sliding directly over the Tempests on the port side," wrote Beamont's biographer. "He glanced quickly over his shoulder for the reassuring, companionable sight of the rest of 3

Squadron slanting down the sky with him. The sun was right behind. It was the perfect 'bounce'."

Eight hundred yards behind and still overtaking, he switched on the illuminated gunsight and the camera gun. "Black crosses were growing plainly visible on the target. How long can this last? he wondered. How unsuspecting can they be! He selected his target . . . he had to get this Hun."

At last the Germans realized the peril they were in. "Black smoke spurts from their exhaust as they ram open wide their throttles, and reverse violently across the path of the Tempests in a scurry for the cloud tops." It was too late. "Beamont rudders his gunsight on to the last aircraft in the formation. Bead slightly above the cockpit. Halfway along the wing for fifteen-degree angle deflection. Now! His thumb tightens and the Tempest shudders with the recoil of the cannon. Hell! He'll never forgive himself. He has missed." But in his desperation to get away, the 109 pilot twisted back under Beamont's guns. "This time there is no mistake. The range is less than two hundred yards . . . dusty puffs of shell bursts rise from the 109's tail, fuselage and cockpit, and the sight of them stokes a concentrated desire, an overwhelming compulsion to destroy. The climax of the hunt is hot in his blood."

Then Beamont's windscreen filled with smoke and he pulled up sharply to avoid collision. He rolled the Tempest over and looked down to see the Messerschmitt "still on the same heading, but with yellow flames streaming from the cockpit to the tail. For a few seconds he watches, fascinated. Slowly the port wing

323

crumples and folds back, and the 109 drops vertically, trailing thick oily smoke, jet black against the whiteness of the cloud." A few seconds later Beamont was hit himself, but managed to return to base in one piece. A few months later he was shot down and taken prisoner, proof that the Luftwaffe, although utterly dominated, showed the same manic doggedness as their comrades on the ground.

In the main, however, in the Normandy campaign, the fighter pilots would wreak havoc with abandon. Beamont may not have written the purple words above, but the prose is authorized and it reflects the joy Allied airmen felt at leading the charge to what now seemed inevitable victory. Lightnings, Mustangs, Tempests, Typhoons, Thunderbolts and Spitfires roamed the skies, arriving at any time, and literally out of the blue, to bomb and blast, generating a fog of dread that hung over every German soldier, so that no one paused for a smoke or to empty their bowels without having one ear cocked for the menacing note of a Packard or Napier or Merlin engine and an eye trained for the rapidly growing speck in the sky.

The mayhem they caused is recorded in the cine-gun film. Even in grainy black and white you can sense the surge of rockets as they power away from under the wings of the Typhoons, either singly or in devastating salvos, trailing ribbons of white smoke as they race towards earth to explode in the targets hidden in the fields, orchards, lanes and hedgerows of bucolic, summer Normandy.

No one was safe, not even the German commander Erwin Rommel. At 6p.m. on 17 July, after a day-long tour of the Front, he was heading for the Army Group B headquarters. Allied aircraft had just been busy and the road was piled up with wrecked vehicles. His driver turned off on a side road but, according to his aide Captain Helmuth Lang, as they approached Livarot, "suddenly Sergeant Holke our spotter, warned us that two aircraft were flying along the road in our direction. The driver, Daniel, was told to put on speed and turn off on a little side road to the right, about a hundred yards ahead of us, which would give us some shelter. Before we could reach it, the enemy aircraft, flying at great speed only a few feet above the road, came up to within 500 yards of us and the first one opened fire.

"Marshal Rommel was looking back at this moment. The left-hand side of the car was hit by the first burst. A cannon shell shattered Daniel's left shoulder and left arm. Marshal Rommel was wounded in the face by broken glass and received a blow on the left temple and cheekbone, which caused a triple fracture of the skull and made him lose consciousness immediately." The driver lost control and the car hit a tree stump and turned over. The unconscious Rommel was thrown out. As he lay "stretched out in the road" about twenty yards from the car, a "second aircraft flew over and tried to drop bombs on those who were lying on the ground". Rommel survived, only to be made to commit suicide in October 1944 for his connection with the 20 July Plot to assassinate Hitler. Such was the plethora of Allied air activity in the area that three pilots from three separate squadrons were later to claim the credit for having dished the Desert Fox.

Bomber Command threw its thunderbolts into the cosmic chaos. Its size, power and efficiency now made its gallant but puny efforts at the start of the conflict a distant memory. On the night of 8–9 June, 617 Squadron went to work with a new weapon. It was the 12,000 lb "Tallboy" bomb, another product of the mind of the inventor Barnes Wallis. The Tallboy was made of strong, light molybdenum steel, twenty-one-feet long, tapering to a point that was as sharp as a pencil and fitted comfortably into the bomb bay of a Lancaster. Wallis had given his bomb a perfect aerodynamic shape and arranged the fins so that they would impart an increasingly rapid spin. As Tallboy passed through the speed of sound it attained a velocity that drove it a hundred feet into the earth. Wallis had established that shock waves rippled more powerfully through earth and water than they do through air. Thus, the bomb did not have to score a direct hit to destroy a target.

The objective that night was the main railway line running from the south-west — where German units were held in reserve, including the soon-to-be-notorious Das Reich division — and Normandy. The aim was to bring down a bridge and collapse a long tunnel in the area of Saumur on the Loire to block the flow of reinforcements. Four Lancasters from 83 Squadron were to drop flares and deal with the bridge. The tunnel was reserved for 617. The target was marked by Leonard Cheshire, Dave Shannon, an

Australian veteran of the Dams Raid, and Gerry Fawke in Mosquitoes. Nineteen Tallboys were dropped, collapsing not just the tunnel but the whole hillside above it.

Four days later Hitler ordered the first of his "revenge weapons", the V-1 flying bombs or "doodlebugs", to be despatched to fall randomly on London and the South East. It was a measure of desperation. The assault was unexpected and had a particularly demoralizing effect on a population who were starting to believe the war was nearly over. Great effort went into dealing with the V-1. For the next two months, half of Bomber Command's operations went into trying to neutralize the rocket launching sites, until the Allied ground advance eventually swept over them. The sites were well-hidden, buried under thick layers of concrete and heavily protected, and about 3,000 Allied airmen would die in the campaign to destroy them.

In that time the Germans managed to fire 2,579 V-1s at England, half of which fell in the London area. Fighter squadrons were on guard over the approaches to London and managed to shoot down a total of 1,771. The Tempests proved to be particularly adept executioners, accounting for 638.

In the great effort to break out of the landing zone, air power could change the course of a major battle. On 7 August 1944 the German counter-attack at Mortain in the Falaise pocket was stopped by Typhoons dropping bombs, and, above all, firing rockets which delivered the same punch, it was said, as a broadside from a destroyer.

The Luftwaffe was incapable of mounting a serious challenge to Allied air supremacy, but it could never be completely written off. On 16 December the German army launched its last desperate counter-offensive in the Ardennes. Operation Bodenplatte had been intended to provide limited air superiority to cover the thrust, but it was repeatedly delayed by bad weather. It was not launched until New Year's Day 1945, when, having somehow scraped together more than 750 fighters and enough fuel to keep them airborne, the Germans mounted a surprise attack. To the astonishment of the Allies, waves of aircraft arrived over seventeen airfields in the Lowlands, destroying 150 aircraft and killing forty-six, most of them ground crew members. It was an impressive act of defiance, but made no difference. German losses were heavy and unsustainable. About 270 German aeroplanes were destroyed. Adolf Galland, the fighter ace who became a Luftwaffe general, regarded this as the pointless, last gasp of his force. "In this forced action we sacrificed our last substance," he wrote. "The Luftwaffe received its death blow at the Ardennes offensive."

The Allies now had the air to themselves. The power they had accumulated was demonstrated by an event that would become synonymous with the indiscriminate destructiveness of the strategic air campaign. On the morning of Monday, 13 February 1945, Roy Lodge, a twenty-one-year-old bomb aimer with 51 Squadron, and his crew were told they were on "ops" that night. They got on with routine preparations, while waiting to learn the target. That afternoon in the briefing room,

328

Lodge recalled, "the CO addressed us with, 'Gentlemen, your target for tonight is . . . Dresden.' " The news produced some groans and whistles. The target was distant, requiring a round trip of eight and a half hours. Lodge, a Cambridge undergraduate before volunteering for Bomber Command, read later that some of those who took part experienced beforehand "a sense of foreboding, as though they felt some terrible act was about to be committed". For him and his crew, however, "Dresden was just another target, though a long, long way away."

The British — and the Americans who also took part in the operation — were acting at the request of the Soviets, who were concerned at the build-up of German troops in the town, threatening their advance. Operation Thunderclap would turn out to be a catastrophic success. Two waves of aircraft, more than 800 in all, dropped 2,600 tons of bombs. Roy Lodge, in the second wave, was a hundred miles from Dresden when he saw the horizon throbbing with light. "As I drew closer I saw the cause of the glow," he wrote. "Ahead was the most enormous fire. Ahead, and then below us were great patches, pools, areas of flame." Lodge's crews were meant to be dropping markers, but it hardly seemed necessary. "We added our own long line of flares to those already across the target. I saw white flashes of bomb explosions and more sparkling incendiaries. As we completed our run across the target and turned away on our homeward journey, I could see the pools of flame were joining up in one huge inferno."

The firestorm Lodge witnessed consumed about 25,000 people. Coming so close to the end of the conflict, the vast toll of mostly innocent lives sparked unease, then embarrassment, then guilt. Churchill was soon seeking to distance himself from the massacre, noting in a memo to Portal and the Chiefs of Staff Committee at the end of March that "the destruction of Dresden remains a serious query against the conduct of the Allied bombing". It was the start of a process that was to make the strategic bombing campaign an awkward subject in the post-war years, and historians overlooked the vast contribution made by Bomber Command to the Allied victory and the liberation of Europe. For decades it meant that the honour and respect due to the 55,000 young men who died in its operations were withheld. Even today it is rarely admitted that it was the scale of destruction suffered by Germany — largely wrought by the bombers — that brought about the Germans' conversion to the path of peace and democracy.

Dresden cast a tragic shadow over the RAF's extraordinary achievement. At the start of the war only Fighter Command could be said to be in a condition to face the tasks ahead. By the end of the conflict all branches were operating with superb efficiency, laying waste an evil enemy and protecting the innocent over land and sea. By VE Day the RAF had more than 9,000 aircraft on charge, and more than a million men and women in its ranks, from all across the British dominions. The contribution of the ground crews, "the forgotten ones" as Philip Joubert called them in his book commemorating their deeds, was vital. In the words of John Terraine, a great historian of the RAF, many would "rather die than admit to any pride in their part in what they would like to present as a most almighty 'eff-up' from beginning to end".

As for those who flew, "in those young men we may discern the many faces of courage, the constitution of heroes; in lonely cockpits at dizzy altitudes, quartering the treacherous and limitless sea, searching the desert's hostile glare, brushing the peaks of high mountains, in the ferocity of low-level attack, or the long, tense haul of a bombing mission, in fog, in deadly cold, in storm, on fire, in a prison camp . . . in a skin-grafting hospital." It is hard to disagree with his judgement that in Britain's great battle for the freedom of the world, it was the RAF that held the traditional place of honour in the order of battle on the Right of the Line.

With Germany's collapse Bomber Command turned from taking life to giving it. From April onwards, Lancasters and Mosquitoes flew nearly 3,000 missions on Operation Manna, delivering 7,000 tons of food to the starving population of Western Holland. This was followed by Operation Exodus to airlift the 75,000 British servicemen in German prisoner-of-war camps.

Then began the same great dismantling that had followed the end of the last conflict. In their hundreds of thousands the non-professionals who made up the vast majority of the air forces handed in their uniforms, received back a demob overcoat, sports coat, flannels and pair of shoes and stepped out into the real world. It was a battered and shabby world and not particularly welcoming. But it was what they wanted and what they had fought to save.

CHAPTER
SIXTEEN

Jet

At 11.01 on the morning of 9 August 1945 Leonard Cheshire was in the nose of an American B-29 bomber, heading for the Japanese city of Nagasaki. "Suddenly," he wrote later, "it was there." In the distance, a diamond shard of intense light expanded into a sheet of brilliance. Cheshire was flying as an official British observer, but due to the pilot's reluctance to endanger his passenger, he did not get as close to the seat of the explosion as he would have liked. What he did see was a vast cloud of smoke, ash and dust rising out of a boiling sea of fire. It had an "evil kind of luminous quality . . . the colour of sulphur".

"Fat Man", the atomic bomb the United States dropped on Nagasaki, killed about 35,000 people outright. "Little Boy", dropped three days earlier on Hiroshima, killed 70,000–80,000 people. Neither wreaked as much destruction as the conventional bombs dropped on Tokyo five months earlier, which started a firestorm that took about 100,000 lives. It was the nature of the new weapon and its obvious potential that was significant. The world had entered the nuclear age and the shape of military aviation would also change to accommodate this new and awesome fact.

A second, more benign development would also affect profoundly the nature of flying, both military and civil. Before the Second World War had reached its end it was clear that the future belonged to jets. Britain had been at the forefront of this development, thanks largely to the efforts of one man. Frank Whittle was born in 1907 in Earlsdon, a suburb of Coventry, a city with a long tradition of engineering. His father, Moses, was a foreman in a machine-tool factory, who left to start his own business. When it failed, young Frank was forced to leave school. He spent much of his time learning about gas and steam engines in the local library. He applied to join the RAF as an apprentice, but, at a shade over five feet tall, did not meet the regulation height. He persisted, and was let in on his third attempt. It was a tribute to the Trenchard system that his talents were recognized and in 1928 Frank Whittle was sent off to Cranwell as an officer cadet.

He won a reputation as a stunt pilot. It was his intellectual qualities, though, that attracted most attention. In his graduation thesis he came up with the ideas that would make his name and ultimately transform flight. He asserted that for aeroplanes to reach speeds of 500 mph or faster they would have to fly at much greater heights than they did at present, to take advantage of the reduced drag resulting from lower air density. Neither propellers nor piston engines functioned well in thin air. A new kind of engine was needed.

The notion of a jet engine had been around for some years. The principle was relatively simple. Air was compressed, fuel was fed into it and ignited. The resulting explosion produces gases, which, if directed backwards, generate thrust. The great problem was how to compress the air in the first place.

Eighteen months after writing his thesis Whittle came up with a solution. He calculated that there could be enough energy produced at the explosive stage to not only provide thrust but to also to turn a turbine which would drive an air compressor. Thus was born the "turbojet" and Whittle took out a patent in 1930. He passed the idea on to the Air Ministry, which showed little interest. The patent lapsed.

Four years later Whittle was at Cambridge, sponsored by the RAF, and resumed work on his ideas. He re-filed the patents, and since the university had no aeronautical laboratory facilities he sought outside backers to take his research forward. He joined forces with two retired RAF officers and, with assistance from investment bankers, in March 1936 he formed British Power Jets. After pausing to take a first-class honours degree, Whittle got to work designing a prototype. In April 1937 the first turbojet was ready for testing, and by the following year its fan, which controlled the thrust, was measured revolving at speeds of up to 12,000 revolutions per minute.

At a University Air Squadron dinner Whittle met Henry Tizard, the chairman of the Government's Aeronautical Research Committee. Tizard quickly grasped the importance of the invention and pressed it on the Air Ministry. With tragicomic predictability the bureaucrats reacted with suspicion rather than gratitude, invoking the Official Secrets Act and the fact that Whittle was a serving officer to bilk him of a fair price for his invention. By the time work started on an airframe, manufactured by the Gloster Aircraft Company (chosen on the basis that they did not have many orders on their books at the time) and with an engine made by Rover, the Second World War had started and the project did not get the energy and resources it required. An experimental Gloster fighter flew in May 1941, attracting Winston Churchill's enthusiasm and demands for development to be speeded up. Other priorities intervened, however, and the war was almost over by the time the first Gloster Meteors took to the skies.

The Germans had already developed their own jet fighter, the Messerschmitt 262 Schwalbe (Swallow). It had a beautiful, streamlined design and its two underslung engines could speed it through the air at about 560 mph — too fast, initially, for its guns to be brought to bear effectively. It went into service in July 1944 and by the end of the war was reckoned to have shot down about 540 Allied aircraft.

The first Meteors arrived at Fighter Command's 616 Squadron at the same time and went into action the following month against V-1s, shooting down fourteen by the time the flying bomb threat was over. The earliest version suffered from several design defects and it was not until the end of January 1945 that it was fit for service in Europe. The Meteor and Schwalbe never met in aerial combat and the forty-six German aircraft claimed on behalf of the British jet were all destroyed in ground attacks.

Refinements and improvements ironed out the initial problems. By 1946 sixteen squadrons were equipped with Meteors. The Government had handed over the Whittle jet to the Americans during the war, but they had been slow to develop it. In 1946 Britain found itself at the leading edge of a transforming technology and it was anxious to advertise its dominance and to reap the commercial benefits.

Jets were all about speed. In late 1945 Group Captain H.J. "Willie" Wilson roared over Herne Bay in Kent at 606 mph to establish a new world air speed record. The Americans set about mounting a challenge with the Lockheed Shooting Star. To push the prize beyond their reach, the RAF's High Speed Flight, founded in June 1946 to explore the boundaries of jet power, made another attempt to ratchet up the record.

Jet test pilots found themselves in a similar situation to that of the first aviation pioneers. The aircraft were immeasurably more sophisticated and powerful. The element of risk, however — of not knowing what your aircraft might or might not do — was just as acute. The consequences if things went wrong were even more drastic. In the case of engine failure, the canvas, wood and wire contraptions of forty years before might well flutter to earth without mishap. Jets plummeted, and ejector seats were not fitted in the early models.

The uncertainties were related by Squadron Leader Bill Waterton, a handlebar-mustachioed, pre-war RAF professional and wartime fighter pilot, who, together with the HSF commander Group Captain Teddy Donaldson, flew Meteors on the next attempt on the speed record in the summer of 1946. Huge publicity surrounded the event, fanned by the Air Ministry, which was anxious to raise a glow of national pride from the ashes of post-war ennui. Success depended on optimum weather conditions — the warmer the better. August was cool and drizzly and there were endless postponements. Eventually, on the afternoon of Saturday, 7 September 1946, conditions brightened enough for the pair to have a go. Donaldson took off first, at 5.45p.m., and landed fourteen minutes later. Waterton followed at eleven minutes past six. The international regulations proscribed that the test course was short and the altitude was minimal, less than 1,100 feet. Waterton's Meteor Mark 4 was "a lovely craft, easy to fly, docile, and as smooth as silk". That was at relatively low speeds. As it approached 600 miles an hour the port wing tended to dip and no amount of trimming seemed able to cure the fault.

At first things went well. "I opened the throttles fully to 15,200 revolutions per minute," he wrote later. "The engines bit into the densely packed air, chewed and swallowed it, then spat it out at supersonic speed through the red-hot tails of the jet pipe nozzles. I felt tensely confident." Then, as "the air speed indicator crawled up to 580. *The cow's putting port wing down as usual . . . Behave yourself you slut!*"

As he broke through the 600 mph mark the wing dug in deeper. It took all the strength in his arms to keep

338

the stick straight and all the weight of his fourteen stones to jam on the rudder and counteract the leftward drift. After a sweaty few seconds he roared inland at Brighton and touched down, content to have survived. Later he learned that Donaldson had raised the bar to 616 mph. Waterton had managed to record a speed only two miles an hour behind him. Success did not mollify his indignation at the pressure he felt had been heaped on him to take unnecessary risks. The attempt, he judged, might easily have ended in "prestige-shattering, disastrous failure". The Meteor went on to be a staple of the post-war RAF, but safety was never one of its virtues. Nearly 900 were lost and 450 pilots killed in its years of service.

Jets claimed a fair number of lives on the ground. There were no whirring propellers to advertise danger, which sometimes had fatal consequences for the unwary. Colin Walker Downes, who we last heard of watching the dogfights over London in 1940, recalled how "one day, while standing outside the squadron dispersal during a Meteor ground run, I saw an airman walk across the front of the aircraft and in an instant disappear, as if in a magic show, followed by a loud bang as the impeller turbine disintegrated. Running over to the aircraft as the fitter shut down the engines, we found no protective grills over the engine intakes and no sign of the airman, apart from one black shoe lying on the ground."

Flying jets and flying propeller-driven fighters were different experiences. Walker Downes had done both and knew which he preferred. "Gone was the rasping, clattering noise of the twelve cylinders combined with the propeller noise as the propeller heaved the aircraft into the air with the blade tips approaching the speed of sound, before the aircraft settled down to a lengthy climb to altitude. Instead the surge of the jet thrust projected the aircraft rapidly into the air and the rate of climb to altitude was initially quite breathtaking. With the pilot insulated within the pressurized cockpit, the whine of the jet engine penetrating the flying helmet was muted and soon ignored, and the flight was smooth and seemingly effortless."

It seemed to Downes that this was the closest that man had got to experiencing the true sensation of flight. Flying through the tropopause, the atmospheric threshold to the stratosphere, the effects of weather ceased and "one could view one's progress through space, marked by the condensation trails of the jet engine as it traced a broad white chalk line across the sky against a deep azure board. At such times, if flying alone with the radio silent, there was an incredible feeling of not being part of this world, especially if above cloud, and regardless of one's religious beliefs, the effect was one of wonder."

In America the end of the war came as a relief rather than a cause for celebration. The country retreated into one of its intermittent bouts of isolationism, from which it was only reluctantly aroused when the extent of Soviet hostility towards the West was recognized. Even so, Washington was reluctant to share nuclear technology with its old ally, and Britain was forced to make its own way into the atomic age. By the end of

1947 a nuclear arms programme was under way to develop an independent bomb. The RAF would have the job of delivering it. It was now all too clear which enemy the bombs would be aimed at. The partnership between the free and communist worlds had started to fall apart even before victory was declared. Stalin had made it clear that the Soviet Union would be expanding eastwards. A dark red shadow fell across Eastern Europe. West Berlin alone stood out. In 1948 Moscow began to choke off the road and rail routes into the city, leaving its 2 million inhabitants in the free area the choice of starvation or amalgamation with their communist neighbours.

It was the occasion for the West's first major stand in what by now had become known as the Cold War. From June onwards, American, British and French aircraft established a *Luftbrücke* (air bridge) to relieve the besieged inhabitants. The RAF flew into Gatow in the British sector of West Berlin with Coastal Command Sunderlands, putting down on the Havelsee lake nearby. The USAAF used Templehof in the centre. They established an astonishingly efficient delivery system that was a triumph of air traffic control. At Gatow, four-engined Yorks (the replacement for the Lancasters) and Dakotas landed every three minutes, stayed on the ground for a maximum of less than an hour and then returned to one of the supply axes to reload. The landing schedule was so tight that any aircraft unable to touch down on its first attempt had to return to its base to maintain the smooth rhythm of deliveries. In the ten months it took the West to persuade the Soviets to call off the siege, aircraft flew 27,000 flights and delivered 235,000 tons of freight. Thanks to Allied air power, a great battle of wills had been won. It was only the first of a continuous and titanic contest of resources, technology, skill and nerve that would last for forty more years, with on one side the forces of the North Atlantic Treaty Organization (NATO), founded in 1949, and on the other the Soviet Union and its Warsaw Pact allies.

The enemy was not just the Soviet Union but communism. The ideological nature of this struggle meant that it could be fought by proxies all over the world. In 1950 capitalism and communism went to war in Korea, when the United Nations intervened to prevent the southern half of Korea being swallowed by the communist north. Most of the outside help for the Republic of Korea came from America, with limited support from Britain and others. The Democratic People's Republic of Korea was backed heavily by the Chinese communists and the Soviet Union.

After a slow start, the Soviets were closing the wide technological gap that had opened up at the end of the Second World War. They had learned how to the build the Bomb and had developed their own jet fighters, notably the MiG 15, which at the start of the conflict outclassed the American Shooting Stars and Panthers, and the British and Australian Meteors. It was only with the arrival of the North American-manufactured F-86 Sabre, which, like the MiG, had performance-enhancing swept wings, that the West was able to compete on equal terms.

342

The Korean War (1950–53) produced some of the greatest fighter-to-fighter confrontations in the history of aerial warfare, with aggressive pilots clashing in individual combats that recalled the contests of the First World War. Much of the dogfighting was done along the Yalu Valley on North Korea's frontier with China, which US pilots nicknamed "MiG Alley". There, Sabres tried to intercept Korean and Chinese jets, many of the former flown by Soviet pilots, and prevent them from attacking fighter bombers operating in the south. The most successful unit was the 4th Fighter Interceptor Wing (4 FIW), which was striving to add to the glory its forebears had won flying Mustangs during the Second World War.

A small number of experienced RAF officers were attached to 4 FIW after Fighter Command, anxious to create a cadre of pilots with experience of jet-fighter combat, called for volunteers. British and American aircrew had worked alongside each other, for the most part in harmony, for large stretches of the preceding war, though there were marked differences in outlook. The British stiff upper lip is a cliché, but in those days it was also a reality, underlying the RAF's attitudes to tactics, strategy and demeanour, in the air and on the ground. The cult of understatement was equally potent. Many Britons found the Americans' capacity for self-dramatization laughable, and their attitudes to death mawkish and embarrassing. In 1944 Bill Waterton, the Meteor test pilot, had been stationed alongside an American Lightning squadron and found that "they stayed at their end of the mess and we ours.

343

The coolness was not due to criticisms of one another as flyers, but to fundamental differences of temperament. We felt rather bewildered by the Americans, for instance, when after the loss of an aircraft, tears flowed with beer and their mess bore a maudlin, funereal air that lasted a week. They, in turn, could not understand British distaste for public exhibitions of grief, and were appalled by the RAF's 'Poor old Mike went for a burton this afternoon. Let's have a drink on him.' "

Another perceived American character defect was glory-hunting, which Colin Walker Downes witnessed while flying Sabres with 4 FIW. The wing was based at K-14 airfield on the south side of the Han river, a few miles west of Seoul and in action daily over MiG Alley. High-ranking desk-jockeys were keen to join the ranks of the "MiG maulers" and claim a scalp. Despite their lack of experience or flying skills they would from time to time take command of an operation, to the annoyance of their subordinates, who had the task of keeping the "one-day wonders" out of trouble.

Nor was there any shortage of egotists among the unit commanders engaged in daily combat. The United States Air Force (USAF), which in September 1947 had moved out from under the aegis of the army to become a separate branch of the US military, encouraged a competitive culture with pilots pushing to log the five kills that would make them an "ace". Senior officers would jostle for the "shooting slots" on the offensive sweeps that provided the best opportunities for success.

British pilots like Walker Downes were given the supporting role of "wingman", watching their leader's back and directing him onto targets. One morning, just before the end of the war, he was flying as wingman to Captain Lonnie Moore in the Yalu area when they spotted two pairs of MiGs apparently heading for their home base at Feng Cheng. Moore ordered the "bounce" on the last pair.

"I was to the right and behind Moore and I called him 'clear' as he closed on the trailing MiG," he wrote. "I asked if he was sure the pair in front of us were the last pair and received an 'Affirmative' answer." Moore opened fire at 300 yards and closed to 100 yards, where it seemed that "the stream of bullets must have gone straight up the tailpipe of the MiG, for several pieces came away, followed quickly by the cockpit canopy as the pilot ejected at 1,500 feet." Moore throttled back to avoid overshooting the lead MiG and Walker Downes had to throw his Sabre into a barrel roll to stay behind his leader.

Hanging upside down at the top of the roll he spotted two MiGs closing on them in staggered formation. He called a warning to Moore, who carried on oblivious, intent on finishing the remaining MiG in front of him, which was now approaching the Feng Cheng runway. The pursuing MiGs were now on Moore's tail. He realized his predicament and broke away to the left, leaving Walker Downes heading straight across the airfield at low altitude. As he flashed across it at a few hundred feet "the whole airfield seemed to light up" as the anti-aircraft guns went into action.

The flak burst alarmingly but harmlessly in the sky around, and then he was clear. The MiG that had been chasing Moore was still ahead and, despite the turbulence which set his "flying helmet bobbing against the canopy, while trying to rubberneck, looking for MiGs", Downes managed to range his gunsight "pipper" on the target. He opened fire at 400 yards. It was too soon, but he saw the Sabre's .50 calibre machine-gun rounds sparking off the fuselage as the MiG broke sharply to the left.

Then Downes was sandwiched between two attackers. One latched onto his tail and opened fire. The Russian jets were armed with three cannon, which had the power to bring down a B-29 bomber with a few hits. The shells moved at low velocity, however, and by turning tightly Downes was able to avoid the "red cricket balls" floating towards him. The huge gravitational forces that weighed in during a full power turn were to some extent counteracted by the "G-suit" — worn over the flying suit and lined with hoses, which pumped up to slow the downward rush of blood away from the brain. Even so, his helmet was "weighing like a sandbag on my head as it pushed my goggles over my eyes" and he felt close to "greying out". He glanced back to see his pursuer slamming "into the ground in an explosive ball of fire" — apparently having gone into a high-speed stall as he tried to bring his guns to bear.

Downes dived for the deck at full power and headed south and out to sea where he landed on the sandy beach of a friendly island. He made it back to K-14 at dusk to the surprise of everyone who had assumed he was dead. When he ran into Moore, the American's main concern was whether Downes had confirmed the two MiGs he was claiming to have shot down.

The gung-ho spirit of the American fliers was mirrored in the institutional attitude of their bosses. The USAF and in particular the Strategic Air Command (SAC) exuded aggression and displayed a willingness to embrace the concept of mutual annihilation that underlay the possession of nuclear weapons. The SAC was the air force's bomber wing and it soaked up much of the mighty resources of the US military budget. It was led by "bomber generals", exemplified by the baby-faced, cigar-sucking Curtis LeMay, the architect of the firebombing of Tokyo. LeMay believed that America's entire nuclear arsenal should be employed in a single, obliterating strike if it seemed likely that a Soviet attack was planned — an atomic age version of the "knock-out blow" theory of the interwar years. Throughout the 1950s the SAC stood in a state of perpetual readiness to send its nuclear bombers against a host of Soviet cities as soon as the order was given.

It was a Sisyphean task, requiring constant reconnaissance, monitoring and analysis of the Soviet Union's actions. It was the fate of the RAF during the period to work as a junior partner with the USAF, sharing the exhausting labour of eternal vigilance.

In October 1953 warheads were exploded in the South Australian desert, the start of a process that would produce Blue Danube, Britain's plutonium bomb. The new weapons would be carried by a succession of "V Bombers" — the Vickers Valiant, Avro Vulcan and Handley Page Victor, which acted as Britain's independent nuclear deterrent force until the responsibility passed to the Royal Navy's Polaris missile-equipped submarines in 1969.

America's initial reluctance to share her nuclear secrets waned and in 1958 the US-UK Mutual Defence Agreement was signed, which locked the two countries into a shared nuclear strategy. The RAF was at the forefront of NATO's plans for nuclear war with the Soviet Union. From bases in central and eastern England V-Bombers would be the trigger force for a nuclear Armageddon, and had the capacity to destroy Moscow and Kiev, killing millions before the Americans had entered Soviet airspace. For much of the time the RAF's Cold War duties seemed to those who carried them out like an elaborate game, albeit one that bore the risk of violent death if things went wrong. Both sides broke the rules frequently. RAF aircraft flew deep into Soviet air space on intelligence-gathering missions, collecting radar and photographic evidence of military sites, and despite some narrow escapes they got away with it.

In autumn 1962, however, the feeling of unreality that pervaded the Cold War evaporated and the unimaginable prospect of a nuclear war became horribly plausible. At the end of October, President John F. Kennedy received hard evidence that Soviet missiles were about to be deployed in Cuba, a hundred miles from the Florida coast. He warned that the delivery of the weapons would be opposed by force. Any clash had the potential to escalate into an all-out nuclear conflict in which Britain — as America's nearest ally and partner in her nuclear strategy — would be in the front line. During the weekend of 26 October 1962 the V-Bomber force was brought to the highest levels of readiness. At four air bases forty Vulcans stood with their bombs on board, their crews waiting alongside at fifteen minutes' readiness.

"The aircraft were all ready to go," remembered former Wing Commander Peter West, an electronics officer on a Vulcan based at Coningsby in Lincolnshire. "We were fully kitted out with our flying gear. All we had to do was get in, put our straps on, press the button and the engines would start up."

The crisis passed, however, and for decades the British public remained in ignorance of how serious the drama had become. Over the next few decades fear of nuclear obliteration retreated from the national psyche. As the era of the Bomb passed and nuclear weaponry moved into the realm of intercontinental rocketry, the notion of superpower conflict once again became too big to comprehend. After the dying skirmishes of the colonial era — in Suez and in Aden — the prospect of a conventional war seemed equally remote. By the early 1980s, aside from its Cold War preoccupations in Germany, Britain's military energies were mainly spent trying to control the rebellious natives across the water in Northern Ireland. In both theatres, life had settled down into a familiar and predictable rhythm. In 1982 it was shattered by an eruption in a group of islands most Britons had perhaps heard of, but would be hard-pressed to locate on a map.

CHAPTER
SEVENTEEN

Fox Two Away!

From the outset, the Falklands conflict seemed a freak of history. It was fought to hang onto a scrap of empire — yet the principle underlying the action was the very un-imperial one of self-determination. It came at a time when imperial sentiment had anyway all but vanished and Britain's armed forces were being reshaped to suit the needs of a post-colonial world. It was fortunate that they had not yet been transformed to the point where a major exercise in power projection was no longer possible. Victory did nothing to arrest this process, however. The war remains a historical firebreak, a last demonstration of classical, twentieth-century war-fighting before the arrival of the hi-tech military age.

It was also the last time in which the Royal Navy would play the major role in a war involving Britain. The fleet was still of a size that it could organize the transportation of thousands of soldiers 8,000 miles across the ocean, deliver them into battle and sustain them on the ground. Equally importantly, it was equipped with an air force that could protect them throughout the operation. The air war over the Falklands was fought largely by naval aviators flying off

351

aircraft carriers. Long before the ground troops went ashore the airmen were in action against a formidable and determined enemy, who had the advantage of operating from their own soil. The British aviators had to succeed if the campaign to recapture the Falklands was not to end in bloody and ignominious failure.

Air power sustained the campaign at every stage. The first military response to the arrival of thousands of Argentinian troops on the Falklands on 2 April 1982 was the despatch the following day of RAF transport aircraft to Wideawake Airport, the British air base on Ascension Island, lying in the equatorial waters of the South Atlantic, a thousand miles off the coast of Africa. They were followed two days later by the first of the Nimrod maritime patrol aircraft, which would scour the seas for Argentinian submarines.

The spearhead of the Task Force's air component was the Fleet Air Arm's Sea Harriers. Three squadrons — Naval Air Squadrons 800, 801 and elements of 899 which reformed as 809 — headed south on the aircraft carriers HMS *Hermes* and HMS *Invincible* after sailing from Portsmouth on 5 April. Their job was to protect the Task Force from aerial attack. The RAF's 1 (F) squadron, equipped with GR3 Harriers, was also sent to support the troops on the ground. The fixed-wing component was augmented by 170 helicopters — mostly Sea King and Wessex — tasked with searching and destroying enemy shipping as well as rescue and transportation duties.

The air war opened three weeks before the landings. On 30 April the British government declared a

200-mile total exclusion zone around the Falklands, and any Argentinian vessel entering it risked attack. Late that evening, eleven fully loaded Victors — enjoying a new lease of life as aerial tankers — took off from Ascension. Their job was to provide in-flight replenishment for a sole Vulcan carrying twenty-one 1,000 lb bombs, which was bound for Port Stanley airport, 3,886 miles away. Another Vulcan flew behind in reserve. The Black Buck raids — as the five bombing and missile missions against the airfield at Stanley and the Argentinian radar defences were called — were amazing logistical feats. They required skill, precision and huge resources. The attack bomber had to be refuelled seven times on the outward journey and once on the return, burning 22,000 gallons in all. The tankers needed in-flight refuelling themselves to stay in the air. The operation involved a round trip of more than 9,000 miles — sixteen hours' flying time. This made it the longest bombing mission in history.

There were a thousand things to go wrong and, inevitably, many did. As the lead Vulcan XM 598 climbed to cruising altitude, the captain, Squadron Leader John Reeve, noticed the cabin was not pressurizing properly — the result, as it turned out, of a perished window seal. The bomber was forced to turn back and it now fell to the reserve Vulcan, 607, to carry out the mission. The pilot, Flight Lieutenant Martin Withers, informed the crew with the laconic observation that "it looks like we've got a job of work, fellas".

The bomber arrived in the target area just before 4a.m. local time, to the astonishment of the

Argentinians. It swooped down to 300 feet for its approach, then climbed to attack height, delivering its stick of twenty-one bombs at a 35-degree angle across the runway. It then roared away, unscathed, to the north for a rendezvous with a tanker, after flashing the signal "superfuse" to indicate a job well done. It had, indeed, been quite a feat. To laymen, however, the results did not seem proportionate to the enormous effort and vast outlay of resources. Only one bomb had hit the runway. When this news reached the *Canberra*, steaming southwards towards the islands, the sailors, marines and paras on board reacted with delighted derision. Regret at the limited damage the raid had inflicted was more than outweighed by pleasure that a rival service — the "Crabs", as they called the RAF — had apparently ballsed things up. In fact, it was always understood by the air force that bombing runways rarely had lasting effect and the single bomb did at least render the Stanley airstrip unusable to Argentinian fast jet fighters — though not to C130 transports supplying the garrison. The four Black Buck raids that followed produced similarly modest results and the series was essentially a side show that served to remind the world that the RAF had a part to play in the enterprise.

The main role in the air battle belonged to the aircraft and pilots of the Royal Navy. From the earliest days, naval aviators had lived in the shadow of the Royal Air Force. In both world wars they had carried out their duties with the same dedication and skill as the RAF, but had not received their fair share of recognition or acclaim, perhaps because most of their activities took place out of range of public or media notice. Fleet Air Arm jets had conducted thousands of operations off light fleet carriers throughout the Korean War and its helicopters buzzed over the jungles of Malaya, operating against communist terrorists throughout the Malayan emergency. Navy fighters also provided fighter cover and carried out air strikes during the Anglo-French intervention in Suez in November 1956.

In all of these actions naval aviation had always been a junior player in an ensemble dominated by the RAF. The circumstances of the Falklands conflict gave the naval air squadrons a unique opportunity to take centre stage and they relished this chance. The theatre of war was at the other end of the world from the United Kingdom, with the rocky speck of Ascension Island the only friendly landfall between the two locations. As the Herculean exertions required for the Black Buck raids demonstrated, conducting protracted land-based operations would be impossible logistically. Fortunately, the Sea Harriers aboard the carriers — and the men who flew, directed and maintained them — were more than equal to the challenge of defending the Task Force in the air, as well as attacking the Argentinian enemy on land.

The first demonstration of their abilities was given on 1 May, a few hours after the Vulcan and Victors had departed Falklands air space. Once again the airfield at Port Stanley was the target, as well as the airstrip at the settlement of Goose Green. The task of bombing was given to 800 Naval Air Squadron, operating off *Hermes*, while 801 Squadron from *Invincible* flew top

355

cover to protect them from attack by Argentinian interceptors. The raiders all returned safe and sound, a fact reported by Brian Hanrahan, the BBC reporter aboard *Invincible* and operating under censorship restrictions with a phrase that would lodge itself in the British folk memory: "I counted them all out and I counted them all back again."

Throughout the day the Sea Harriers flew Combat Air Patrols (CAPs) around the islands. This was their staple activity throughout the remaining forty-four days of the war. The purpose was to intercept raids by the Argentinian Air Force, operating from airfields on the mainland, several hundred miles to the west. The Fuerza Aérea Argentina was not organized to fight a major military power. It was designed rather for war with its neighbour Chile, with whom it had a history of territorial disputes.

The British naval air squadrons mustered twenty-eight Sea Harriers between them. They were facing a fast jet force with a notional strength of about fifty McDonnell Douglas A-4 Skyhawks, thirty Daggers (the Israeli Aircraft Industry's version of the French Mirage 5 multi-role fighter) and seventeen French-built Mirage IIIEAs. The Argentinian navy air fleet comprised eight Skyhawks, six Italian Aermachis and four French Super Etendards, equipped with the devastating Exocet air-to-surface missile. The Argentinian ground forces on the islands were also supported by two dozen Pucarás, powered by twin piston engines, which, although slow, were very effective ground attack aircraft in the hilly terrain of the Falklands.

The numerical advantage was not as daunting as it looked on paper. The Skyhawk fleet was in poor shape, suffering from an arms embargo imposed by the United States to punish Argentina for its protracted "dirty war" against left-wing revolutionaries, dissidents, trade-unionists and students. A decision was made not to base fast jets on the islands — the wisdom of which seemed reinforced by the Vulcan raids. They operated instead from air bases strung along the coast at distances of between 660 and 430 miles from the islands. Most of the jets had no in-flight refuelling to extend their time over target and there were only two tankers to service those that had.

As to performance, the Sea Harriers had the edge. They were ingeniously designed to take off and land vertically — a requirement imposed by the decision taken in 1966 to scrap plans for a new generation of large aircraft carriers. The four vector nozzles on the "Shar" meant they could lift off and land on small deck spaces. The Shar's top speed of 700 mph was slower than the supersonic Mirages and Daggers. It was, however, considerably more manoeuvrable, and pilots used the nozzles as brakes to "Viff" (Vector in Forward Flight), enabling it to dodge pursuing aircraft and missiles. It was also armed with the latest AIM-9 sidewinder missiles (the Argentinians had only the short-range version).

The experience of flying in a Sea Harrier was memorably described by an Argentinian aviator and writer, Maxi Gainza, who, seven years after the war, was taken for a flip over South Wales by 800

357

Squadron's David Morgan. "It is quiet inside a Harrier," he wrote. "Even at 450 knots [517 mph], the engine sound coming through the helmet is faint — like that of a seashell cupped to the ear. The ride was velvet smooth, there being little turbulence, and for minutes at a time I could sit and enjoy the scenery unreeling through the haze ... Then, suddenly wham! An invisible pile-driver would pound me into the seat, triggering the G-suit's vice-like hold around my lower body, while my head turned to solid lead. Grinding my neck vertebrae in the effort of looking up, I would see ghostly green symbols dancing on the Head-Up Display and beyond it, the horizon tilting to near vertical and whirling away like a fruit machine — trees, streams, sheep, houses ..."

The initial contacts suggested the Argentinian pilots were fully aware of their disadvantages. The first came at dawn on May Day when the air defence controller on board HMS *Glamorgan* spotted two "bogeys" approaching from the west. He notified the Combat Air Patrol being flown by Lieutenant-Commander John Eyton-Jones of 801 and Flight Lieutenant Paul Barton, an RAF pilot attached to the squadron. But as they approached the delta-winged Mirages the Argentinians turned away, apparently warned by the surveillance radar on the ground. The British pair returned to their back-and-forth patrolling, whereupon the Mirages crept back, only to turn tail when it looked like they would be confronted again. This feinting continued until the Argentinians finally seemed to commit to an attack. They swooped down and the Shars accelerated towards them. Just before they met, the Mirages broke away and turned towards land. The pursuing Harriers found they were flying straight into tracer from ground batteries. Whether it was a deliberate trap or happenstance they would never discover. They headed out to the safety of the sea before returning to relate their experiences to an eager audience of their fellow pilots, awaiting their turn to test themselves against the opposition.

The second pair, Lieutenant Commander Robin Kent and Lieutenant Brian Haigh, also ran into two Mirages, one of which appeared to fire a missile that passed by harmlessly, before heading for home. It seemed to 801 Squadron's commander Nigel "Sharkey" Ward that "the Mirages were obviously not too keen on mixing it, otherwise full combat would have developed. Their tactics appeared to be to enter any intercept from high level with a lot of energy or speed. When they were met head-on they would release ordnance, turn away and return to base." The tactics made him feel "a little frustrated. I wanted to see a result."

Soon Ward himself was airborne, flying alongside Lieutenant Mike Watson, one of five pilots on loan from 899 Naval Air Squadron. Their CAP station was off Volunteer Point, a long peninsula north of Stanley.

"As we set up the patrol in battle formation at 12,000 feet, we could see little of the islands with only one or two rocky mountain peaks jutting through a layer of low cloud," wrote Ward.

There was a flurry of excitement when the *Glamorgan* air controller vectored them onto some slow-moving aircraft, but they lost them in cloud. Then they were directed at some high-flying Mirages, but they, too, vanished before an interception could be made. It was not until the afternoon that the Sea Harriers drew blood.

By now the islands lay under a mattress of white cloud, but the skies above were a shimmering icy blue. Lieutenant Steve Thomas and Flight Lieutenant Paul Barton were cruising up and down, awaiting instructions, when the *Glamorgan* controller alerted them to two Mirages approaching high and fast from the west. Down below on *Invincible*, Ward listened in as the drama unfolded.

"Initially the Mirages played the same tactics as in the morning, closing towards the CAP pair and then retreating when menaced," he wrote. "But the Argentine pilots must have become as bored as we were by these cat-and-mouse games, and must have been adding up the odds for and against them." They appear to have calculated that they held the tactical advantage, for "they were higher and faster and, when used to good effect, this extra energy of position and speed could be made to pay dividends in a dogfight. They also were looking down against a white, cloud-top background, which made it much easier for them to see their targets when in visual range — the [Sea Harriers] would stand out as distinct white dots against the cloud."

Conversely, the Shar pilots would find it hard to pick up the tiny shapes of the Mirages against the clear sky, now darkening as dusk descended. These factors seem

360

to have made up the Argentinian pilots' minds, for they tipped into a steep dive towards the CAP pair. As the *Glamorgan* controller called the diminishing range between the two pairs, Thomas and Barton climbed towards the attackers, straining to get them into radar contact so they could activate their Sidewinder missiles.

The Sidewinder was already a quarter of a century old, but its brilliantly simple and adaptable design meant that it was capable of endless refinements and it remains in service to this day, the most effective heat-seeking missile in aviation history. The Shars were equipped with the improved "Lima" variant, which had an "all-aspect" capability allowing it to be fired from any position, even head-on, while still managing to manoeuvre behind the victim to home in on its jet pipe.

Thomas was the first to pick up a contact: two thin blips on his screen showing the Mirages ten degrees high and seventeen miles distant. He took over from the *Glamorgan* controller, in the same way as his Fighter Boy forbears would have done from the section controller once they had sighted "bandits" forty-two years before. He decided to approach the Mirages head-on. Barton steered to the left, so as to swing round behind them. This was a manoeuvre they had practised repeatedly. Everything was unfolding in instruction-manual fashion. The only question was whether the Argentinians would turn away. But no, on they came, closing on the Sea Harriers at a rate of a mile every three seconds.

At four miles the lead Mirage showed as a tiny dot on the Head-Up Display, projected on his windscreen, framed by the four arms of the radar-acquisition cross. Thomas switched on his missile. The signal that the Sidewinder had locked onto the heat of the target engine was a low electronic growl, but none came. The Argentinian pilots seemed to have throttled back to reduce their heat signature and stymie a head-on shot. Thomas began to worry that the Argentinian racing towards him may by now have locked his own radar-guided missiles onto him. Just as he flashed below the delta wings of the oncoming Mirages two trails of smoke streaked past his cockpit.

He pulled his Shar round to the right to make another approach. Now Barton was approaching the pair from the side. One was trailing the other, apparently oblivious to the danger he was in. The electronic signal told Barton his missile was primed. He pressed the firing button and called the NATO launch signal — "Fox Two away."

According to Ward's account, based on his debrief of his men, "the missile thundered off the rails like an express train and left a brilliant white smoke trail as it curved up towards the heavens, chasing after the Mirage, which was now making for the stars, very nose-high. Paul was mesmerized as the angry missile closed with its target. As the Sidewinder made intercept, the Argentine jet exploded in a vivid ball of yellow flame. It broke its back as the missile exploded and then disintegrated, before its remains twisted their way down to the cloud and the sea below."

Steve Thomas was now in pursuit of his own Mirage and managed to get his Sidewinder on target just as his quarry disappeared into the cloud below. He could not confirm a definite kill, but it seemed a probable. In fact, the missile had proximity-fused near the aircraft, which managed to limp to Stanley airfield, only to be shot down by "friendly" anti-aircraft fire. The pair headed back to *Invincible* and "it was quite definitely a hero's welcome when the two landed back on board". There was more good news from *Hermes*. Flight Lieutenant "Bertie" Penfold, an RAF pilot attached to 800 Squadron, had downed a Dagger which had been taking part in an attack on HMS *Glamorgan* and HMS *Arrow* off Port Stanley. In the early evening, 801 Squadron claimed another victim when Lieutenant Alan Curtis shot down one of a group of three Canberra bombers over the sea.

The score at the end of the first day of air combat was four Argentinian aircraft shot down and four aircrew killed. There were no British losses. The pattern was set for the remainder of the war. Argentinian fighters did not manage to shoot down any of their British opponents. The six Sea Harriers and three GR3s lost were brought down by gun or missile fire or were lost as the result of accidents.

This lack of success was not due to any failure of resolve or skill on the part of the Argentinian pilots, who still managed to inflict devastating damage on the British fleet, despite being armed with unguided and incorrectly fused bombs. Their courage was magnificently in evidence on Friday, 21 May 1982, when the Task Force at last went ashore. I watched from the deck of the P&O liner *Canberrra*, which had been pressed into

363

service as a troop ship, as Skyhawks and Daggers flashed into San Carlos water at what seemed like mast-height, pursued by missiles twisting up from the navy ships moored around us. Among the attackers that day was Captain Hector Sanchez, the Skyhawk pilot who survived the battle which opens this book, when Commander David Morgan downed two of his comrades. Like most of those who were involved in it, he fought his war in the air without hatred.

"I have nothing against the British," he told Maxi Gainza in 1989. "We shot at one another, but we were both doing our job and I respect them for it." Later he would meet Morgan to share a drink and exchange memories, in much the same way that RAF and Luftwaffe veterans of the Battle of Britain had met to shake hands and reminisce. Such human encounters belonged to an era that had already passed. The Falklands conflict saw the end of the tradition established over the trenches of the Western Front when men matched their machines and their flying skills in mortal combat. Inexorably, technology was coming to dominate the practice of aerial warfare and a future beckoned in which human beings would play an ever-diminishing part.

CHAPTER
EIGHTEEN

Per Ardua ad Astra

In the late summer of 2008 soldiers of the Parachute Regiment led an operation to clear the way for the delivery of a generator turbine needed to boost electricity supplies to southern Afghanistan. They were tasked with securing the route along which the convoy carrying the machinery would be driven. The last stretch of the journey to the hydro-electric station at the Kajaki Dam in Helmand Province was bandit country, a web of irrigation ditches, fields and compounds, thick with insurgents. Several hundred Paras were moved into the area. Even so, air power was essential if the ground was to be secured. The operation that followed provided a demonstration of the nature of aerial warfare in an age where highly advanced technological societies clash with a primitive enemy.

On the morning of 30 August 2008 the convoy had safely crossed the desert and mountains and was ready to move onto the rock-strewn, dusty track that led through the cultivated area to its final destination. The night before it had seemed that an attempt by the Paras to secure a ceasefire with the local Taliban by means of bribery might succeed. When they arrived at an agreed rendezvous to formalize the deal, however, there was no sign of the rebels. The deal was off.

The commanding officer of 3 Para, Lieutenant Colonel Huw Williams, still felt that a show of force might persuade the insurgents to lie low. At his request, a fighter-bomber made an ear-splitting pass at 250 feet over the lush fields, dotted with baked mud compounds.

The demonstration had little effect. When the soldiers moved off down the road, they soon came under attack. Artillery, rocket and mortar fire was called down on the Taliban positions. Despite the bombardment, spasmodic shots still sounded from one compound. It was time to call in the air force. Accompanying the soldiers was an RAF officer, Flight Lieutenant Adam Freedman, a slim, lively Londoner, who was serving as a Joint Tactical Air Controller. His job was to call in the locations of enemy positions so they could be dealt with by bombs or missiles, delivered by fast jets or helicopters.

Freedman relayed the co-ordinates over the radio. A few minutes later a 500 lb satellite-guided bomb erupted on the insurgent position, followed minutes later by another. The shooting stopped. Of the American B-1 Lancer that had dropped the bombs there was no sign. It was flying far too high to be seen by the naked eye, let alone be threatened by any weapon to be found in the Taliban's armoury.

The RAF does not feature much in the iconography of the Afghan war. It is the army which seems to be doing all the work. The public imagination is dominated by images of lines of patrolling troops moving cautiously through mud-walled villages and the rattle of firefights in maize fields. Air power is unseen and perhaps unappreciated. Without it, however, the army could not function. As the Chief of the Air Staff, Sir Stephen Dalton, pointed out, the patrolling soldiers on the TV news are totally reliant on air power, "depending on situational awareness provided by unseen and unheard surveillance aircraft, the assurance of firepower support from on-call fighter aircraft and unmanned systems over the horizon; the mobility and resupply capability provided by tactical air transport". As they gingerly put one boot in front of the other, constantly bracing for the boom and blast of an exploding IED, they will also be "bolstered by the knowledge that, if necessary, medical evacuation helicopters are on hand to ensure that battle casualties will be delivered to first-class hospital care within the critical 'golden hour' ".

In two respects the super-sophisticated aircraft are fulfilling the same function as their wire-and-canvas forbears of nearly a century before — providing accurate information about the battlefield and firepower in support of their comrades on the ground. But others are relatively new, particularly the reliance the army now places on the air force to get them to and from the battlefield, and to transport them around it and supply them during operations.

The attack aspect of military flying is no longer the domain of men alone. In 1992 the Government announced that women would be allowed to fly jet aircraft and two years later a woman pilot, Flight Lieutenant Jo Salter, joined 617 Squadron, the illustrious Dambusters, taking part in operations to enforce the no-fly zones over Iraq.

In the conflicts Britain has been engaged in recently, flying fast jets has become a progressively less dangerous experience, at least as far as the threat from enemy fire is concerned. At the time of writing, twenty-one RAF personnel have died in Afghanistan since 2006. Some were killed by roadside bombs. Most were the victims of a crash when an elderly Nimrod fell out of the sky during a reconnaissance mission as a result of mechanical failure. None of the deaths was caused by an aircraft being brought down by enemy bullets or missiles — though that possibility always remains.

By the end of the twentieth century the insulation of the jet jockey from not just the battlefield but the world was almost complete. Flight Lieutenant John Nichol, a navigator who began his service in the Cold War era, always found it difficult to answer the question "What's it like flying in a Tornado?" because "It's like nothing else. In the grey, pre-dawn drizzle you clamber up into your big, ugly, mechanical monster, snuggle down into your seat and snap shut the canopy. Now you are in a different world, enclosed, autonomous, completely shut off from the outside, with a beautiful, cosy, electronic whine in the background."

Nichol was based in Germany and on his morning flight he would look down through gaps in the cloud to see "the rest of the world coming to life, waking up and going to work. Lines of cars in traffic jams stretch out below you, their lights on, wipers too probably, the drivers smoking, getting frustrated, checking their watches, listening to the bad news on the radio and a miserable weather report. And you have escaped their drudgery and trudgery and cannot but feel sorry for the poor bastards, while you are high in the blue, in heaven with an electronic whine. It is hard sometimes not to feel superior. This is why some fast jet jocks, especially single-seater pilots, develop unmatchable egos and feelings of godlike supremacy."

In January 1991 Nichol and his pilot Flight Lieutenant John Peters were brought down to earth during a low-level day-light raid in the opening phase of Operation Desert Storm. They were operating alongside US Air Force and Navy jets against targets in southern Iraq. Their objective was the Ar Rumaylah Air Base in the desert west of Basra, which was strongly defended by anti-aircraft batteries and Soviet-made SAM-3 and SAM-6 surface-to-air missile sites. The pair were struck by a succession of catastrophes. First, the Tornado's bombs failed to release over the target. They managed to shake them free and were heading for home, when they were hit by a SAM. The Tornado was in flames from stem to stern and there was nothing for it but to eject.

"We both hauled up on the handles between our legs," wrote Peters. "There was a faint mechanical thud through the seats. Automatically, straps whipped around me, drawing my arms and legs firmly in against the seat frame to prevent ejection injury."

369

For a few agonizing seconds, nothing happened. Then, "the rockets fired. A giant grabbed us by the shoulders and ripped us upwards at thirty times the force of gravity . . . rag dolls tossed high into the air: a massive noise from the seat rocket motors, a deafening wind rush, a sensation of tumbling over and over in space. The slipstream was crushing, even through the flying kit, 400 miles per hour strong . . . there was a feeling of falling, endlessly falling, somersaulting end over end, then the drogue gun fired out a small stabilizing parachute, to stop the whirling through the air. Immediately, as the seat became upright, the main parachute deployed. There was a jarring 'crack' as the canopy snapped open, a massive jerk as it caught the weight . . . the seat cut free automatically, falling away to earth. I opened my eyes. I was hanging under the blessed silk of the parachute . . . floating down into the deathly silence of enemy territory."

Peters and Nichol were captured, interrogated, beaten up and displayed on Iraqi television. After seven hellish weeks they were released after Saddam Hussein's adventure in Kuwait ended in defeat and humiliation. In all, twenty-nine Allied aircraft were brought down, most of them by SAM missiles. The danger of air-to-air interception passed when the Iraqi air force defected en masse to Iran, or the figure would surely have been higher.

The lessons learned from the 1991 Gulf War and the counter-measures adopted meant that, thereafter, the threat from ground defences was greatly reduced. Between the end of that conflict and Britain and

America's return to war with Saddam in 2003, their aircraft enforced no-fly zones to prevent him from using air power against the Kurds in the north of the country and the Shias in the south. In that time, British and American aircraft flew more than 300,000 missions and sustained not a single casualty. The air war that led the overthrow of Saddam in 2003 came at virtually no cost to the allies. Two British aircraft were shot down, but as the result of deadly American mistakes, rather than enemy action.

NATO aircraft also found themselves facing ageing Soviet technology when they attacked Serbian targets in the spring of 1999. The Yugoslav pilots showed exemplary pluck, coming up to face their enemies, but they presented no real threat. Missiles — even the old-fashioned and poorly maintained types in the Serbs' armoury — still posed a danger, however, and an American F-117 stealth bomber and F-16 fighter bombers were brought down by SAM strikes.

By the time the West launched its air war against the regime of Colonel Gaddafi in March 2010 the procedure developed in two Iraq wars and the Kosovo intervention had a well-practised smoothness, which quickly eliminated the threat from the ground. In the opening phase, more than a hundred Tomahawk cruise missiles rained down on all the key points in Libya's air defence infrastructure, so that operations to dominate the regime's forces could carry on virtually unhindered.

Technological advances mean that air strikes are now far more devastating and carry far less risk than they did even in the 1990s. The advent of the laser-guided

371

bomb, then of satellite-directed weaponry, means that ordnance can now be delivered with uncanny precision. The result is that the volume of bombs dropped has shrunk. One bomb can now be used to destroy a target where fifteen would have been needed just twenty years ago, and perhaps a thousand during the Second World War. Aircraft no longer have to get close to the objective to increase their chances of hitting it, and the weather and the fact that it is day or night are increasingly irrelevant. As accuracy has soared, risk has fallen. The increasing use of Unmanned Aerial Vehicles — UAVs or "drones" — as weapons platforms has removed the possibility of operator casualties altogether. Precision and lethality, however, only have value if they are directed at the right targets. The interventions in Bosnia, Iraq and particularly Afghanistan have been blighted by horrific intelligence blunders, resulting in "smart" bombs blowing to scraps the very people the mission was purportedly launched to save.

The one area of military aviation where risks are regularly taken is that of flying helicopters. In Iraq, American rotary aircraft proved alarmingly vulnerable to ground fire, even from such primitive missiles as Soviet-designed rocket-propelled grenades (RPGs).

In Afghanistan in the early days of the British deployment to Helmand Province, Chinook pilots flying in troops to remote and embattled locations frequently came under small-arms, machine-gun and RPG fire as they landed their machines. Flight Lieutenant Chris Hasler, a twenty-six-year-old Canadian flying with the RAF's 18 Squadron, underwent a particularly harrowing experience when inserting 3 Para soldiers on an operation to seize a key insurgent leader in Helmand in July 2006. As he approached the target area with more than thirty men on board reports came in that the enemy was waiting for them. The Chinooks carried on regardless. Hasler raced into the landing zone behind two helicopters piloted by a Royal Navy pilot, Lieutenant Nichol Benzie, and his boss, Wing Commander Mike Woods. As Benzie touched down the shooting started. When Hasler's turn came to land he "wanted nothing more than to pull in power and get away from that place as fast as possible". But the first Paras were now scrambling down the ramps at the rear of the lead Chinooks. Hasler realized that "if I didn't put my own troops on the ground to bolster their strength they would surely be cut to ribbons".

He continued his approach "for what seemed like years". There was so much incoming fire and floating ribbons of tracer that he "didn't realize how fast I was going until it was almost too late". To slow down, he pulled up while only a few yards from the ground, putting the underbelly of the chopper flat on, so that it acted as an air brake. If the angle of approach was more than twenty-six degrees, he risked digging the rear rotor into the ground and a catastrophic crash. But he just "managed to check the nose forward to under twenty-five degrees, half a second before we touched". It was a hard landing, but they were down. Hasler's first reaction was "jubilation that I hadn't killed everyone on board".

Then there were other things to worry about. A heavy machine gun was hosing bullets from a position about a hundred yards away to the left. One of the RAF crewmen tried to return fire from one of the Chinook's door-mounted GPMGs, but "was having a tough time . . . the enemy had sent out groups of women and children ahead of them while they fired over their heads at us".

Operational procedures dictated that a helicopter should spend no more than thirty seconds on the ground, even if there were still troops on board. Hasler had been down for more than a minute and his crew and co-pilot yelled at him to lift off. He was unaware that three men were still on the ramp, struggling to unload mortar bombs. As the Chinook rose skywards, rather than head back to safety the soldiers jumped for it. Hasler poured on the power and the helicopter lifted "like a cork", chased by "big green bulbs of tracer swishing past my co-pilot's head at what seemed like only inches away". Hasler was awarded the Distinguished Flying Cross for his Afghan exploits.

This organic integration with army operations is just one of the RAF's twenty-first-century functions. Once again its primary duty is one that emerged early in the history of British military aviation. Just like the RFC and RNAS, which took to the skies over London to try and shoot down the looming Zeppelins and Gothas in the First World War, the RAF carries the responsibility for defending Britain from enemy air attack. Since the attacks on the World Trade Centre of 11 September, 2001 a force of Typhoon fighters is held at constant, round-the-clock "quick reaction alert", ready to scramble within five minutes to intercept any aircraft that enters the United Kingdom's airspace without authority. During the heightened threat period of the London Olympics in 2012 they were joined by Sentry airborne warning radar aircraft.

Since the end of the Cold War the RAF has moved from a static posture, operating from bases in the United Kingdom and Germany, to becoming essentially an expeditionary air force. This means it is in a position to project British air power — usually in alliance with American and European partners — to operations across the globe, both military and humanitarian. Following the earthquake in Pakistan in 2005, for example, C-17 and Hercules transports were in action almost immediately, flying in food and vital supplies.

The RAF is the world's oldest independent air force. It has played a central part in the nation's history throughout the twentieth century, and could reasonably be said to have saved it when, in the summer of 1940, the skill and courage of its airmen averted the possibility of defeat and enslavement in the greatest air battle ever seen. The RAF's contribution to Allied victory was enormous and its losses, particularly in Bomber Command, were heavy. In the post-war years it was at the heart of our system of defence against the threat of attack from the Soviet Union, and since then it has been intimately engaged in every conflict the country has faced.

The RAF is universally admired for its technological sophistication and skill, and respected for the power it

375

yields. It is the biggest air force in Europe and the second largest in NATO after the USAF. The cost of maintaining it — especially in a time of global recession — has meant that just as in the early days of its existence it is compelled to restate frequently its *raison d'être*. The RAF's best argument is that its technological virtuosity makes it uniquely capable of reacting to the multiple dangers emanating from conventional and unconventional adversaries across the globe. It is now faced with the challenge of defending our interests in space, where the satellites that control 90 per cent of all military capabilities reside. It has also to develop defences against cyberspace attacks, which seem likely to be a new theatre in future wars.

At first sight the identity and preoccupations of the modern air force might seem to bear little relation to those of the bold aviators who in August 1914 climbed into their fragile craft to head out over the English Channel on their way to the battlefields of France. Yet there is a direct, linear connection between the two, which modern airmen cherish.

"Every RAF squadron has a history linking it back to units from its formation," said a young serving officer who has done intensive service in combat roles. "Our history is relatively new and so is perhaps remembered more vividly."

The RFC, the RNAS and the RAF were born of new technologies. To survive, to succeed, it was essential that they stood ready to exploit every new scientific development that brought the prospect of advantage. That attitude ensured that the reputations of the RAF, along with the Fleet Air Arm and Army Air Corps, have stood so high for a hundred years. It is matched by the spirit of the men and women who have served over the last century, a unique mixture of boldness, ingenuity and optimism that remains as fresh and inspiring as it was in the heady days of the pioneers. *Per Ardua ad Astra* . . .

Acknowledgements

This book has benefited from many conversations with many people over the years, some historians, some aviators with first-hand experience of the events described. I am particularly grateful to the late Peter Brothers, Eric Brown, Sebastian Cox, the late Billy Drake, the late Christopher Foxley-Norris, Lawrence Goodman, Tony Iveson and Rob Owen for helping me to at least partially comprehend what it is to fly in battle.

Wings has also been enriched by the work of many fine aviation historians. I am indebted to, among others, the late Ralph Barker, Joshua Levine, Nigel Steel and Peter Hart and John Terraine.

My task has been made much easier by the enthusiasm, cheerfulness and professionalism of the Atlantic team. To Toby Mundy, Angus McKinnon, Ian Pindar, Margaret Stead and Orlando Whitfield, my heartfelt thanks.

Target Tirpitz

Patrick Bishop

Tirpitz was the pride of Hitler's navy, the largest and most powerful battleship in Europe. To Churchill she was "the Beast", a menace to Britain's supply lines. To those who sailed in her she seemed impregnable, an "Iron Castle" that could withstand any bomb or torpedo. Tirpitz rarely fired her monster guns. She did not need to. This warship haunted the imaginations of the men directing Britain's war. Plan after plan was hatched to send her to the bottom.

In the end it was Bomber Command who finished her off. In the autumn of 1944, Wing Commander James "Willie" Tait, led Lancasters from 617 Squadron — the famous "Dambusters'" — and 9 Squadron on a series of raids that stretched endurance, skill and bravery to the limit. It ended with the destruction of the battleship that had come to symbolise the hubris of Hitler's Germany.

ISBN 978-0-7531-5316-1 (hb)
ISBN 978-0-7531-5317-8 (pb)

Operation Fortitude

Joshua Levine

The greatest hoax of the second world war

Operation Fortitude tells the thrilling tales of an ingenious deception that changed the course of the Second World War. The success of D-Day was made possible by those not even present on the Normandy beaches. General Patton spent D-Day on British shores commanding a phantom army. Spanish double-agent GARBO sent messages relaying supposed intelligence from his fictitious spy network. And R. V. Jones, the head of British Scientific Intelligence, masterminded the dropping of tinfoil confetti from Lancaster bombers, creating the impression that a flotilla of Allied ships was heading on a different course entirely.

Even as the Normandy landings were happening, Hitler remained convinced they were a diversionary tactic to force him to move his troops. So, thanks to Fortitude, D-Day was a triumph; without it the war might well have had a very different outcome.

ISBN 978-0-7531-5297-3 (hb)
ISBN 978-0-7531-5298-0 (pb)

Behind Enemy Lines

Sir Tommy Macpherson with Richard Bath

With three Military Crosses, three Croix de Guerre, a Légion d'honneur and a papal knighthood for his heroics during the Second World War, Sir Tommy Macpherson is the most decorated soldier in the history of the British Army.

Yet for 65 years, the Highlander's story has remained untold. Few know how, aged 21, he persuaded 23,000 SS soldiers of the feared SS Das Reich tank column to surrender, or how Tommy almost single-handedly stopped Tito's Yugoslavia annexing the whole of north-east Italy.

Still a schoolboy when war broke out, Tommy quickly matured into a legendary commando. Twice captured, he escaped both times, marching through hundreds of miles of German-held territory to get home. With a dizzyingly diverse cast of characters, Behind Enemy Lines is an astonishing story of how an ordinary boy came to achieve truly extraordinary feats.

ISBN 978-0-7531-5283-6 (hb)
ISBN 978-0-7531-5284-3 (pb)

Battle of Britain

Patrick Bishop

From the bestselling author of Fighter Boys and Bomber Boys, Battle of Britain is a magisterial account of a defining episode in modern British history: the epic struggle of RAF Fighter Command with the Luftwaffe in the summer of 1940.

From the shock defeat and evacuation from Dunkirk in May/June 1940 to Fighter Command's assertion of superiority over the Luftwaffe in mid-September of that year, Patrick Bishop charts the key staging-posts of Britain's fight for national survival. The day-to-day progress of the battle — its dogfights, its heroes and victims, its impact on flyers and civilians alike (from the Luftwaffe's "Black Thursday" of 15 August, to the opening day of "the Blitz" on 7 September) — is evoked in a richly compelling and moving narrative. Eye-witness descriptions and extracts from diaries and journals evoke the often horrific reality of war in the air.

ISBN 978-0-7531-8778-4 (hb)
ISBN 978-0-7531-8779-1 (pb)

Bomber Boys

Patrick Bishop

The 125,000 men from all over the world who passed through Bomber Command were engaged in a form of warfare that had never been implemented before. Between 1940 and 1945 they flew continuously, stopping only when weather made operations impossible. There was nothing romantic about their struggle. Often barely out of boyhood, they lived on bleak bases, flying at night on long, nerve-wracking missions that often ended in death. In all, 55,000 were killed, counting for nearly one in ten of all the British and Commonwealth war dead.

In this powerful and moving work of history, Patrick Bishop brilliantly captures the character, feelings and motivations of the bomber crews and pays tribute to their heroism and determination. They were among the best of their generation, who were called on to carry out one of the grimmest duties of the Second World War. Bomber Boys brilliantly restores these men to their rightful place in our consciousness.

ISBN 978-0-7531-5675-9 (hb)
ISBN 978-0-7531-5676-6 (pb)

ISIS publish a wide range of books in large print, from fiction to biography. Any suggestions for books you would like to see in large print or audio are always welcome. Please send to the Editorial Department at:

ISIS Publishing Limited
7 Centremead
Osney Mead
Oxford OX2 0ES

A full list of titles is available free of charge from:

Ulverscroft Large Print Books Limited

(UK)
The Green
Bradgate Road, Anstey
Leicester LE7 7FU
Tel: (0116) 236 4325

(Australia)
P.O. Box 314
St Leonards
NSW 1590
Tel: (02) 9436 2622

(USA)
P.O. Box 1230
West Seneca
N.Y. 14224-1230
Tel: (716) 674 4270

(Canada)
P.O. Box 80038
Burlington
Ontario L7L 6B1
Tel: (905) 637 8734

(New Zealand)
P.O. Box 456
Feilding
Tel: (06) 323 6828

Details of **ISIS** complete and unabridged audio books are also available from these offices. Alternatively, contact your local library for details of their collection of **ISIS** large print and unabridged audio books.